Qualitative Research and Social Change

Also by Pat Cox

CHILD SEXUAL ASSAULT: Feminist Perspectives (*co-edited*)

Also by Thomas Geisen

MIGRATION, MOBILITY AND BORDERS: Issues of Theory and Policy (*co-edited*)

Also by Roger Green

VOICES FROM THE MEAD: People's Stories of the Kingsmead Estate

Qualitative Research and Social Change

European Contexts

Edited by

Pat Cox
University of Central Lancashire, UK

Thomas Geisen
University of Applied Sciences, Northwestern Switzerland

Roger Green
University of Hertfordshire, UK

First published 2008 by
PALGRAVE MACMILLAN

Palgrave Macmillan in the UK is an imprint of Macmillan Publishers Limited,
registered in England, company number 785998, of Houndmills, Basingstoke,
Hampshire RG21 6XS.

Palgrave Macmillan in the US is a division of St Martin's Press LLC,
175 Fifth Avenue, New York, NY 10010.

Palgrave Macmillan is the global academic imprint of the above companies
and has companies and representatives throughout the world.

Palgrave® and Macmillan® are registered trademarks in the United States,
the United Kingdom, Europe and other countries.

ISBN-13: 978–0–230–53727–9 hardback
ISBN-10: 0–230–53727–8 hardback

This book is printed on paper suitable for recycling and made from fully
managed and sustained forest sources. Logging, pulping and manufacturing
processes are expected to conform to the environmental regulations of the
country of origin.

A catalogue record for this book is available from the British Library.

Library of Congress Cataloging-in-Publication Data

  Qualitative research and social change: European contexts / edited by
Pat Cox, Thomas Geisen, Roger Green.
    p. cm.
  Includes bibliographical references and index.
  ISBN 978–0–230–53727–9 (alk. paper)
   1. Social sciences – Research – Methodology. 2. Social change –
Research. 3. Qualitative research. I. Cox, Pat, 1950– II. Geisen, Thomas.
III. Green, Roger, Dr.

H62.Q352 2008
001.4'2—dc22   2008029970

10 9 8 7 6 5 4 3 2 1
17 16 15 14 13 12 11 10 09 08

Printed and bound in Great Britain by
CPI Antony Rowe, Chippenham and Eastbourne

Contents

Part III   Issues in Research

Acronyms

EU	European Union
IALS	International Adult Literacy Survey
ILO	International Labour Organization
OECD	Organization for Economic Co-Operation and Development
OMC	Open method of coordination
PISA	Programme for International Student Assessment
UNESCO	United Nations Educational, Scientific, and Cultural Organization

Contributors

Zvi Bekerman teaches anthropology of education at the School of Education and the Melton Center, Hebrew University of Jerusalem. He is also a Research Fellow at the Truman Institute for the Advancement of Peace, Hebrew University. His main interests are in the study of cultural, ethnic, and national identity, including identity processes and negotiation during intercultural encounters and in formal/informal learning contexts. Since 1999, he has been conducting a long-term ethnographic research project in the integrated/bilingual Palestinian-Jewish schools in Israel. He has also recently become involved in the study of identity construction and development in educational computer-mediated environments. He is the Editor (with Seonaigh MacPherson) of the refereed scholarly journal *Diaspora, Indigenous, ad Minority Education: An International Journal* (LEA, 2007).

Pat Cox is researcher and senior lecturer at the University of Central Lancashire, UK, in the Department of Social Work. Her research, both national and international, focuses on children, young people and their families, particularly those who are disadvantaged and excluded. She has authored and co-authored a number of book chapters and journal papers. Recently she was an invited member of the Delphi Expert Consultation Panel for the Department of Health and Institute of Mental Health (UK) for the Victims of Violence and Abuse Prevention Programme (VVAPP). Currently she is a member of the Research Advisory Group: Migration, Families and Childhood at the University of Trier, and is the recipient of a national award for a research project about asylum-seeking families' experiences of the child-protection process.

Diana Wendy Fitzgibbon qualified as a Probation Officer in 1989, having previously worked in a range of caring professions in health and social services. Since qualifying as a Probation Officer, she has worked in a number of generic teams, a bail and probation approved premise and HMP Pentonville. She also spent a number of years researching social policy and development issues in the European Parliament. Diana Wendy graduated in 2002 with a Masters in Criminology from the Middlesex University Centre for Criminology and since April 2003 has been Senior Lecturer in Criminal Justice Studies at the University of

Hertfordshire. She has just submitted her PhD on Risk Assessment and the Deskilling of Probation.

Thomas Geisen, PhD, is working as a researcher and lecturer at the University of Applied Sciences Northwestern Switzerland/School of Social Work and holds academic degrees in social work, sociology, and political science. His main fields of interest are work/labour relations, migration, violence, and social theory in which he has widely published. He is co-founder and co-worker of the Institute for Regional and Migration Research (IRM) (www.irm-trier.de) and is editing the series; 'Contributions to Migration and Regional Research', IKO Verlag, Frankfurt.

Roger Green, PhD, is Director, Centre for Community Research, University of Hertfordshire. He developed an interest in communities after spending a number of years working in London first as a youth worker, then as a community development worker, followed by retraining as a qualified social worker. A sociologist, specializing in applied social research, and community activist for over 25 years, Roger is best known for his work on marginalized groups and communities, in particular his pioneering participatory action research project on the Kingsmead Estate in Hackney, East London for the past eleven years. He is a trustee and advisor to several community projects, and regularly provides expert advice to Government Departments, Local Authorities, NGOs, and Housing Associations on community development issues.

Stephen Hicks is Reader in Health and Social Care at the University of Salford. He has written a number of articles in the field of lesbian and gay parenting, and is co-editor of *Lesbian & Gay Fostering & Adoption* (1999), *A Bibliography of Family Placement Literature* (2005), and co-author of *The Relationship between Child Death & Child Maltreatment* (2004).

Paul Hoggett is Professor of Politics and Director of the Centre for Psycho-Social Studies at the University of the West of England. He has longstanding interest in the role of emotion and unconscious forces in political behaviour and his current ESRC project focuses on the 'emotion work' required of regeneration workers as they negotiate the ethical dilemmas of their jobs. He is the UK Editor of the journal *Organisational and Social Dynamics*.

Katrin Kraus, PhD, is researcher and lecturer in the Department of Vocational Education at the University of Zurich (Switzerland). Her main research interests are vocational and further education and social change, international comparison, and policy analysis. Further interests include conceptual questions, the philosophy of (vocational) education, and the theory of social space. She has published books and articles on employability, the German concept of 'Beruf' (vocation), competences, the policy of lifelong learning, European policy, demographic change, and cross-cultural cooperation. Publications include *Vom Beruf zur Employabiltiy? Zur Theorie einer Pädagogik des Erwerbs* (Wiesbaden, 2006) and *Re-working Vocational Education: Policies, Practices and Concepts* (Bern, 2008, forthcoming; edited with A. Heikkinen).

Marjorie Mayo is Professor at the Centre for Lifelong Learning and Community Engagement at Goldsmiths, University of London UK. Her research interests focus on strategies for participation and empowerment, both at the local level in relation to community regeneration and development and education with a current focus on community participation. She recently worked with colleagues at the University of the West of England on an ESRC funded project to explore the ways in which professionals identify and address ethical dilemmas in the context of regeneration programmes.

Chris Miller is Professor of Social and Community Development and Director of the Centre for Local Democracy at the University of the West of England. He is Editor of the *Community Development Journal*. He is shortly to take up a post as Professor of Social Work at the Flinders University, Adelaide, Australia.

Carolyn Taylor is Senior Lecturer in Applied Social Science at the University of Lancaster. For several years she has taught on various qualifying and post-qualifying social work programmes in the North West of England as well as Masters in Research programmes and a professional doctorate in health and social care. Her research interests include the study of professional cultures and practices using discourse and textual analysis; a particular interest is the production and use of documentary sources in health and welfare organizations. She is the author (with Sue White) of *Practising Reflexivity in Health and Welfare: Making Knowledge* (Buckingham, Open University Press, 2000).

Michael Wrentschur, PhD, works as a researcher and lecturer at the University of Graz, Institute of Education, Department of Social Pedagogy. He studied Sociology, Education, and Economics at the University of Graz and at the Humboldt University in Berlin. He is joint Director Courses and Studies in Theatre Pedagogy and Theatre Work. His fields of work include Social Cultural Work and Participation;

Theatre Work in Social Fields; Drama and Theatre-based Methods of Social Research. Michael Wrentschur is also the artistic director of Inter*ACT*, a non-profit organization for Theatre and social-cultural activities located in Graz. His activities there encompass leading workshops, projects, and productions in social and political theatre work.

Introduction: The Importance of Qualitative Research to Social Change – Preliminary Considerations

Pat Cox, Thomas Geisen, and Roger Green

The context of research

In recent years, there has been an increasing amount of interest in countries across the world in the undertaking, findings, and application of social research, together with a groundswell of debate and discussion about methodology and methods applied in social research. The 'paradigm wars' (Halfpenny, 2001), especially those relying on the relative merits of quantitative and qualitative methodologies and methods for their focus, continue apparently unabated: it is also possible to identify a more pragmatic stance towards this debate. Here pluralism in methods and methodology is seen as the one-size-fits-all approach, referred to by some as triangulation (for example, Flick, 2002). At the same time, this 'new' acceptance of qualitative approaches as a valuable contribution to social research brings into question not only the reason for this acknowledgement but also the question of its strength. Flick (2002) identifies social change as an important issue in the rise in practice and interest in qualitative research:

> Rapid social change and the resulting diversification of life worlds are increasingly confronting social researchers with new social contexts and perspectives...traditional deductive methodologies...are failing...thus research is increasingly forced to make use of inductive strategies instead of starting from theories and testing them...knowledge and practice are studied as local knowledge and practice. (Flick, 2002, p. 2)

Underpinning this insight into the weaknesses of traditional deductive methodologies in social research is an epistemological position in which the relevance of complexity and context for understanding the social world is highlighted. Therefore, following Kuhn's (1970) acknowledgement that knowledge is context dependent, numerous qualitative researchers have agreed that there is 'no god's eye point of view' (Putnam, 1981) and that it is impossible that there should be a 'view from nowhere' (Nagel, 1986). Given that 'context' is an extremely relevant condition for social research, the relationship of social research and social change becomes significant in social research. From a critical perspective, the relation between them must be understood not as a linear relation but as one which is intricate and ambivalent: social research seeks to understand social change but at the same time social change also influences and guides social research. Therefore, from the position of critical qualitative research there is a need not only to find answers to the question of how social research can best contribute to the understanding of the social world: as or possibly more important, is a second question: What is the contribution of social research to social change? This question is not neutral; it is a question about the assessment of approaches within and practices of social research: Does this approach contribute to improving social conditions by means of emancipatory praxes? Does it result in relevant and reliable data which can be taken up by those who have some responsibility for law or public policy, health, welfare, or education; in short, those with responsibility for implementing social change?

Many of the current demands for social research findings are driven by steady changes in a world dominated by capitalism. In his analysis Marx (1960, p. 465) emphasized that the permanent and revolutionary change of all social relations is an inherent condition of capitalism. And it is the capitalist mode of production in which permanent change seems to be the only reliable consistency, damaging or destroying established social relationships based on mutuality, continuity, reciprocity, and solidarity (Touraine, 1971). For social research this situation is demanding, since social stability and continuity are both fragmentary and under pressure (Haug, 1991). On the one hand, there is an immense growth in affluence, not only in the Western world and in Japan – the established centres of capitalism – but increasingly also in the new boom areas of capitalism in China, India, and Southeast Asia. This growth has been the driving force for a fierce race for raw materials, first for oil and more recently also for food. This is paralleled by a rapid growth in poverty in both the majority and minority worlds. In politics neo-liberalism has become established as the predominant ideology in the United Kingdom and in the United States, and has now become influential in, and been adopted by, other western European countries and by some in eastern Europe. This ideology and its variants also impact upon qualitative social research endeavours, see Andrews (2001).

One of the most obvious consequences of these increases of both affluence and poverty/superfluity (Castel, 2002) is migration. The 'age of migration' (Castles and Miller, 2003) is also an age in which wealth results in high mobility and transfer of different kinds of labour-forces (Geisen, 2004a, b); both being deployed and deploying themselves for production and re-production. This dynamic brings about another significant feature, the simultaneity of the global and the local; the 'glocal' (*Glokalisierung*), see Bauman (1996, p. 661). All these developments present challenges for social research, testing its limits in undertaking research in a world of instability, discontinuity, and fragmentation in social relationships; key features of social life in what Giddens (1991) has termed as the 'late modern age'.

Research now occurs in rapidly changing global and local contexts. Poverty and the social exclusion of individuals, groups, and communities of peoples is rife across the globe and many migrate in search of a different and a better future (Cox, 2007; Nguyen, 2005) The outcome for qualitative researchers is that there is an ever-growing range of 'lived experiences' (Van Maanen, 1988) to understand and to make visible within the world, particularly where these 'lived experiences' are less stable and fulfilling than others.

Currently, the majority constituency of social science qualitative research is people who are marginalized, dispossessed, and excluded from societies' mainstreams. However, Gouldner (1973) criticized sociological sentimentality towards members of marginalized groups and 'advocacy' research which described and 'displayed' them, but which did not change their situations. Gouldner also noted that research was 'tamed by being harnessed to the State in welfare and research funding modes' (Stanley, 2000, p. 57). In this Gouldner highlights two key issues: that peoples who are marginalized are also peoples most exposed to exploitation and oppression and that they are very likely to be among the most scrutinized and researched in pursuit of knowledge production.

Concern about how social science and its associated research activities risk becoming tools of the powerful continue to exist; see, for example, Henriques et al. (1984), Mergner (1999, 2005), and Walkerdine (1997).

Such concerns mean that researchers need constantly to analyse how we are implicated in the development and production of knowledge and of its deployment and to be aware of how findings become – or may become – commodified.

As Plummer notes:

> what has happened recently is a concern that 'research knowledge' only makes sense if we can acquire understanding about the active processes through which such knowledge becomes produced. (Plummer, 2001, p. 208)

The purpose of this book – critical reflections

Contributions to this book seek to reflect critically upon relationships between research and social change, aiming to stimulate thinking and critical debate on the interconnections between them. Reclaiming the concept articulated by critical theorists that research should do more than represent *what is*, the contributions emphasize that, irrespective of theory, methodology or method, qualitative research can and should work for society and help to bring about beneficial social change. This book derives from the editors' and contributors' experiences of undertaking qualitative research with individuals, groups, and communities across the world. The aim of the book is to explore and analyse the relationships between research theory, praxis, and social change through a focus on exploration and examination of the interconnections between theories, methodologies, methods, and the potential for social change. Such explorations form the subject matter of each chapter.

Within the social science research and social research communities (academics, research students, researchers, service users and carers, community groups, professional practitioners in agencies) there are ongoing debates concerning the relevance and the status of social research with regard to the uses made of research findings. Compared with the emphasis upon, and attention paid to, the outcomes of research, the capacity of research to inform and improve social life and bring about social change is rarely addressed in research accounts. We think that the product of social research – its potential and actual benefit to individuals, groups and communities in a society – should be seen as the final link in a process that begins with the developing of a research interest and question, continues with the application of a theoretical perspective and moves through considerations of methodology and method.

Qualitative research approaches, throughout the 1990s and more latterly, have made valuable contributions to theory and praxis in social research and social science. However, the continuing dominance of the positivist paradigm and quantitative methods has meant that contributions to social change made by qualitative research are rarely analysed and have been relatively neglected in research literature to date. Even if researchers are not concerned with the impact of their research practice while undertaking it, such an influence is always there. Being concerned about this means therefore viewing the research process as a process of interaction in which findings are co-produced by people involved and participating in the research process. Therefore, there is an urgent need for research, especially for that research practice which understands itself as critical, to reflect upon its immediate influence which occurs before any outcome is 'produced'. For example, what does it mean for the research process and its outcomes if the research process itself is democratic and participatory? Taking into account that much social research is undertaken with marginalized peoples in vulnerable situations, it is important for researchers to think about what the effects of both emanicpatory practices – and their opposite – might be? Do research practices, however well intended, reinforce and confirm peoples' social situations (see above, Gouldner, 1973)? From whom is information collected and to whom does the researcher give it? The question can be asked: What do research subjects get back from the research process? This question, of course relates not only to research practice; it has implications for social relationships more generally. Therefore, one of the main reasons for writing this book is to encourage such critical debate and engagement about research, amongst ourselves, and with and amongst our readers.

Critical reflections on the links and interconnections between theories, methodologies, methods, and social change should be an indispensable component of research and accounts of/narratives of research, wherever and however it is/they are undertaken. For example, to add to the questions raised just above: how are research subjects involved in research endeavours: are they treated merely as research subjects or do they have a voice in the research process? How do they perceive research and what does this mean for development and social change? How do the interconnections between theory, methodology, method and social change vary? How are they realized and to what degree? While the impact of quantitative research can result in change in public policy (top-down change), qualitative research may result in social change for individuals, groups and communities, which may be bottom-up, as well as top-down (Cox et al., in press; Green, 2000).

What is different about this book is its substantive focus on the exploration of the links between theory, methodology, method, and social change in qualitative research. Some of the chapters are more theoretical in orientation; in others, the authors explore interconnections through examples of their own research projects. Thus, the subject or focus of the book is addressed in a variety of ways, ensuring that the book appeals to readers with a range of research interests and experiences. Editors and contributors are from across the world and our work represents therefore a range of differing traditions in theorizing about and undertaking critical and qualitative research. This is an essential part of the book's appeal: readers who are less familiar with some theories, methodologies and methods than with others can learn something of other approaches to research directly through the words of the researchers writing here, rather than in a 'contextless' text book.

Many research texts concentrate either on theoretical and methodological approaches, or on method used, or on outcomes (sometimes all three). What the editors and contributors of this book provide, in a more innovative way than existing publications, are explorations of interconnections of theory, methodology and method in qualitative research with social change, including change for research subjects, for communities, and sometimes for researchers themselves. The book both models and encourages reflection and reflexivity and will be of interest both to novice researchers and to those who are more experienced. Ethical issues are not specifically addressed in each chapter, as there are a number of texts on ethics in research already in existence: however, ethical behaviour in research is implicit throughout the book.

Content of the book

The book is arranged into three complementary parts with three chapters in each (see below). We have made a decision not to impose a formal editorial structure, or too much editorial influence on the contributions and thus each is very different in style and in how the authors address their subject matter. We believe that the differences in style and content will encourage and sustain reflection and debate for some time to come.

The title of Part I is 'Exploring Concepts and Approaches' and in these chapters each contributor addresses in particular the application of theory in undertaking qualitative research to bring about social change.

The first chapter in this section is Pat Cox's chapter: Changing Research, Research for Change: Exploring the Perspectives of Complexity

Science. In this chapter, Pat Cox explores the contribution of complexity science and complexity science concepts to research and social change, including questions of theory, methodology and method.

Building on Witkin's (2002) assertion that in today's climate of onto-logical and epistemological uncertainty is the potential for creativity, changing levels of awareness, and establishing new priorities, she analyses the nature of values and knowledge underpinning research and examines the application of complexity science to research and research processes. She explores the potential of complexity science to move beyond the positivist and interpretivist paradigms and to contribute to the development of a new epistemological framework for research practice and processes that centralize relationships and understanding and learnings as well as knowledge and which may initiate different forms of social change.

Ambivalence is a concept which relies on the epistemic assumption that an object, situation, or action cannot fully be described and analysed using a single category, because it contains at least two notions contrary to one another. It became well known as a theoretical concept through post-modern theorists (Zygmunt Bauman, 1995) and post-colonial theorists (Stuart Hall, 1994a, b). Within the concept of ambivalence, social change cannot be equated with the improvement of social conditions, or with the steady continuation of political freedom. Thomas Geisen argues that the concept of ambivalence can make a fruitful contribution to social research, since it facilitates a plurality of perspectives, practices, and rationalities, based on the plurality of human existence and human actions. From this perspective the researched are part of the research process, since valuable insights can only be reached by organizing the research process as cooperative and dialogical practice. In this chapter, he explores characteristics of the concept of ambivalence and discusses its relevance for theory, methodology, and research practice and process.

Stephen Hicks and Carolyn Taylor challenge the notion that discourse analysis is unable to address issues relating to social change, recognizing that discursive approaches present fundamental challenges to Enlightenment thinking by their rejection of grand narratives of social change and their focus upon language as social action. Selecting two differing approaches – discursive psychology and a Foucaultian analysis – Hicks and Taylor outline key tenets before offering examples of how discourse analysis can be used to address issues of social change: the first example explores the minutiae of everyday 'race' talk; the second deploys a genealogical method to research sexuality and social welfare.

In the course of their discussion the authors offer a critical assessment of the complex terrain of discourse, drawing out similarities and differences in the two approaches and emphasizing their contribution to researching social change. They thus argue for a more nuanced understanding of the concept of social change and underline the potential of detailed empirical work in this area.

Part II is 'Welfare Issues and Community Development'. Here contributors focus on research in and with communities and with those who work in them, with a particular emphasis on involving research subjects more deeply in research praxis.

In the first chapter of this part, Roger Green discusses and analyses the lessons learned from an ongoing participatory action research project with residents on an estate in East London. The research aims to involve local residents and organizations in supporting collective community action to tackle the poverty, marginalization, and social exclusion they experience everyday. The research remains ongoing and has been effective in supporting funding for a number of community projects and initiating a community development process for social change and re-empowerment. The chapter focuses on how the contextualization of applied social research methods in a community which has historically experienced disadvantage and exclusion over many years, mounts a challenge to what Freire (1970b) has termed the 'culture of silence', with its oppressive and passive acceptance of the status quo.

Michael Wrentschur brings new insights to debates about qualitative or quantitative methodologies, arguing that neither can provide a complete answer to a specific practical, ethical, and political research problem: how can people, who are affected by certain issues be empowered to research their own experiences and possibilities for change? How can body and mind, knowledge and actions, be integrated into the research process? The author discusses these questions, using the example of a social-cultural theatre project with homeless people in Graz, Austria. Following the concept of the 'Theatre of Oppressed' and 'Legislative Theatre', developed by Augusto Boal, theatre is used in this example as an artistic approach to facilitate a participatory and empowering research process and as a tool for social change. The effects on the participants and on the socio-political contexts are analysed, as is the role of the researcher and the specific quality of 'knowledge' in these processes. In conclusion, Michael discusses the potential of theatre as a tool for social research.

Moving on from debates between critical rationalists and postmodernists, psychosocial approaches enable researchers and researched to co-produce meanings, whilst retaining continuing processes of critical reflection. Through psychosocial approaches, research teams are developing new ways to explore the interactions between individuals' agency and socially constructed contexts. In this chapter, Chris Miller, Paul Hoggett, and Marjorie Mayo explore how such approaches provide a different focus to the study of social change, using the exemplar of research into how policies are impacting upon front-line professionals in human service professions who are engaged in community involvement in urban regeneration programmes. They demonstrate how psychosocial approaches provide more participative ways of gaining new insights into the ways in which individuals both experience and grapple with the dilemmas associated with social policy changes and the impact of emotions in the workplace.

Part III is 'Issues in Research'. In this part, each contributor addresses an issue or issues arising from their own experiences of undertaking and of teaching research.

Diana Wendy Fitzgibbon's chapter concerns the effectiveness in practice of the current pre-occupation in social welfare and probation practice with risk assessment and criminal justice. Following a review of the main themes in research in this area, the author examines methodological issues arising from an evaluation of the E-OASys used by the Probation service in the United Kingdom. The research focuses on a limited number of cases from the London area, exploring whether E-OASys had identified those offenders with mental health problems, those most at risk and whether or not this led to effective case management both to reduce risk and to provide support to clients. A follow-up study contrasted the findings of this random group with those revealed by examining a number of 'Serious Further Offence Reports', also from within the London area. In the final section of the chapter, Diana Wendy Fitzgibbon analyses the strengths and limitations of this particular research methodology for yielding knowledge that is relevant to policy concerning risk reduction and client support.

Undertaking research and teaching research are two important components in the production and dissemination of knowledge. Zvi Bekerman discusses the many, longstanding – and frequently hidden – ways in which both education and education research have maintained existing social divisions, instead of being a force for bringing about social change. This is an engaged account of the author's own commitment to research that makes a difference, both in the academy and in the social world. In this chapter, he reflects upon his experiences as a teacher of anthropology and education, and analyses reasons for difficulties he encounters when trying to share with students the paradigmatic perspectives which he believes might help overcome the predominance of traditional empirical perspectives in the social sciences in general and in education in particular.

A linear policy model underpins the new evaluative paradigm in policy research conducted by international organization such as the OECD or the EU, argues Katrin Kraus in her chapter. Additionally, the changing role of the nation states as political actors par excellence of the nineteenth and twentieth century challenges policy analysis in education. Against this background the chapter offers with the 'policy circle', a model that facilitates better understanding and analysis of policy as a process in highlighting crucial phases like agenda setting or negotiations and important elements, such as actors, interests, or power. The chapter draws attentions to the necessity of multi-perspectivity and multilayered approaches in order to face the complexity of political processes and to work out contradictions between education policy and pedagogical practice. Differences between official and hidden agendas can be addressed only by contextualizing political process diachronically as well as synchronically. The critical question is who is given voice by the selection of sources for policy analysis.

We editors began this project, this book, in October 2004, following discussions between ourselves that began at a conference and have been sustained in the main by emails, with phone calls and occasional coming together at conferences. We were certain that the proposed focus on the interconnections between theory, methodology, methods, and social change would resonate with others undertaking qualitative research, as they do with us.

Personal experiences and anecdotal evidence from amongst qualitative researchers we know suggests that there is little, if any, encouragement for such considerations and engagement in reports of findings from qualitative research and that some journals discourage it. One of the striking issues to emerge as the book developed and we editors read the draft chapters sent to us was that, given the institutional pressures on all of us to 'do' research, how strong is the commitment among qualitative researchers to take the time to pause, to consider, and to engage critically with their own work and the epistemological and methodological frameworks which underpin it. Throughout all the chapters runs a sense that we live and research in challenging times and that researchers must be responsive to this, including questioning our own roles in knowledge production.

Taken together, the chapters provide a strong argument for the worth of the contribution of qualitative research to learning about life, work, education, communities, criminal justice, and relationships in the twenty-first century. In a climate in which much research is becoming subordinated to managerial, policy, and political agendas, these chapters raise issues which are both practical and moral and which renew qualitative research's engagement with understanding the social world and its potential for social change.

Part I

Exploring Concepts and Approaches

1
Changing Research, Research for Change: Exploring the Perspectives of Complexity Science

Pat Cox

Introduction

In our introduction, we editors write about the indivisible relationship between research and the societies within which research is undertaken. It is our contention that researchers should aim to reflect upon this relationship throughout the research process. It is my contention that this should include reflection on the roles of researchers and our influence on research relationships. My epistemological position draws from that of critical and feminist theorists in viewing research as a means of questioning, challenging, and changing 'what is', rather than merely describing it (Habermas, 1973; Harding, 1986; Smith, 1999).

One of the challenges for qualitative researchers in the twenty-first century is how to maintain our commitment to understanding relationship, dialogue, uncertainty and learning, and enabling disparate voices to be heard, when within many national and global contexts the emphasis is on categorical statements, knowledge, agreement, and unity. Also, how might qualitative social researchers challenge the 'taken-for-grantedness' of the activities of transnational capital and its multiple damaging effects on lives and relationships through their commodification; how might we contest the discourses of individual achievement which disguise much of the hollowness of contemporary life in the richer countries of the world; how can we stay focused on what matters and how to continue to care that some things do not; that safety and security are not rights enjoyed by all.

That there is a need for us to maintain a permanent critical engagement with the social world should not be doubted. Among others, Walkerdine notes: 'the place of research within the apparatuses of social regulation' and that

> Social science has been central in the management of populations, and so we have a responsibility in taking apart those truths to construct narratives of our own, no matter how difficult that might be. (Walkerdine, 1997, p. 76)

A corollary of this requirement for permanent critical engagement is a sense of moral responsibility on the part of social scientists and qualitative social researchers (Scambler, 1998) to respond to societal injustice. I would like social scientists and researchers to respond regularly as a group or groupings to inequality, injustice, and the misapplication of political power both here in the United Kingdom and elsewhere in the world: see, for example, Andrews (2001); Denzin and Lincoln (2003a); Lincoln (1995); Steele (2004); Stanley (2000). Poulos (2003) notes the importance of 'compassion, responsibility and commitment' (p. 241), all attitudes which are relevant for a critically engaged emancipatory research practice.

In their preface to *Collecting and Interpreting Qualitative Materials*, Denzin and Lincoln (2003b) assert:

> There is a pressing need to show how the practices of qualitative research can help change the world in positive ways. So at the beginning of the twenty first century, it is necessary to re-engage the promise of qualitative research as a generative form of inquiry (Peshkin, 1993) and as a form of radical democratic practice ... to show how the discourses of qualitative research can be used to help imagine and create a free, democratic society. (p. xi)

In this chapter, I analyse the contribution of complexity science to praxis and processes in qualitative research, focusing mainly on the UK context. Concepts from complexity science can be applied to developing a particular epistemological approach to qualitative research, one which centralizes learnings rather than knowledge acquisition; as I see it there is potential in its application to research endeavours, which can further the initiation of social change. It is my opinion that the application of complexity science enables us to think differently about research and to establish new conceptualizations and emancipatory praxes.

I seek a critical engagement with complexity science, although I don't argue that it answers everything, and I am applying it here not as a metaphor, which is merely descriptive, but as a model which has explanatory worth. Like Varela (1989), I look for and acknowledge examples where there is resonance, rather than an exact fit. I draw also on social theory where I see some resonance with complexity. I am aware of the dangers of appearing uncritically to transfer concepts between different disciplines, but wish to argue that complexity science can *unify* – in the sense of identifying commonalities – rather than impose a *unitary* framework on, different aspects of research processes and praxes (Brah, 1993, p. 31) and can facilitate unexpected considerations of social change.

I begin with a summary of the context of qualitative research and proceed to outline a very brief history of complexity science and definitions of some key concepts. I follow with the application of these concepts to various aspects of research processes and praxes and then explore how applying complexity science concepts to qualitative research can lead us to think differently about processes and outcomes. I consider the implications of applying complexity science to research for forms of social change related to research itself and close with a short discussion and conclusion. For the purposes of this chapter, I refer to researchers based in university departments, although I know that there are many located elsewhere, including community-based researchers and service users and carers (Beresford and Evans, 1999). Following Kvale's (1996) example, I refer throughout to 'research subjects'.

The context of qualitative research

There is disagreement about whether our times are modern or postmodern (Latour, 1993) or something of – and beyond – both:

> The contemporary period cannot be reduced to either modernity or postmodernity ... To go beyond modernity and postmodernity is also to move beyond the limits of the European/western project of the Enlightenment to new constructions of human experience in a world which is neither modern nor postmodern. (Delanty, 2000, p. 5)

In social science research, positivism has been challenged widely, including by Weber emphasizing 'interpretive understanding of social action' (1978, p. 4); by critical social theorists such as Habermas (1984, 1987) and by Lyotard (1984) in his critique of grand narratives. Within the interpretivist paradigm, qualitative researchers have highlighted the impossibility and implausibility of research that is free from both theoretical preconceptions and emotional engagement (Denzin and Lincoln, 2003b; Gouldner, 1970, 1973; Richardson, 1997; Shacklock and Smyth, 1993). Damasio's (2006) research on the interconnections between brain and emotions demonstrates that emotions are necessary both for rational thinking and for rational behaviour in social settings. Thus, Damasio provides some *post hoc* support for previously intuitive understanding of qualitative research, expressed in Mies' (1983) assertion of the need for a 'conscious partiality' on the part of the researcher for their research subjects. Damasio's research is relevant to my discussion: research cannot and should not be free from emotional engagement in relation to social change – 'commitment', as Gouldner described it (1970, 1973).

In addition, just as the dichotomy of reason and emotion is challenged, the mind-body duality comes under social scientific scrutiny. Within both social theory and social policy, arguments for the relevance of studying the body gather momentum: see, for example, Ellis and Dean (2000); Prout (2000); Turner (2000). Studying the significance of emotions in social life is underway in social theory (Williams, 2001) and in social policy (Hoggett, 2000). These developments are entering into and influencing qualitative research, in the growing recognition that both we researchers and our research subjects are inseparable from the influences of our bodily experiences and emotions – 'whole persons'. Like many who are persuaded by feminist theories, I do not wish such explorations to return us to essentializing notions of biological destiny; nor should they be recycled to justify dominance or subjugation, such as that practised by some adults against children (Summit, 1988). However, previously the body has been an 'absent presence' in both these disciplines, and so I extend a cautious welcome to these attempts at integration, examining how they might engender new ways of viewing the 'taken-for-grantedness' of social life. Examples of research inclusive of these influence are Frank (1995, 2000, 2004); Bochner (2003); Ellis (1993, 1998, 2003); Ellis and Bochner (2003); Richardson (1997, 2003); Sparkes (1996). In Kuhnian terms, the conditions for another paradigm shift are already present: it may be time for a new 'methodenstreit' – Kiel and Elliott (1997, p. 296).

Complexity science: Brief history and description

Awareness of the relevance of complexity science for social science has grown in the United Kingdom and North America recently (Stevens and Cox, 2007; Wallerstein, 2000; Wallerstein et al., 1996) although in Italy it has been integral to social theorizing and discussion for longer (Geyer, 2003). Sweeney (2002) asserts that debates about complexity science are: 'universal ... exploring *the fundamental nature of explanation, representation and interpretation of knowledge*' (Sweeney, 2002, p. 19, my emphasis).

Complexity science originates in the natural sciences – in a number of them quite closely in time – and my account of its relevance to qualitative research begins with study by nineteenth-century mathematician Poincaré (1914) and the concept of 'deterministic chaos' – that is, the impossibility of predicting the orbits of the planets for all time because the orbits change in unknown ways. This concept of deterministic chaos does not describe complete chaos or randomness: it encapsulates the impossibility of forecasting exact change or movement, even though previous experience (whether of observing planets or plant growth) means that observers can anticipate change of some sort. However, they cannot specify the exact *form* the change will take. 'Poincaré's finding is central to ... complexity theory' (Morowitz, 2002, p. 10). There are other relevant findings across a range of scientific disciplines, but there is no space to describe all of them here. Examples include: in biology, von Bertalanffy (1971) with his work on 'General Systems Theory', which moved away from reductivist approaches to the study of natural phenomena; and in the field of thermodynamics research by Prigogine (1980, 1997); and in cybernetics by Wiener (1948) have also contributed to the continuing developments in complexity science.

It may seem paradoxical to draw from the natural sciences in discussing qualitative research. However, some mathematicians, physicists, and astronomers now engage both with the edge of understanding (Rees, 2006) and with that which is unknown and currently unknowable: for example, string theory, which as yet cannot be verified experimentally (Greene, 2005); while Porter (1994) notes that Prigogine's work has been applied beyond the discipline of physics within which it was originally developed. Such theoretical explorations may seem remote from the concerns of researchers and of many of our subjects but they demonstrate that in fact our attempts to engage critically with the social world are limited by current knowledge, and that the boundaries of this knowledge are constantly being challenged and changed, which may and can have unforeseen consequences for our research – see also above, Damasio's research (2006).

Complexity science concepts and their application

It is important to note that complexity science is not the same as chaos theory, although the two are often elided (McDaniel, 1997). The emphasis in chaos theory is on how the complex arises from the simple (Cilliers,

1998), while complexity science focuses on the emergence of order from complex systems: see, for example, Prigogine (1980, 1997). One of the difficulties experienced here in defining complexity concepts, is that language is linear, whilst complexity science itself is multifaceted. Concepts are deployed slightly differently by various authors, although some commonality exists. Burton (2002) summarizes:

> Complex systems consist of multiple components. Such systems are understood by observing the rich interaction of these components, not simply understanding the system's structure;
>
> The interaction between components can produce unpredictable behaviour;
>
> Complex systems interact with and are influenced by their environment;
>
> The interactions between the elements of the system are non-linear; that is to say the result of any action depends on the state of the elements at the time as well as the size of the input. Small inputs may have large effects and vice versa;
>
> The interactions generate new properties, called 'emergent behaviours' of the system, which cannot be explained through studying the elements of the system, however much detail is known;
>
> In complex systems such emergent behaviour cannot be predicted;
>
> Complex systems are open systems: when observed, the observer becomes part of the system. (Burton, 2002, p. 2).

The complexity science concepts which I have selected as most relevant for thinking about research are: complex adaptive systems, non-linear relationships between systems, agents, networks and feedback, and emergent properties.

Complex adaptive systems

Complex adaptive systems are open systems which are both dynamic and organic, existing at the boundary of order and chaos (Gribbin, 2004, p. 157). One change in one component of a complex adaptive system may result in an enormous change, or a small change; alternatively, it may result in no change at all. Cohen and Stewart (1994) and Merry (1995) emphasize that complex adaptive systems transcend reductionism, with Merry emphasizing that the complex system cannot be understood by reducing it to its parts (Merry, 1995).

According to Waldrop (1992), Holland et al. (1975, 1986) write that the concept of complex adaptive systems can be applied to understanding cultural and social systems as well as biological ones: therefore societies, communities, and families all can be described as complex adaptive systems on the edge of chaos (Stevens and Cox, 2007). Mainzer asserts that

> The crucial point of the complex systems approach is that from a macroscopic point of view the development of political, cultural or social order is not only the sum of single intentions but the collective result of non-linear interactions. (Mainzer, 1996, p. 272)

Byrne (1998) defines a complex adaptive system as being 'the domain between linearly determined order and indeterminate chaos' (1998, p. 1), relating this definition to his social scientific commitment to understanding how societies are formed and how they alter (Stevens and Cox, 2007); issues very pertinent to qualitative research practice seeking to influence social change.

Qualitative research endeavours to *re*-produce (to varying degrees) the feelings, experiences, and lives of individuals, families, groups, and communities, all of whom are complex adaptive systems. Application of this concept to qualitative research process and praxis therefore means that we researchers must be always mindful of the constantly evolving nature of the (complex adaptive) systems being researched, including being mindful that we are all members of a number of complex adaptive systems, both large and small, all of which are constantly evolving also.

Non-linear relationships and non-linear understanding

Developments within complex adaptive systems are non-linear and we need to apply non-linear understandings. The concept of non-linear relationships implies that an increase in one variable may not result in a uniform increase in another variable: 'A linear system is more or less equal to the sum of its parts; a non-linear system may be either much more, or much less than the sum of its parts.' (Gribbin, 2004, p. 49). Cilliers notes that in complexity science there is the demise of history as the 'master key': in relation to research this has implications for any certainty we may seek about future outcomes and future relationships and developments (Cilliers, 1998, p. 122).

Therefore, applying the concept of non-linear relationships to research is to acknowledge that an increase in input on the part of the researcher – more interviews or more in-depth questions – may result in richer or clearer data; it may result in very different data, and equally, it may not result in either. Issues of relationship development, data collection, and analysis and how findings are understood in such a shared undertaking, such as collaborative research with a community group are impossible to anticipate in their entirety as we lack 'information about the starting conditions' (Gribbin, 2004, p. 49).

A qualitative researcher asking questions of young women in a community about why they don't use a particular sports facility by asking them about their reasons for non-use, about what might encourage them to go, and then coding the reasons by most frequently mentioned first, is employing a form of linear understanding along the lines of: *because this, and this, or this, therefore, resulting in that.* However, applying complexity science establishes that this is an inappropriate method of researching intricate phenomena. Individuals, families, groups, and communities all experience changes within themselves and simultaneously, changes within their environments. Changes in the feelings, thinking, or behaviour of researchers may also occur concurrently, and all such changes need to be considered. Non-linear understanding means that we researchers must be attentive to every detail, including those which are apparently insignificant, for these may turn out to be most influential for the system (Stevens and Cox, 2007).

All of this is not to imply that researchers should not be paying attention to rigour at every stage of the research: it is just that there is seduction in believing that if we concentrate on the content of research – meeting ethical requirements; type of method; type and number of questions; number of research subjects – there will be 'good' data and findings that are relevant to our research question – a linear outcome. Yes, we must address content – and we must be prepared for the unexpected:

> We must become good improvisers. There are some trades, jobs, professions and tasks whose workers come to be good at working with ambiguity. Good scientists are always working just beyond the edge of what they know. They feel their way, trust their instincts, and make frequent leaps of faith. Instead of assuring the workers that the ambiguity and uncertainty will go away once we 'get things under control', managers in complex adaptive systems must teach them to live with ambiguity and embrace surprise. (McDaniel, 1997, p. 34)

Here, if 'researchers' is substituted both for 'scientists' and for 'workers' and 'research project managers' is substituted for 'managers', then we have a sense of how complexity science provides a model for researchers working, 'at the edge of what (we) know'.

Agents

Complex adaptive systems comprise a large number of 'agents' within themselves, 'The individuals that make up the whole are designated agents' (Morowitz, 2002, p. 13). Agents have the capacity to share information amongst themselves, with others in their environment and to adjust their behaviour as a result of the information that they process. Agents have differing amounts and various sources of information and no one agent understands the system in its entirety. Agents have agency (in the social theoretical sense of the word).

Researchers and research subjects considered as agents

We researchers and our research subjects can exchange information amongst ourselves and with our environment and adapt our own behaviour as a function of information that we process. We and our research subjects interact with one another and our environment; we develop and adapt as the environment changes, sometimes for reasons that we ourselves do not entirely recognize. However, we lack full knowledge of the functioning of the whole system, of which we all are a part.

We researchers are therefore involved in sense-making activities with our research subjects and with limited and constantly changing information. In applying complexity science to our understanding of qualitative research processes, researchers would try to design research to allow for such adaptations and maintain awareness of, and adjust to these adaptations, as they occur.

Networks and feedback

An important feature of complexity science is the manner in which things interact with one another – networks and interconnections between simple parts. Gribbin notes that complexity is based on a simple idea: 'the sensitivity of a system to its starting conditions and feedback' (Gribbin, 2004, p. 3).

Rather than seeing the research process and our 'researcher relationships' with our research subjects in terms of hierarchies, applying complexity science allows us to view these interrelationships as networks. And, if and how connections between events are made – or not made – influences research findings and outcomes in very different ways. Applying the concept of networks and feedback, feedback of research findings in complex adaptive systems can be directed to where it applies and is needed: 'feedback in complex systems goes directly to the elements running relevant parts of the system and problems are explored openly, rather than in an atmosphere of blame and sanction.' (Blackman, 2003, p. 4). The implications of research findings to social change in policy and practice can be jointly discussed and jointly owned.

Emergent properties

Emergent Properties are brought into being because of localized interactions between connected units: they are characteristic of the whole system. 'Novel behaviours...are the emergent properties of the system, properties of the whole. They are novelties that follow from the system rules but cannot be predicted from properties of the components that make up the system.' (Morowitz, 2002, p. 13). Cohen and Stewart (1994, p. 436) assert that emergence is a rule rather than an exception.

Research and emergent properties

Governments, international, national or local charities or foundations may know the particular aspect of social life into which they want to have research undertaken. They commission the research; but neither they nor we can predict what data is generated from the interactions between ourselves and our research subjects (Griffiths, 2002, p. 155); nor can they or we explain it through studying ourselves and our research subjects.

From knowledge towards learning and understanding

Qualitative research is an undertaking to learn about and understand the emotions, experiences, and lives of our research subjects. If we do not address the importance of research processes, research may still occur but it will not be a meaningful experience for anyone involved in it. The concept of complex adaptive systems reminds us that each individual researcher is a part of larger complex adaptive systems too. This concept can be applied to understanding our part in the processes of a research undertaking: it can encourage us to examine our role as researchers; our impact on the processes; and seeing what we can learn from this examination. Existing research thinking on this uses the concept of reflexivity – see, for example, Plummer (2001) – which for me fits well with consideration of complex adaptive systems:

> The term reflexivity is used in a methodological sense to refer to the process of critical self-reflection on one's biases, theoretical predispositions, preferences and so forth...reflexivity can be a means for

critically inspecting the entire research process... Reflexivity in a methodological sense can ... (also) ... point to the fact that the inquirer is part of the setting, context and social phenomenon he or she seeks to understand. (Schwandt, 2001, p. 224)

Conceptualizing non-linear relationships within research demonstrates how little control we can exert through our research designs. Our relationships with co-researchers and with research subjects may have as great or a greater influence on outcomes than what we do. And the concept of emergent properties promotes understanding of how – although we can anticipate that our research interactions will generate data of some kind – we cannot predict or fully explain what emerges.

Finally, we can combine both the concept of complex adaptive systems and the concept of agents to recognize that we and our research subjects are feeling, thinking, embodied subjects, all of us acting with agency in situations of limited awareness.

Uncertainty is fundamental to complexity science (Geyer and Rihani, 2001) and I argue that it is also fundamental to research: meaning is reached not through achieving a fixed state of knowledge but through working with *and* through ambiguity; *learning* and making and re-making sense of what is going on. We researchers (agents) tend to seek explanations because they fit, but then we exclude other forms of equally valid knowledge. Pressure to produce knowledge leads to a focus on outcomes, not on process. If we shift the emphasis from seeking research outcomes that are knowledge-oriented, to achieving continuous mutual understandings and learnings, then we accept that we can never know everything, as Hazelrigg observes, what we can know and do is finite: 'what the human creature is not, no matter what the strength of will, is omniscient and omnipotent'. (Hazelrigg, 1995, p. 102).

Complexity and social change

Part of the social change I seek is a sea change in how research is conceptualized and undertaken. Complexity science reminds us of our limits and limitations. We should do research that seeks social change; however, applying concepts such as non-linearity reminds those of us who undertake research which we hope will be empowering or transformative, that good intentions and emancipatory research practices cannot guarantee tranformative outcomes. We can work towards social change but must acknowledge that it may not happen directly because of our efforts, nor when we expect it to: it may not happen in our lifetimes. Small-scale qualitative studies may prove more influential than large-scale ones; research undertaken by those who use health and social care services and their carers may be just as influential as that carried out by professional researchers, see Cox et al. (2008/9). While recognizing that our efforts may have results that are small-scale and finite, we therefore work towards change, constantly asking ourselves: 'Are things better than they were?' (McTaggart, 1996, p. 245).

According to Prigogine (1980, 1997), complexity science repudiates dichotomies, so applying it as a model for understanding research would mean that there is no clearly defined boundary between researcher and researched; between those of us with access to particular forms of knowledge and those of us without that access. However, some knowledges clearly are valued more highly, or less highly, than others (Grover, 2004; Harding, 1991; Hill Collins, 1991; Pole et al., 1999). Using the concept of our shared membership of complex adaptive systems, maintaining dialogue, communication, and acknowledging reciprocal influences between agents (researchers and research subjects) can lead to the emergence of shared learnings; with power coming not from the academic domain alone but emerging from the experiences of partnership in our research relationships (Latour, 2000, p. 116). Lee comments on the need for a synthesizing approach to knowledge rather than a reductionist approach and looks to complexity as a possible solution (Lee, 1996, p. 198). Thus could complexity science assist in researchers seeing – and reaching – beyond Cartesian dualisms of subject and object, knower and known.

'Complex systems are open systems: when observed, the observer becomes part of the system' (Burton, 2002, p. 2). Here I am using this concept to think about the issue that researchers always influence in some way, and become part of, the complex adaptive systems we engage with. Acknowledging our part in such systems reveals that an attitude to research that is about the model of the autonomous researcher forging a career – a concept which derives from the sort of individualism seen in Western free-market liberalism and in rational choice theory – is misguided. We cannot 'do' research and walk away – we must have 'commitment' (Gouldner, 1970, 1973); we must have a sense of responsibility for the effects of our actions (Sparkes, 1993). Thinking and using 'I' and 'We' in accounts of research would reflect our shared membership of complex adaptive systems.

The concept of agents; our varying amounts of information about parts of systems which we may share with others, together with an ability to adjust our actions as a result of information shared, assists in consideration of by whom research findings are disseminated. Many researchers are located in higher education or other professional settings and are thus 'discursively privileged' (Alcoff, 1991, p. 19); most of our research subjects are not thus privileged. Debates about the appropriation of the 'other' in research – Opie (1992) – and about the complexities in attempting to speak about others, but not *for* them, are many and thoughtful: for example, Moore (1994); Said (1989); Scott (1991) and Trinh (1989). However, eschewing omniscience is not the same as refusing political engagement or commitment and if we undertake research in order to engage in transformative projects, we must ensure that findings about the lives of peoples who are oppressed and who lack security and safety, reach the eyes and ears of those with power to make a difference to their situations: 'While we cannot fully control how research findings are heard, seen, understood, and interpreted': 'a *partial* loss of control does not entail a *complete* loss of accountability' (Alcoff, 1991, p17, emphases in the original).

Not to speak, argues Alcoff is to renounce our own agency: 'a retreat from speaking for will not result in an increase in receptive listening in all cases... such a retreat... significantly undercuts the possibility of political effectivity' (Alcoff, 1991, p. 19). And Spivak (1988, cited in Alcoff, 1991, p. 21) criticizes assumptions made by some: 'self-abnegating intellectuals' that 'the oppressed can transparently represent their own true interests'. She asserts the need for a 'speaking to' in which the intellectual (here the researcher) neither abnegates their discursive privilege, 'nor presumes an authenticity of the oppressed, but still allows for the possibility that the oppressed will produce a 'countersentence' that can then suggest a new historical narrative' (Alcoff, 1991, p. 22).

Alcoff (1991) recapitulates Spivak (1988) in thinking that this is not as straightforward as it sounds, and urges researchers and others to examine critically our own need to speak, to develop conditions for 'speaking to' and with, thus remaining open to transformative possibilities – or, as Denzin and Lincoln have it, 'radical democratic practice' (Denzin and Lincoln, 2003b, p. xi) .

Most of us are – or feel – constrained to present our research findings in a 'tidy', linear fashion, effectively rendering the complex simple. Research presentation, including much qualitative research, almost always follows a convention which is reductionist, yet such a presentational style is antithetical to the multifaceted nature of complexity science; often there is little sense of 'conceptualising the immanent dynamism and open-endedness of the world' (Gardiner,

1993, p. 778). Opie raises important questions about how we do or don't include our research subjects in research accounts and how we write:

> If one accepts [the] ... argument that all data is inherently unstable, how much is this instability and otherness of the participants fully acknowledged in the research report and therefore recognized as affecting any conclusions? What does it mean to write critically but less authoritatively when the act of writing is so strongly associated with authority and centrality? (Opie, 1992, p. 57)

Complexity science directs us towards different forms of writing – which, while existing research practices remain hegemonic – may have to be in addition to, rather than instead of, the required reports of findings. Although not drawing upon complexity concepts, Schwandt, (2001, p. 224) writes about 'messy texts' which

> reject the 'finished' appearance of a realist tale written by a detached observer. They reflect an open-endedness, incompleteness, the full presence of the writer in the text, and the continual movement back and forth between description, interpretation and multiple voices.

Writings like these would be closer to the spirit of complexity science than many current accounts. Some researchers, including Ellis and Bochner (1996); Lather (2001); Lather and Smithies (1997) are already developing research narratives similar to these described above. And Richardson's (1997, 2003) thinking about writing research suggests that, for her, it is a process that has some similarities with the concept of deterministic chaos.

As noted by Robert Jensen in another context:

> predictably the search for causation and the use of science leads most everyone to say that we just don't know enough to say for sure. But a shift in emphasis and method offers a way to state not The Truth (or conclude we don't yet know The Truth), but a way to tell true stories and begin to make trustworthy moral and political decisions. (Jensen, 1998, p. 101)

Discussion

Delanty's thinking about 'new constructions of human experience in a world which is neither modern nor postmodern' (Delanty, 2000, p. 5) indicates the necessity to consider how these experiences might be researched. There is a need for research which reflects 'multiple genuine perceptions of one and the same reality' (Mendez et al., 1988 p. 147).

Complexity science challenges positivist epistemological thinking by undermining the idea that there is always knowable truth out there to be discovered through research; it also augments interpretive and deconstructionist methodologies by reminding us how much is not knowable and how knowledge is often culturally and temporally specific (Medd, 2002). An early influence in the interpretivist paradigm and in qualitative research is Weber (1978), with his emphasis on different forms of 'verstehen' – 'aktuelles' and 'erklärendes'; the latter being the one most researchers seek. Application of complexity science reminds us of, and returns us to, the origins of qualitative research – with an epistemological framework that is about processes of exploration, understanding, and learning.

Alvesson and Sköldberg (2000, p. 4) note that, rather than methods, epistemology is one of the 'determinants of good social science'. As I have argued throughout this chapter, complexity science requires of us researchers that we look and see in a different way to that which we now do: 'thinking in [the] new way' (Bateson, 2000). With an epistemological framework of complexity science, the methods for undertaking qualitative research remain the same as they are currently, but our choosing *which* methods is influenced by a different understanding of research relationships, praxes and processes, and so should be more considered than perhaps is usual. Bateson's comments on this process are apposite:

> I distrust the applied scientists' claim that what they do is useful and necessary. I suspect their impatient enthusiasm for action, their raring to go, is not just a symptom of impatience .... I suspect that it covers deep epistemological panic. (Bateson and Bateson, 1987, p. 15)

Understanding our shared membership of complex adaptive systems encourages the recognition that we and our research subjects cannot be understood separately from the influences of bodily experiences and emotions – no longer transcendent, detached – and thus links to ongoing developments in social theory and policy and in qualitative research more generally.

As noted above, Sweeney asserts that debates about complexity science are 'universal ... exploring *the fundamental nature of explanation, representation and interpretation of knowledge*' (Sweeney, 2002, p. 19, my emphasis).

Together with understanding, explanation, representation, and the inter-pretation of knowledge are included in what we qualitative researchers and our research subjects look for in our research endeavours: we don't look for certainty and predictability (Waldrop, 1992)

Complexity science allows for the possibility of both certainty and uncertainty. It can encompass the complex and subtle interactions between environment and adaptation and can assist in identifying general processes that govern adaptive processes in different sorts of systems. Rather than either the search for quantifiable fundamental laws or the undermining of any truth claims, it allows for an acceptance of order while acknowledging uncertainty, emergence, and the need for interpretation. It allows researchers to recognize not only what is present and observable, but also to recognize tacit and subjective knowledge (Polanyi, 1967) which inform social processes and the (non-linear) 'pattern which connects' (Bateson, 1979).

In its repudiation of dichotomies, complexity science provides a model for conceptualizing and undertaking research that links us researchers inextricably with our research subjects. This emphasis on the relational dimensions of complexity science as model for research praxis echoes Gramsci's (1971) concept of prefigurative politics, where activists endeavour to model non-exploitative relationships and prac-tices, corresponding to the improved social world we aim to achieve (see also Kaufman, 2003). In seeking different, less instrumental forms of research relationships, we begin to see how 'the discourses of qualita-tive research can be used to help imagine and create a free, democratic society' (Denzin and Lincoln, 2003b, p. xi).

Conclusion

In complexity science there is always potential for change in systems, even if we cannot anticipate when and how they will occur. The appli-cation of complexity science to qualitative research enables us to think about how we might transcend the boundaries of the academy and develop more extensive networks and partnerships. In the struggle between the transformative potential of prefigurative politics and the established order (Gramsci, 1971), the application of complexity science concepts to qualitative research indicates possibilities of a more eman-cipatory praxis, underpinned by an epistemological approach that emphasizes understandings and learnings rather than knowledge. Deploying complexity science renders a teleological (ends justifying means) attitude to research obsolete and assists in conceptualizing our previous less-than-perfect research differently becoming the change we want to see, while acknowledging that further change may be necessary; and thus drawing from Taylor's (1989) concept of 'epistemic gain': 'movement from a problematic position to a more adequate one within a field of available alternatives (rather than epistemology's mythical movement from falsity to truth)' (Calhoun, 2000, p. 538). Such a conceptual framework can indicate how to bring about change starting with research itself.

Researching without certainty and in pursuit of social change is a challenge for qualitative research in the twenty-first century. 'Like Columbus, we have to take the chance that the mapmakers were wrong' (Summit, 1988, p. 52) and acknowledge that we are experiencing a possible Kuhnian shift in inquiry, one in which relationships and outcomes can never be fully anticipated and one which comprises both challenges and opportunities for a renewed critical engagement with the social world.

2
The Notion of Ambivalence: Human Action and Social Change beyond Analytical Individualism

Thomas Geisen

Introduction

There has been much debate in social research about the understanding of social change. At first glance it seems that conflicting positions are dominant, which define social change as that which is determined by societal development and seen as a process upon which the influence of human action is very limited. The determining aspect of the social was profoundly expressed by Karl Marx, who emphasized that while human beings make history they do not exist in free and chosen conditions and so the tradition of all 'death generations' is like a nightmare on the brain of the living (Marx, 1960, p. 115). An alternative to this perspective of the human being bound by social conditions brought into being by previous generations is the notion that social change is the result of human action. Indeed, the longing for a better life and for a better world becomes efficacious. Accordingly, human action is seen as a thriving force through which social change is propelled. Walter Benjamin argued that such actions could be detected and identified in history. Past events show the capacity of human beings to achieve social change and improve social conditions but can fail – this was seen by Benjamin as a weak messianic force which is passed from previous generations to the current one (Benjamin, 1977, pp. 251–252).

Both positions emphasize different aspects of the relation between past and present. Whereas Marx emphasized the influence of the past on current conditions, Benjamin believed that social emancipation could be similarly impacted from the past. Gottfried Mergner (1999, p. 13) sees herein the relation between the objective social condition and the subjective everyday practice, new perspectives, and the remnants of ruling power, as well as resistance and adjustment. These contradictions do not demonstrate a mere transient emergence. Rather, they are deeply inscribed into social life and can be characterized and labelled as ambivalence (Geisen, 2003).

Starting with some general thoughts on social change and social research, this chapter seeks first to discuss analytical individualism as one of the central theoretical assumptions in social research. Limits and consequences of analytical individualism are revealed. In the second part of this chapter, the concept of ambivalence will be discussed and explored as a complementary theoretical and methodological approach for qualitative research because it avoids the pitfalls of analytical individualism by applying analytical pluralism. Finally, the theory of 'social limits to learning' (Mergner, 1999, 2005) will be presented and discussed as a method which incorporates the concept of ambivalence.

This chapter argues that the approach and concept of ambivalence social research leads to a better understanding of human action, and by doing so provides an important contribution to social change.

Social change and social research

Social change, interventions, and subjectivity

The modern longing for fundamental social change is expressed in the deep hope of humanity for a world and life which is better than the current one. One expression of this longing for social change are the many stories in which reality is often described and referred to by a magic storyteller, as a means through which secret wishes and dreams for a miraculous change become truth. For the modern world, the dishwasher-story where hard work and volition enables a poor dishwasher to transform himself into a wealthy man can be seen as an emblematic icon of capitalist society. Referring to the Christian tradition, the Bible often uses this kind of story telling to show a turning point in which the faith of man is changed by God through a single event, such as the 'Road to Damascus' – a fundamental change from Saul to Paul – illustrates such a turning point. Each perception is different in crucial ways. Whereas in the modern story, humanity is the creator of social change, in the Christian tradition social change comes about by forces which lie outside the control of human beings. However, the similarity between these stories regarding social change is striking. Both interpret social change as a one-dimensional consequence of intervention and action. In this perspective, reality is already dichotomously ordered.

Analytical individualism

In scientific terms, the distinction between intervention and action is described as that between the subject and the object. For Kant the subject is defined by cognition and action while the object is defined as the aim of an action of human cognitive faculty (Kant, 1995). Hegel's critique of Kant referred to this clear distinction between subject and object, and he argued for the dialectical character of both. In other words, subject and object are influenced by each other (Hegel, 1988). In the dialectical approach, the distinction between subject and object receives a temporal character. This means that the split between subject and object is somehow blurred, while at the same time each keeps its constitutive character. The underlying assumption behind this analysis is the ascription of certain values to an individual, for example the individual is understood as a subject that dominates objects by their actions or the individual is understood as an object embraced and dominated by others, and is led into the core of modern culture which is based on the assumption that humans are independent individuals endowed with rationality.

Based on the assumption of the independency and rationality of the human being, social theory developed a perspective in which the individual is predominant and at the centre of analytical thinking. As a result, in theory and practice analytical individualism has become a core element of modern society. Analytical individualism refers to one or more persons and by doing so reduces them to a single category – the individual, the social group, the community, the society – in which either the individual becomes detached from its manifold relations towards others and becomes seen as a human being in 'isolation'; or the differences between many individuals disappear and those individuals merge to only one 'individual', for instance the peer group or the community. The 'isolated' individual – as a single person yet also as the member of a group or community or of society itself – has been put as the centre of interest in social research. Analytical individualism in this context refers to the attempt of ordering a plurality of deeds and values in its relations to the individual object under scrutiny. The individual is the result of a process in which it is constructed and endowed with a unique coherence and character by ascribing certain deeds and values towards it. However, in each 'individual' the antagonism between the 'ego' and the 'community' works as a contradiction between the values and expectations of antagonistic ethnicities (Jouhy, 1996, p. 86). Jouhy argues that it is not sufficient to oppose the category of 'corporate feeling' to 'egocentrism'. Moreover, there has to be a developed criterion which helps to evaluate and appraise the criteria of value within antagonistic 'ethnicities' which claim to be 'communities' within society. They have to be evaluated and appraised on an individual basis (Jouhy, 1996, p. 86).

Given that categorization is at the basis of analytical individualism, there are difficulties in understanding plurality. The focus on the individual(s) diminishes the simple fact that there can only be an individual if there is a collective and/or plurality of others existing in contrast. For the modern understanding of the world – dominated by an individualistic world perspective – this criticism is far-reaching, especially with regard to the nature of social change.

This can be illustrated by using the two examples from the beginning of this chapter about the dishwasher and Saul and Paul. These stories represent the different understandings of how social change can occur. In the dishwasher story, social change occurs as a fact and emanates from social life itself and the inwardness of the life processes referred to as labour. The ongoing and perpetual use of the labour force is what guides social change. Hannah Arendt emphasized this by arguing that 'social change' is something that happens because the social is part of the circular processes of life itself (Arendt, 1994, 1996). Further when humans create their own world from natural resources and external forces, the life-processes from which social change is driven have lent some of these forces to the human world.

In comparison, the Saul/Paul story is an emblematic example of when only a single deed – in this instance, one that was carried out by God – leads to a fundamental change. Transferring this to the human world, it illustrates how social change can be actively created by humans through a process in which they take possession of the world and in doing so make it their own by creating an enduring world and establishing continual relations between each other through individual and mutual action as Arendt argues by emphasizing activities of work and human action. According to Arendt the fundamental ambivalence of social change is bound to the natural life-process itself, while also resulting in human action. Whereas the life-process demands labour as its basic human activity, Arendt showed that the importance of thought and action in the processes by which human beings give meaning to the world at large and through individual interactions with others in their common world. The ambivalence of social change as a perpetual motion of life and as a result of human action also influences research, methodology and methods, since the meaning-giving processes are most important for understanding.

Qualitative and quantitative approaches in social research

Assumptions of social change and reality have influenced the development of methodology and methods in social research, where the quantitative and the qualitative approaches can be distinguished. In both approaches, individuals with their actions and meanings become the objects of research. Whereas the quantitative approach towards social research is based on the predominance of probability in the actions of the many, the qualitative approach focuses on the meanings given to actions by the individuals. Here different patterns become identified and are understood as 'objective possibilities' (Weber, 1988, p. 194). Both approaches in social research differ fundamentally from each other. The quantitative approach essentially searches for similarities and general patterns in the actions and thinking of people, relies on numbers, and tends to neglect the characteristics of the single case.

In contrast, the qualitative approach focuses its inquiries on the possibilities and limitations of individual action and looks to understand the special characteristics of each single case. Since qualitative approaches do not focus on numbers but on single cases, the problem of generalization appears. Often this is solved by developing a typology. Here 'ideal-types' (Weber, 1988, p. 194) represent common patterns and/or strategies which have been identified in different single cases. The ideal-types can be interpreted as different ways of understanding and action which can be found in society given the same context and conditions. There is, however, another important difference between the quantitative and qualitative approaches: Quantitative approaches search for probabilities and rely on continuities, whereas qualitative research highlights discontinuities and bring attention to new phenomena. In other words, qualitative research makes both current structures and new phenomena visible.

There is ongoing and controversial debate and criticism about the different approach of quantitative and qualitative research to methodology. The main criticism of the quantitative approach is its standardization which limits the possible responses from an interviewee into pre-defined answers. The qualitative approach addresses this point by allowing interviewees space to present their own varied opinions and perspectives and situate them in a specific social context. However, it attracts criticism because of its lack of true representation or its opportunistic character, so stories from the interviewees are strongly dependent on the current interpretation of the situation in the interview itself and therefore do not provide reliable insights of past events or current issues.

The strength of the qualitative approach is its ability to uncover and give sense to complex situations whereas the quantitative approach seeks to quantify or precisely measure the extent and existence of a given phenomenon in a society. This has consequences in the underlying systematic of the research. Whereas the quantitative approach seeks an explanation and follows a systematic process of causes and consequences, qualitative social research follows the hermeneutic approach, a research tradition which is characterized by the reconstruction of the meaning given in a specific social context. The hermeneutic understanding is not simply based on the study of events and reconstructing their context of meaning, but also on the analytical process in which the researchers try to understand their research findings. By extension, Giddens characterizes the qualitative approach as a 'double hermeneutic' (Giddens, 1997) where interpretation and understanding are not only necessary for conducting the research process and analysing its findings but also for theories used in the analysis of empirical data. In social research, both empirical findings and social theories need to be understood in terms of its value targets and its underlying assumptions and perspectives. Under this dictum, there is a need and demand in social research for reflecting upon theory, methodology, and methods. For research which seeks to analyse and understand social change while at the same time endeavouring to deliver knowledge to inform social change it is necessary that the underlying theoretical assumption(s) of research and its consequences are duly reflected.

Plurality and ambiguity

This means that analytical individualism, which seeks to identify action, thinking, and meaning on the basis of the assumption of an isolated individual as the central focus of social search, has to be overcome because plurality in society becomes theoretically reduced to a mere functional means and is therefore too easily available for hegemony and dominance. Recent theoretical debates on post-colonialism, feminism, and post-modern conditions shed light on the fact of social plurality in society contrary to the discourse on analytical individualism (Bauman, 1995; Benhabib et al., 1993; Bhaba, 1995; Bronfen et al., 1997; Butler, 1993; Institut für Sozialforschung Frankfurt, 1994; Zima, 1997). These debates do not only analyse and contest the predominance of 'the West over the Rest' (Hall, 1994a, b), but they also argue for the necessity of a new perception and understanding of plurality. Postmodern theories give new access to the understanding of plurality in the human world.

By means of deconstruction, it confronts a modern kind of mastering plurality by way of categorization, with analytical individualism seen as one of its by-products. In its consequences, categorization means the process of a manifest and consistent ascription of meaning towards a phenomenon. In such cases, decidedness becomes the character of an action of which heterogeneous and ambiguous meanings become excluded. Therefore, in modernity the individual is understood to be a coherent individual who overcomes and solves ambiguities.

Zygmunt Bauman refers to the fact that categorization seeks to produce unambiguity (Bauman, 1991). However, at the same time at which mastery of ambiguity has been sought, ambiguity itself becomes even more visible which leads to cyclical increase and emphasis of categorization. In understanding social change and research methodology and methods, an understanding of social reality should be based upon the processes of categorization in which ambiguities are neglected or perceived as temporary and conquerable. Here, the notion of progress can be understood as a development in which contradictions become solved and transcended.

In social research, the process of mastery and the overcoming of ambiguities have often become ascribed to individuals as their singular achievement. The production of unambiguity can therefore be seen as the underlying assumption and judgement in social research. In the quantitative approach, unambiguity is produced by processes of abstraction and by focusing on probability. Qualitative research, however, tries to understand the individual by seeking to understand the complexity of their situation and actions. It is an approach which tries to improve understanding under conditions of plurality. Therefore, it is not by accident, that interest in qualitative research (which had its first huge impact as early as in the 1920s and 1930s) has grown during the past two decades worldwide and in the European context since the 1990s. Further, the qualitative approach is not an approach per se which is free of systematization, as illustrated in the processes through which a type is constructed from a particular case (Kelle and Kluge, 2007) and not least the way in which researchers apply qualitative research methods and interpret ambiguity in their findings. This is not so much a question of methodology and methods but a question of the theory which guides researchers in their quest for understanding. Therefore an important (pre-)condition for understanding in social research is the quest to make ambivalence visible.

Consequences of analytical individualism for qualitative social research

In the quantitative approach, analytical individualism is difficult to avoid because of the inherent limits discussed above. Similarly, the qualitative approach is not completely free of such limits due to its reductionist thinking and outlook. These limitations result because analytical individualism not only refers to methods and methodology but more so to social theories. Here the key question is: What relevance is given to the identified contradictions in the empirical material and how do they become interpreted with reference to social theories? Here the epistemological question regarding the emergence and structure within the empirical material can be identified and the relevance given to them for understanding is ascertained. The following discussion focuses solely on qualitative research, questioning how the limitations of analytical individualism can be overcome.

Ideal-types and generalizations

Qualitative social research is directed towards the identification of a phenomenon and the reason it is using certain terms and concepts. In doing so, distinctiveness is seen as a core element for describing and understanding the given phenomenon. According to Max Weber, distinctiveness and directness are important criteria for using a term in social research (Weber, 1988). By starting with the use and application of theoretical terms in the description of social reality, social research in Weber's view leads to the construction of ideal-types. These are different from reality in the sense that they are theoretical descriptions for measurement and judging and not applicable to phenomena in reality. Reality is thus measured and judged through a process in which the researcher applies the theoretical assumption of a clearly constructed situation or abstract category towards a plural and heterogeneous social situation or event. The ascription of a specific, typological set of explanations towards a situation which was constituted by individual action and the consequent ascriptions of meaning towards this situation can be identified as analytical individualism. The term and concept both refer to the individual and their actions.

Weber argued that there is a difference between ideal-types and reality; however, this does not affect the validity of the ideal-type. Rather it can be seen as a confirmation of its existence, since ideal-types are constructed in a two-fold process which combines both inductive and deductive methods. In qualitative research, the construction of ideal-types in such a twofold process is based on the results of abductive reasoning (Pierce, 2004) where the best explanation is derived from the available empirical evidence. Qualitative research methods differ in the ways they create (ideal-)types. In Grounded Theory (Glaser and Strauss, 2005), 'generalization' seeks to develop a typology by integrating similar cases into one single ideal-type; other qualitative approaches have developed a different method of generalization. In Biographical Research (Rosenthal, 2005), the construction of a typology refers to the exemplarity during the course of biographical development while Objective Hermeneutics (Wernet, 2000) seeks to identify the general within a particular case by analysing the latent structures of meaning. Independent from more concrete methodology and methods, objective hermeneutics is common to all research methods where during the process of data collection generalization or gaining of generalized knowledge takes place. The benefit of these qualitative methods is that they show very clearly the importance that subjective meaning is given with regard to reality and individual action.

Limits of interpreting interviews

There are, however, limitations which can be seen in the interpretation of narratives. In qualitative research the data-material is based on narratives which are produced in the research process. The focus on the narratives entails the dilemma that 'narratives' have to be of 'good quality', and something as stated by an interviewee. But as we all know, some people are good story-tellers and others are not, and what does this mean for qualitative research? What do we do in research with narratives which are not 'good quality'? Such limits of narration are controversial and they are discussed at length under the banner of 'narrative competence' (Küsters, 2006) where it is argued that this competence is influenced by the 'social background' (Fuchs-Heinritz, 2005) of the interviewee. However, it is also clear, that these kinds of limitations are always inherent in social research and therefore no particular method can be blamed for this shortfall. In such cases, Ethnographic Research (Crang and Cook, 2007) which combines different types of data collection including participant observation seems a workable solution to overcome some of these limitations.

Another limitation of qualitative research occurs during the interpretation process of the data where the aim is to analyse latent structures of meaning in a narrative. Some of the methods in qualitative research, for example in objective hermeneutics (Wernet, 2000), try to find out the internal and systematic structure through which regularities in the meaning-giving life-processes are discovered. Here the aim is to gain knowledge about the regularities of understanding and action. Given that options in a real-life situation follow certain rules, objective hermeneutics seek to identify these very rules while also seeking to understand the subjective dealing with these rules in each specific case. However, this approach follows a problematic structure where the 'real' interpretation is not given by those that are being researched but rather is left to be detected or picked up by the researcher from the textual material each party produces during the research process, for example in narrative-interviews (Glinka, 1998), or from existing material, such as letters. In doing this the right and the opportunity for the interpretation of research findings is taken away from the individual under scrutiny and is fully given over to the researcher(s).

In qualitative research specifically during the process of data-production, the dialogical situation is predominant, and in research practice, the analysis process can often be characterized as a mono-logical process in which interpretations are produced only by one person or a group of researchers. This means, that as while the process of categorization – another possibility to describe systematic analysis and interpretation – begins, the dialogical situation ceases. Sometimes findings and results from the research process are returned to the research subjects for discussion. The difficulty here is that those absent from the process where categories were developed have difficulties participating in the subsequent analysis process and in being understood. In such 'uninformed' communication, the danger of the (re)confirmation of working relationships characterized by dominance in the research process is obvious. It becomes even more relevant if the research focuses on marginalized social groups, where the structural situation of powerlessness impacts more upon social research.

For the research process, this means a detachment of the research findings from the researched subjects. Action research tries to avoid this disconnection by establishing a collaborative research process in which those being researched are established in the role of 'co-researchers' (McIntyre, 2008) from the outset. This process can be seen as a process of reification and dispossession in which the researched become mere objects of the researchers and the research process. The danger of 'reification' and 'dispossession' is also prevalent in the phenomenological hermeneutic tradition of social research (Schütz, 1993), where the research process can result in a 'substitution' or 'assisting' interpretation by which 'objective meaning' is produced (Schütz, 1993, pp. 186–190).

Another drawback can be found in the biographical approach of Rosenthal (2005), which distinguishes between the 'experienced' and the 'narrated' biography. Here there is also a risk of 'reification', when the dualism of experience and narration is mistakenly understood as a praxis of proving and identifying what has been wrong in the narration and tries to explain this by telling the 'real' story.

An example of the problems of 'reification' and 'dispossession' in qualitative research, taken from the author's own research project, is seen in research practices which aim to detect and identify causes of motivation and action assumed and hidden in the contradictions of the empirical material. Such research practices, focus on 'faults' in the narratives, and so often neglects the purpose and value targets openly presented and told in the narrative. One rationale often used in such situations by researchers is the devaluation of such narratives as mere 'theorizations'. Another difficulty for social research is how to deal with narratives which refer to ideologies and tend to be characterized as individual 'theories'. What is their relevance for the research process, especially for analysis? During analysis of the interview material, some of the researchers argued that the reconstruction of the 'right-wing' attitude and understanding was not relevant to the aim of research, which was focused on 'family-education and right-wing extremism'. A 'right-wing' attitude and understanding was implicit here in the detached behaviour of the young interview subjects and interpreted as a form of camouflage of other social difficulties and problems. In such an understanding and practice of research, this kind of information is devalued and qualified only at a 'surface' level. This leads to misunderstandings because it is at the surface level that value targets which guide individual thinking and action are named and become understood by the researchers. With devaluation of their concrete attitudes and neglect of their own understanding – called 'theoretization' or mere ideology – of the given situation, the subjectivity of the researched is questioned; they are seen as mere objects, forced and driven like certain constellations and family situations into right-wing extremism. From a theoretical perspective the neglect of 'theoretizations' given by the researched – it can be argued that this is a kind of 'second order' interpretation of the researched themselves – is also the neglect of the processes in which the ascription of certain values towards social reality become visible and concepts for the future become formulated.

In any case, it can be stated that as soon as the dialogical principle disappears from the research process, the dominance of the researcher's own interpretation over that of the researched prevails. Logically speaking, this procedure cannot be criticized since its basic assumption is that behind the individual scenario there is a general structure which unifies all those with a similar social background and individual circumstances. For example, this means that when Objective Hermeneutics are applied to marginalized individuals, not only claims to interpret a single situation, but also to identify core characteristics of situations in which the marginalized individuals live. Behind the individual, a society is visible. Therefore, according to Objective Hermeneutics the individual himself/herself as a free actor disappears and becomes a mere actor of the social. By eliminating subjectivity, analytical individualism is finally referred as the 'meta-individual'.

Critique of analytical individualism

This example of Objective Hermeneutic shows that analytical individualism as a theoretical concept explains the process in which the perspectives humans take into the world are understood from an individual position. But the 'individual' can be very different, depending on how that individual is constituted in the process of social research. This means that the individual can be a single person, a group, or even society as a whole. Analytical individualism refers to the fact that findings become interpreted either from or towards a given identified individual. Here, differences become unified in a generalized 'individual' – a person, an ideal-type, or a society. Research processes based on analytical individualism tend to neglect the fundamental plurality and heterogeneity which is the central characteristic of human life. Plurality and heterogeneity are not only the central characteristic of the many, living together and having different kinds of relations between each other, but they are also central to the understanding of the individual itself. Therefore, it is not identity which is central to the understanding of the human but difference and its validation. Analytical individualism neglects those differences and their associated validations, and instead views positive development where unity and coherence can be identified and made 'visible'. In contrast, contradictions and ambivalences are interpreted as critical events with a negative and disruptive influence on a life story and for personal development.

In the discussion on research methodology, methods and practice so far, there has been an attempt to characterize and criticize the term 'analytical individualism' in current social research as a practice which does not sufficiently consider or indeed tends to neglect the social plurality and complexity that exists. This deficit is deeply inscribed into social research and its methodology. On the one hand, 'analytical individualism' focuses either on the individual or the social group, or on the social group or the society. As a result, the individual as a con- flicted unit in which dominant and latent feelings and imaginations are merged is neglected and remains invisible. This means, that the components of ego-centrism and corporate feeling, of ethnocentrism and universalism which the individual contains are not reflected (Jouhy, 1996, p. 78). Further, consequences and conclusions become one-sided and do not allow the 'as-well-as' option. Such an alternative is mostly perceived and analysed as problematic. But only the 'as-well- as'-approach allows the researcher to recognize and understand why actively produced contradictions should not be considered a hin- drance but rather as a productive means for the individual to deal with different demands constantly approaching and confronting them in the social world.

On the other hand, the processes of value targeting of things and actions goes beyond the scope of 'analytical individualism' because it is not only directed towards different things and actions; it varies and is often contradictory depending on a given social settings; for example, particular communities, institutions and organizations, or society. Contradictions in social embeddedness are crucial for the understand- ing of social action since they represent plurality. Here understanding results from a process of co-production of knowledge in which differ- ent perspectives inform and support an individual's understanding and actions. These contradictions – being constantly produced and managed – can become apparent through a research practice which seeks to identify and analyse the different processes of value targeting and of the allocation of subjective meaning towards things and action. Such an approach is directed towards the improvement of existing research methodology and methods and is ideally based on the under- standing of the complexity of the social as ambivalent.

The concept of ambivalence as a concept for analysing pluralism

The concept of ambivalence

Ambivalence describes the synchronistic presence of opposing ambitions and the term and concept have been introduced into social sciences by psychoanalysis. Freud understood ambivalence as a concept which could be applied to an event or action in which a 'double meaning' is apparent and is applicable in opposite directions. One of his examples was the word 'tabu' which had a double meaning of 'sacred' and 'impure'

(Freud, 2000, p. 357). He also posited that ambivalence was a key structure in understanding the relationship between father and son in patriarchal societies (Freud, 2000, p. 258). In the context of early childhood, ambivalence was discussed as a changing relation of love and hate which the child develops towards desired objects. As things progress, this ambivalence does not disappear but instead its presence is split up into a conscious and an unconscious part. Brenner (1990) emphasizes that early ambivalence does exist to a certain degree throughout our whole life, but weakens progressively as we reach adulthood. Following Freud, Brenner (1990) argues that early life experiences of ambivalence become partly sublimated by culture and partly suppressed and become part of the unconscious. Cultural processes and practice support such processes of dealing with both early and later life experiences of ambivalence, with patterns of dealing with ambivalence in childhood influencing responses in later life.

The 'conflict of ambivalence' becomes accelerated when humans must live together (Freud, 2000, p. 258). According to Freud, culture is intrinsically ambivalent. In social theory, the concept of ambivalence espoused by Freud was often understood as a dialectical principle (Bernfeld, 1971, p. 52). But 'dialectic' implies that there is an aim to displace the contradiction which was previously identified (Goldschmidt, 1993, p. 42). However, Freud's 'dialectic' is different, it is a dialectic which is not fixed by the 'thesis-antithesis-synthesis' schema, but rather it is a continuous and irreconcilable schema of 'thesis-antithesis' without the salvation of the 'synthesis' in view. Such a 'dialectic' can be defined as a 'standstill-dialectic'.

With the advent of post-modern theory, the concept of ambivalence regained new prominence in social theory, particularly through the work of Zygmunt Bauman in 'Ambivalence and Modernity' (1991). He argued that the cultural impetus of modernity was to bring about order to diminish ambivalence. However, this process was necessarily ambivalent in itself, since the quest for order leads as much to order as it leads to dis-order and/or ambivalence; in so doing the quest for order continues and may become stronger. Bauman emphasized:

> Taxonomy, classification, inventory, catalogue and statistics are paramount strategies of modern practice. Modern mastery is the power to divide, classify and allocate – in thought, in practice, in the practice of thought and in the thought of practice. Paradoxically, it is for this reason that ambivalence is the main affliction of modernity and the most worrying of its concerns. (Bauman, 1991, p. 15)

The quest for order as a core element of modern society has already been described and emphasized by Horkheimer and Adorno. In the 'Dialectic of Enlightenment' they argue that Enlightenment has become the radical and mystic angst, the pure immanence of positivism. Nothing is allowed to stay outside because the mere conception of outside is the underlying source of Angst (Horkheimer and Adorno, 1988, p. 22). Of course, the precondition here is, that the distinction between 'in' and 'out' already exists. And as such, leads back to the problem of categorization.

Ambivalence, complexity, and social research

According to these issues surrounding ambivalence, a problem for social research becomes obvious: does the quest to make ambivalence visible not lead to the criticized process of ordering and categorizing? Again, this problem might not be solved by social research, since the task of social research is to make different and contesting perspectives visible and to seek a better understanding of the plurality of possible perspectives for analysing social reality. Being able to advance understanding of social reality, categories are needed. Yet categories can always be challenged, and the greater the number of aspects of social life that are analysed, the more, it is argued, categories have to be developed and used to assist understanding and explanation. This means that social research in general relies on plurality in the use of categories. Yet the manner in which social research seeks to reduce this plurality, in its extreme form to a single category from which all others are derived, not only violates plurality but also supports the possibility of its instrumental use for dominance. The analytical reduction of a phenomenon to only a few factors and criteria opens possibilities for clear positions and fast (re) action. By contrast, analysing what is multifaceted in social research can make important contributions in comprehending and making visible modern rule in its practice and function towards the ruled. In this sense, social research is critical in as much as it is improving the understanding of how complex the social and its developments are.

To improve the understanding within social research the approach to ambivalence is highly important, since it seeks to find and identify not only differences but also the meaning and appraisal given to these differences by the individuals in different, competing social contexts. In doing this, the concept of ambivalence supports in theory and practice an epistemological position in which it is not so much objects and deeds that are seen as the most important for understanding but rather the relevance and meaning given to them by the individuals concerned.

Therefore, an approach based upon ambivalence should examine how relations become established through deeds and communication, and attempt to understand the ascribed and established meaning(s). In searching out understandings of ambivalent relations researchers must be sensitive to people in minority positions, as well as to those in dominant ones, developing an understanding of how these positions arise. Such an approach is simultaneously synchronic and diachronic in perspective. With regard to the synchronic perspective, Sartre called this a 'cross-moving totality'; it is both independent and dependent from the diachronic perspective (Sartre, 1964, p. 66). Here ambivalence abandons analytical individualism and seeks to establish an analytical pluralism. In practice this means different scopes structuring human life are combined. First, there are the individuals in their concrete areas of life; second, there are the different communities within which individuals are interwoven; third, the more abstract social space of society which establishes the concrete historical conditions for the individuals and communities; fourth, the global-society which increasingly influences the economy and the living conditions of all societies, and by extension has influence over communities and individuals (Mergner, 1999).

Such a complex approach is highly demanding for social researchers. However, given that such a theoretical perspective can make a valuable contribution to improve social research, some methodological considerations will be presented and discussed in the following section.

Methodological considerations for research based on ambivalence

The basic methodological assumption of ambivalence is its shift from analytical individualism towards analytical pluralism. Analytical individualism is based on the reduction of plurality to a single category from which everything is derived: for example, everything becomes understood and explained from an individual standpoint, from a social perspective, from labour activities or from communicative processes. In contrast, analytical pluralism seeks to analyse the different relations humans have established between each other, not only by theoretical and empirical analysis but also by understanding the meanings given to them by both, the researchers and the 'researched subjects' (Erdheim, 1992, pp. viii–ix). These processes in which meaning is given to an action, deed, or event are characterized by a situation which is synchronic and diachronic at once. This means that situations cannot be characterized by ascribing only one characteristic to them; for example, they are not characterized by commonality or difference, but by commonality and difference. They are ambivalent in a sense that they must be understood in a 'two-in-one' perspective, meaning that they are at the same time in and out, equal and different, united and opposed.

Against this background, pluralism is the result of different backgrounds and understanding which can be applied to a situation because of its ambivalent character. Therefore, the basis of analytical pluralism is the thesis that human relations are established under certain conditions given and taken over by the past, as Marx emphasized for the given conditions and Benjamin for the hope of social change. But at the same time in human action is also the possibility of a new beginning; the capability to establish something new which is unpredictable and cannot be traced back to past events (Arendt, 1994). In these new beginnings, the human aspiration to exceed a situation can be identified. Indeed, it is through this human aspiration to exceed the limits of a given situation that is the origin of social change.

This aspiration towards exceeding existing defined situations was also seen by Sartre as a basic need of humans (Sartre, 1964, p. 75). Understanding human action must also involve the identification of the conditions with a given social context which determines social action, as far as these conditions limit the range of action. However, it is also necessary to analyse the imaginary relation to a certain object-to-be, which is wished to be reached or created by human action. The limitations of a given situation and the individual 'Entwurf' (outline) are the two key components human action is comprised of according to Sartre (Sartre, 1964, p. 75). Therefore increasing the range of possibilities is the aim of the acting human to exceed a given situation. The ambivalence here can be found in an underlying dual-relation: with regard to the 'given'; social practice is negative, but in relation to the 'object to-be', practice is positive (Sartre, 1964, p. 76). Interestingly, Sartre is still very close to the dialectic scheme and he does not apply the concept of ambivalence to that which he qualified as negative and positive. Therefore, there is a need for more distinctions to better understand what is gained and lost if social change takes place.

The great importance of these meaning-giving processes and actions is demanding for social research. It is not sufficient to reconstruct a given situation and corresponding action with its objective limitations and chances. Indeed, social research has to reconstruct the underlying judgement(s) of a situation and the attendant aspiration to understand how the social situation and action came into being in the first place. By taking this into consideration it must also be emphasized that an action in and of itself cannot be judged solely by its purpose but should also be viewed in terms of its result with an understanding that an action intrinsically has different layers of truth – a product of contradictions (Sartre, 1964, p. 80).

Often there is a choice between different and even conflicting options, which raises another difficulty for research in discovering just what range of possibilities exist. For the reconstruction and understanding of social action it is important not only to find out why certain options are taken but also to determine what options are rejected and why. This is of particular relevance when there are highly conflicting options involving moral judgement. In such cases, it is important to understand the inner debates and conflicts which lead to a final conclusion and action or set of actions and brought about a given situation. This is an ongoing task in human life since human beings are continuously confronted with ambivalence.

'Solving' a situation by choosing a given option for action means that not only has one situation been exceeded but possibly others affected by this action are exceeded at the same time. On the one hand this fact relies on an understanding of a situation as a phenomenon which is composed of different layers – and therefore conflicting aspirations are structural and logical inherent in a situation. On the other hand, an action taken to solve or react to one situation cannot be limited to this situation only but may also be relevant to others.

Ambivalence and the 'limits to learning'

There is a twofold methodological consequence of applying the concept of ambivalence to social research. First, any concrete action has to be understood as the result of a situation which was of ambivalent character. Social research seeks to analyse and understand this concrete situation not only by reconstructing the previous situation, the options of action that were available in that given situation, but also by searching and understanding the transcendent aspect in the action which takes place. Second, although dealing with ambivalence is an ongoing and never-ending process, by resolving current situations humans can use their experiences based on previous situations. They have evolved their capacity of dealing with ambivalent situations to fulfil their individual demands and needs. In other words, seeking to get fulfilment for individual needs and demands, processes of learning take place on how to deal with the conflicting demands that arise in ambivalent situations. As a result of these learning processes, patterns of action become established which support the problem-solving capability in an ambivalent situation. Sartre (1964, p. 82) calls such a process occurring over an individual's lifetime the development of character.

Ultimately, however, the learned solutions must always be tested for their problem-solving capacity in new situations to prove that they can be adapted to the new demands that are encountered by individuals and the society. Here 'learned' solutions may no longer be relevant and new learning takes place. But Mergner (1999, 2005) emphasizes limits to learning. Learning is understood here as

> a consciously transformative process of influencing one's own histori-cal reality. ... The ability of human being to take their history into their own hands is revealed in the practical capacity to learn. Any and all learning is shaped and limited by one's own ideas and the forms of communication acquired. Learning thus presupposes the communi-cative dissolution of one's own ossified past (and that of society) in the interest of the individual's own knowledge. The aim of all learning is to recognize the objects, arrangements, and institutions handed down form the past in their human constructedness and to appropriate them anew in one's own interest. (Mergner, 2005, p. 28)

Learning as presented here by Mergner is a process which embraces the fraught relations between past, present, and future. Current action can be understood as a result of learning to compromise between wished possibilities and experienced constraints (Mergner, 1999, p. 24). Following this approach, social research can be understood as a practice which seeks to reconstruct and understand human action as learning processes between given constraints and possibilities. This theoretical approach of 'social limits to learning' (Mergner, 2005) can be character-ized as ambivalent in the sense that it does not seek to diminish them.

Concluding remarks

In this chapter, analytical individualism was criticized because of its limited focus; it therefore does not reflect the complexity in which human beings operate and sustain their relations. Therefore, there is a desire and need for analytical pluralism to broaden this understanding. Qualitative research supports this need by reconstructing meaning and biographical development. However, ambivalence is a factor that is often not understood in its existential dimension, indeed it is perceived as the core problem of social change. In recent times the concept of ambivalence, first used in psychoanalysis, has regained attention and is often discussed in post-modern theories. But, it is its potential for social research that has so far not been explored.

If we consider the question of which method can best be applied to the reconstruction and understanding of ambivalence the biographical method seems most adequate but not necessarily sufficient. In qualitative research, different methods are used for biographical analysis, for example Grounded Theory (Glaser and Strauss, 2005), the biographical approach of Rosenthal (2005), and the biographical narratives resulting from narrative-interviews (Glinka, 1998). This latter approach is very helpful in reconstructing and understanding the diachronic perspective of the biography, but the synchronic structures and contradictions, out of which ambivalence results, are difficult to reconstruct and understand, using biographical methods alone. Consequently, more dialogical approaches are needed as used in action research (McIntyre, 2008); in ethnographical approaches (Crang and Cook, 2007); or in ethnopsychoanalysis (Erdheim, 1992). Using these methods understanding is enriched and improved and the synchronic dimension can be better explored. This means, that the relevance of ambivalence and how it is dealt with by individuals can be investigated and analysed by research.

Drawing from the social theory of Sartre, who emphasized the individual's capacity for social change, and Arendt who emphasized the possibility of new beginnings, the individual orientation towards a desired future becomes most important in understanding current action. The individual can reach a compromise between constraints from the past and aspirations for the future and it is the present where the given limitations of a situation become transcended. A theoretical approach which takes on this mandate can be found in Mergner's theory of the 'social limits to learning'. Based on the methodological assumption of ambivalence, Mergner interprets the processes in which individuals try to tackle present tasks in their life as processes of learning. They achieve a compromise between the constraints of a given situation, consisting of past events and actions, with their personal needs and wishes.

Ideally, social research should lead to an improvement in understanding social change by identifying ambivalence. Such understanding must take into account the complexity of social constraints individuals face and the value-orientation within actions taken by an individual to transcend the limits of a given situation. Consequently, this can only be realized through qualitative research methods which use dialogue as a means to improve understanding in a process of co-production between researchers and their 'object of research'.

3
A Complex Terrain of Words and Deeds: Discourse, Research, and Social Change

Stephen Hicks and Carolyn Taylor

Introduction

As the range of chapters in this book demonstrates, qualitative research takes many different forms. In this chapter, we focus on one specific kind that broadly speaking falls within a social constructionist perspective. Discourse analysis (hereafter DA) has developed in a variety of different disciplinary environments including linguistics, psychology, and sociology meaning that it is better regarded as a 'family' of approaches rather than a single, formal method. Additionally, DA has a complex theoretical pedigree which can seem daunting to those new to its concepts. Its influences include hermeneutics, interactionist forms of sociology, the 'ordinary language' philosophy associated with Ludwig Wittgenstein and the speech act theorist John Austin, the work of Michel Foucault and post-structuralist writing (Atkinson and Housley, 2003; Cheek, 2000; Francis and Hester, 2004; Kendall and Wickham, 1999, 2007; Potter, 1996, 2001; Wooffitt, 2005; Wetherell et al., 2001b).

The Discourse analysis (DA) represents one strand of post-modern theory that has provided

> a critique of representation and the modern belief that theory mirrors reality, taking instead 'perspectivist' and 'relativist' positions that theories at best provide partial perspectives on their objects, and that all cognitive representations of the world are historically and linguistically mediated. (Best and Kellner, 1991, p. 4)

wider nexus of desires, hopes and affiliations which characterise everyday human action. (Wooffitt, 2005, p. 37, italics added)

Gilbert and Mulkay made a further significant move in their analysis. Rather than attempting to determine which of the two contrasting repertoires was a 'true' representation of science, they suspended the making of such an evaluation and instead chose to explore *how* the repertoires worked, in what circumstances they were brought into play, and what were the effects. This is what is meant by defining DA as the study of *'texts and talk in social practices'* (Potter, 2004, p. 203, italics in original). A crucial point made by Gilbert and Mulkay (1984) is that language is not simply an inert transmitter of information; rather it is used by social actors to accomplish certain things in particular situations. For example, scientists' contingent repertoires were used to claim superiority for their own research and to undermine critics and/or other research teams and their work. This focus on language-in-use and as performance provides one of the underpinning features of DA to which we now turn.

Discourse as social action

Within DA, as noted earlier, language is treated as a practical activity and an important means for making claims and resisting counter claims. For example, if someone says 'the printer on my computer is broken', the meaning of this statement can change radically in different interpretative contexts:

(a) when said to a flatmate after you lent it to her for a weekend, it may be part of an accusation; implicit blaming;

(b) when said to a tutor or a colleague who is waiting for a paper from you that is late, it becomes part of the process of offering an excuse;

(c) when said to a friend who has a printer compatible with your printer, it may be a request to borrow her printer. And so on (Gill, 1996, p. 143).

Thus, descriptions are not simple statements of facts, to be taken at face value. They are produced in particular contexts and designed to do particular work; they are a form of social action. In the above example, it is not the state of the printer *per se* that determines the statement about it but the local situation in which it is being described and what the speaker aims to achieve. Moreover it is noticeable that such talk is oblique; for strategic reasons we often avoid being direct and explicit in our interactions (Heritage, 1988).

With regard to treating discourse as social action, three main facets should be noted (Wetherell, 2001):

Discourse is constitutive of social life

In many forms of social research, language is taken for granted as representing the world in an unproblematic way (unless error or bias is deemed to have crept in, either intentionally or unintentionally). Interviews, for example, which are the primary sources of data in qualitative research are conventionally accepted as accurately reporting people's thoughts and opinions or as giving direct access to people's behaviours and practices in real time. Discourse Analysis challenges this stance, arguing that language is not an inert container of content or a 'do-nothing domain' (Edwards, 1997). Rather it is constructive: 'words are about the world but they also form the world as they represent it' (Wetherell, 2001, p. 16). Thus, in his study of couple counselling, Edwards notes how one partner will typically present one version of a relationship and its difficulties (or otherwise) in contradiction of the other partner's account:

```
1  Counsellor:   When before you moved over here how was
2                the marriage.
3                (0.4)
4  Connie:       Oh (0.2) to me all along right
5                up to now my marriage was rock solid
6                (0.8) Rock solid. We had arguments like
7                everybody else had arguments, (0.4) but to
8                me there was no major problems. Y'know?
9                That's (0.2) my way of thinking but (0.4)
10               Jimmy's thinking is very very different.
```
                     (Edwards, 1997, p. 154, transcription devices
                                      removed, pauses indicated).

Both partners use counselling sessions such as these to assert both an authoritative account of a relationship and their own moral worthiness, whilst undermining the authority of the other partner's account if it differs materially from theirs. Accounts serve to rebut any claim by the other partner to the moral high ground as the injured party. Accusations of blame and protestations of innocence lie at the heart of talk in relationship counselling.

2.   Discourse involves work

Language occurs in both spoken and written forms and DA concerns itself with both of these. Unlike conversation analysis (CA) with which it has close affiliations (Potter, 1996), DA does not restrict itself to the analysis of talk, usually produced in naturally occurring situations. Discourse Analysis encompasses all forms of text and talk including conversations and interview talk (naturally occurring or otherwise) and documentary forms (including maps, forms, and other visual imagery). The focus of analysis is on the work that discourse accomplishes in a given situation. For DA there is no single description of a person, object or event that simply describes what is 'out there' in a literal, accurate way. There are always different versions that can/will be told depending on the context, as in the computer printer example and discussion of Gilbert and Mulkay (1984).

Within DA, interrogating the nature of versions becomes a primary focus:

Why *this* version or *this* utterance? What does it do? What does it accomplish here and now? And what does it tell us about the wider discursive economy or the politics of representation which influence what is available to be said and what can be heard? (Wetherell, 2001, p. 17)

Accepting the potential for multiple and competing versions leads us into a different terrain of enquiry. Descriptions of things (people, events, and behaviours) become topics for enquiry in their own right; in effect we focus not on what is 'really real' or 'what really happened' but how social actors construct reality in local settings (Gubrium and Holstein, 1997) such as the counselling session referred to above.

In this regard, the argumentative and rhetorical nature of discourse is highlighted (Billig, 1996). Rhetoric tends to be held in low esteem in contemporary society, dismissed as the superficial and gratuitous obfuscation of truths and strongly associated with the political sphere. For DA however, argument and rhetoric are not the purview of politicians (or salespeople) alone, but intrinsic to everyday life. In our social interactions, we engage in acts of persuasion. Implicit in our versions are requests/demands such as 'trust me', 'believe what I am saying', and 'see things my way'. Versions are never just descriptions. They are artfully constructed in particular settings to do particular work. They may not succeed; a version may be resisted or ignored; persuasion is never guaranteed. In the couple-counselling situation cited previously, Connie and Jimmy may reproduce their polarized versions of events and the counsellor may lean towards one or other version or construct a different version. Moreover, Connie and Jimmy may produce alternative accounts of their relationship in different social interactions (e.g., with friends, family, and at work).

3.   The co-production of meaning

The third point follows from the previous two; it is important to recognize the relational aspects of discourse. Not only does the meaning of utterances depends on the occasion of their use but they can also usefully be treated as a 'joint production' (Wetherell, 2001) both in the sense of being a product of culture and of the participants in an interaction as in the example of Connie, Jimmy, and the relationship counsellor (Edwards, 1997). This applies as much to writing as to the spoken word:

> Writing is addressed to someone and writing and reading (interpretation) together make a text for that moment, always open, of course, to other readings so a piece of writing can become other potential texts. (Wetherell, 2001, p. 18)

Texts are created in response to other texts and in anticipation of a further response. They mediate social interaction rather than serving as the simple articulation of inner thoughts and feelings. This point is expanded upon in the next section which explores in more detail a research study from a discursive psychology perspective.

Discursive psychology: A research example

Before we explore an example of research there are certain additional points to be made that indicate the relevance of discursive psychology (DP) and its place in the research spectrum. First, as stated earlier, there are strong affinities between ethnomethodology (EM), CA, and DP. Indeed a recent rapprochement between them is discernible (te Molder and Potter, 2005). Unlike EM and CA which have emerged within the discipline of sociology, DP has been specifically developed within, and as a re-specification of, dominant ways of doing psychology both in terms of methods and of theorizing.

Traditionally psychology has studied topics such as memory and recall, emotions, cognition and the mind, beliefs and attitudes (MacMartin and LeBaron, 2007), primarily using laboratory-based experimental methods. Cognitive studies typically focus on inner processes and mental entities (Chafe, 1990, p. 79 cited in Edwards, 1997, p. 269). In contrast, discursive psychological analyses focus on how versions of mind (e.g., memories, motives, attitudes, and intentions) are produced in language-in-use in everyday and institutional settings (Locke and Edwards, 2003).

Because of its concern with the minutiae of talk and text and its refusal to make prior assumptions about what is going on in social encounters, it could be assumed that DP has nothing to say about social inequalities. It is true that in general, DP, like EM and CA, has little interest in studying the macro, structural aspects of social inequalities or the broader processes of social division and this could be seen as a serious limitation on its part. However, this might not be a fair conclusion to draw for DP has in fact explored how social inequalities and divisions are produced within the discursive practices of participants in particular settings. Examples include studies concerning racism, prejudice, and discrimination (Wetherell, 2003; Wetherell and Potter, 1992); gender inequalities (Gill, 1993; Riley, 2002; Wetherell et al., 1987) and sexism (Gough, 1998).

The following example typifies such work. It is taken from an Australian study of conversational data produced in focus group discussions with 'non-Indigenous majority' students about 'race', disadvantage, and affirmative action for Indigenous Australians (Augoustinos et al., 2005). The interviewer (Int) provides the opening turn, to which student (J) makes a response. The final turn in the sequence by student (A) summarizes the argument against affirmative action.

Int: How do you feel about affirmative action, for example special entry into university for Aboriginals and Torres Strait Islanders and Abstudy? [i.e., Aboriginal studies]

J: I don't think, umm, I don't think it's necessary unless they can prove they have been, umm, sort of treated in a way that's giving them a less a chance (Mmm) I I don't think they should feel as if they're going to get an easy ride. I think they have to try and get in by their own merits (Mmm aha) [...] to a certain point, umm umm yeah not a I mean I'm not taking an extreme view but I think that they should realize that they have some responsibility and I think we should find a way of getting that through (Mmm) maybe education I don't know, education's difficult and if we could get more you know I know it's difficult sort of umm get away without that happening umm so that they might in be a worse position. But I think they have to really put an equal amount of effort at least (Mmm) because we do to get into high school or whatever.

A: By giving them special consideration we're not doing them any favours.

(Augoustinos et al., 2005, p. 322)

The authors situate their work 'within the burgeoning literature on contemporary racist discourse, demonstrating the ways in which non-Indigenous Australians rationalize and legitimate social inequalities by invoking libertarian-egalitarian principles, which allow the unsayable to be said' (Augoustinos et al., 2005, p. 316). They begin from the premise that racism exists and their approach is to illuminate its workings within a particular social context. Unlike some discourse analysts, an overt political stance is acknowledged from the outset. The authors further acknowledge that the above extract is not 'naturally occurring', rather it is co-produced by the interviewer and the students.[1] Thus the interviewer is not treated as a neutral gatherer of the thoughts and feelings of the interviewees, rather s/he very clearly shapes the interview by constructing affirmative action in a particular way as 'special entry into university'. In reply, J makes a series of moves to undermine the argument for affirmative action for Indigenous students. First *de facto* discrimination by reason of membership of an ethnic group is discounted; its existence must be proven rather than assumed. Second affirmative action is glossed as 'an easy ride' (whereas it could have been connoted as a just and fair redistribution of resources in the face of a past wrong). Third, the concept of meritocracy is invoked ('they have to try and get in by their own merits') as the preferred alternative to affirmative action. Combined with the notion of 'an easy ride' it reinforces the association between affirmative action and unfair advantage. Fourth, J attempts to diffuse any suggestion that his views are other than just and reasonable by use of a 'common disclaimer' – 'I mean I'm not taking an extreme view but'. Finally, as Augoustinos et al. (2005, p. 323) indicate: 'the rest of this turn and the next are given over to working up an alternative 'problem' – the failure of Aboriginal people to fully appreciate the moral importance of individual merit'. In the authors' terms, a matter of collective, structural disadvantage is thus transposed into a matter of for individual resolution via effort within the educational system.[2] Whilst not engaging with issues of motive, the authors conclude with a strong claim that opposition of this kind to affirmative action perpetuates structural inequalities and is racist in its consequences in that: 'it protects and maintains white privilege and leaves minority group disadvantage intact' (p. 337).

This issue of making political assertions is a contentious one for DA, given its caution about grand narratives and its conviction that a definitive version of the social world cannot be achieved. Keeping these issues in mind, we now consider another way of approaching discourse, namely that inspired by Michel Foucault.

Foucault and discourse

Foucault's version of discourse differs from that used in DA because he pays far less attention to microanalysis of texts. Instead, he is concerned with ways of thinking about, and acting upon, topics such as 'madness', 'sexuality', 'punishment', or 'crime' that have emerged during different historical periods. For example, he asked how sexuality 'was constituted as an area of investigation', and how 'relations of power had established it as a possible object' (Foucault, 1990a, p. 98). He argued that sexuality refers not to a natural state or set of behaviours, but rather to a system of knowledge/power relations deployed to establish a set of sexual 'types' and their associated characteristics. Further, he asked how subjects are constituted as the objects of knowledge, and so he examined the emergence, in the nineteenth century, of the idea that we all have a 'true sex' (Foucault, 1980a), and of types such as 'the homosexual' (Foucault, 1990a). This has implications both for research and social change: discourse analysis drawing upon Foucault tends to be concerned with highlighting 'usual or habitual ways of making sense', and locating 'these sense-making methods historically' in order to ask about 'their relation to power' (Wetherell, 1998, p. 394). How, for example, might a social work discourse position and define sexual subjects? (O'Brien, 1999).

This means that Foucaultian work is less concerned with textual minutiae, and, for some discourse analysts, this is a failing. However, DA has itself been criticized for being obsessed with text and narrative representation at the expense of social and historical context. Foucault's version of discourse is concerned both with social location and with what happens outside of the text. That is, Foucaultian analyses link narrative or textual utterances with wider social discourses of, say, sexuality. Discourse is 'a material practice with definite, public, material conditions of operation' (Kendall & Wickham, 1999, p. 45). Foucault's work is analysed in Gutting (2005); Mills (2003); O'Farrell (2005) and Smart (2002).

The implications of Foucault's work for social change have also been the subject of much debate. For some, Foucault's work is unhelpful because it doesn't offer a clear programme for political or social change and because it seems largely concerned with critique or radical scepticism (Taylor, 1986). However, there are a number of responses in reply to these accusations. First, Foucault's work has inspired a huge amount of debate, discussion, research, and writing across many academic disciplines. It is arguable that Foucault's work has shifted thinking

considerably and this, itself, is a form of social change. In lesbian, gay, and/or queer studies, for example, his influence is major (Halperin, 1995). Second, Foucault himself was involved in a range of political activities during his life (setting up the Groupe d'Information sur les Prisons in the 1970s; anti-war, anti-racism, and gay pride demonstrations (O'Farrell, 2005).

However, Foucault's views on politics and social change were never straightforward. In relation to gay and lesbian politics, for example, he was frustrated by what he saw as a tendency to reinforce rather fixed or essential views of sexuality categories. He challenged gay liberation theory because he was deeply suspicious of the idea of a true sexual self, and viewed this as a constraining form. He was also against the idea of sexuality merely as a set of identity types. This he saw as leading to a liberal equality politics that left dominant accounts of relationships in place:

> We have to reverse things a bit. Rather than saying what we said at one time, 'Let's try to re-introduce homosexuality into the general norm of social relations', let's say the reverse – 'No! Let's escape as much as possible from the type of relations that society proposes for us and try to create in the empty space where we are new relational possibilities.' (Foucault, 2000c, p. 160)

Foucault termed his political position 'a hyper-and-pessimistic activism' (Foucault, 2000b, p. 256), because he wanted to remind us to be always wary and look for dangers in *any* programme of social change: perhaps for this reason Foucault was suspicious of some political theories or manifestos for action. He argued that there was no position free of power relations, no utopian realm, since any subject position (socialist, Marxist, feminist, gay activist, and others) is a result of discourse and always implies power relations of some kind. It is because of this stance that some have dismissed his work as a-political, a notion that DA would find impossible to support since there is no argument that does not contain a form of politics. Foucault's work does not offer a straightforward, systematic account for either social change or research, but his writings do offer a complex (even contradictory) set of ideas that have been taken up in some forms of DA. To illustrate this, we first need to consider Foucault's use of 'discourse' and his 'genealogical' method.

Discourse in Foucault's work

Foucault's concept of discourse refers to a group of statements about '... x ...', usually sanctioned in some way, that display some internal rules,

and that have the effect of, first, constituting 'the objects of which they speak' (Foucault, 2002, p. 54) and, second, performing exclusions so as to discount other statements. Julianne Cheek summarizes this concept:

> Discourses create discursive frameworks which order reality in a certain way. They both enable and constrain the production of knowledge in that they allow for certain ways of thinking about reality whilst excluding others. In this way they determine who can speak, when, and with what authority, and conversely, who can not [*sic*]. (Cheek, 2000, p. 23)

This version of discourse asks us to analyse both the productive and limiting aspects of any knowledge form:

> for Foucault, all knowledge is determined by a combination of social, institutional and discursive pressures, and theoretical knowledge is no exception. Some of this knowledge will challenge dominant discourses and some will be complicit with them. (Mills, 1997, p. 33)

For researchers, this means that all statements – including their own – are a part of discourse, and so should be subject to the same levels of critique as any other data. There is no innocent knowledge position, and certainly no simple correct/incorrect version of events.

Foucault showed how discourse works to exclude some versions of knowledge (Foucault, 1981). He argued that 'procedures of exclusion' are crucial to discourse, and that the first of these is 'prohibition' (Foucault, 1981, p. 52). This refers to those processes by which certain forms of talk are deemed taboo, with sexuality being a key example. As he states, we 'know quite well that we do not have the right to say everything, that we cannot speak of just anything in any circumstances whatever, and that not everyone has the right to speak of anything whatever' (Foucault, 1981, p. 52).

The second exclusionary procedure Foucault identifies is the opposition between reason and madness (Foucault, 1981, p. 53). Here, processes discount some forms of speech as irrational. Finally, the opposition between 'true' and 'false' is the third system of exclusion. For example, a 'good story' often adopts a realistic narrative form, even though it is fictional, or the discourse of science uses a range of 'fact-making' devices, such as 'objectivity' (Foucault, 1981, p. 55); a point also developed in DA work, as noted in our earlier discussion of Gilbert and Mulkay (1984).

Therefore, discourse involves active processes that aim to establish certain knowledge forms as reasonable and others as unreasonable. Foucault's use of discourse refers not just to what may be said, but also to the processes by which statements are allowed, to the power relations that confer authority upon some statements and discredit others, and to the conditions under which they arise.

Genealogy

Foucault's methods changed throughout his writing; he did not specify a particular approach, but he did make a number of statements concerning what he called a genealogical method. He described this approach as 'gray [*sic*], meticulous, and patiently documentary. It operates on a field of entangled and confused parchments, on documents that have been scratched over and recopied many times' (Foucault, 2000a, p. 369). That is, genealogy works with 'the archive', a 'vast accumulation of source material' (Foucault, 2000a, p. 370), and accepts that data are discontinuous, contradictory, and spread across a wide range of fields. Genealogy does not look for causes or origins, but instead is what Foucault called a 'history of the present' (1991, p. 31). This means that it examines a network of ideas with all its faults and fissures, and asks how such ideas emerge in different times and places, how they compete with each other, form linkages, or fault lines.

Genealogy is also concerned with 'the hazardous play of dominations' (Foucault, 2000a, p. 376), or systems of subjection that occur within discourses. As noted earlier, genealogy avoids the idea of an objective knowledge, asking instead how the idea of a universal law or object of study came to be established and how particular ideas are brought into being and put to use within discourse – think of the emergence and use of concepts such as 'gender', 'race', or 'sexuality'. A genealogy should also attend to the range of discourses about '... x ...', so that non-legitimized knowledges, or what Foucault called 'reverse discourse' (Foucault, 1990a, p. 101), must be analysed. In his work on sexuality, for example, Foucault argued that, at the same time that nineteenth-century discourses on homosexuality within psychiatry, sexology and medicine attempted to define and control 'the homosexual'; homosexuality 'began to speak on its own behalf, to demand that its legitimacy...be acknowledged, often in the same vocabulary' (Foucault, 1990a, p. 101).

Thus genealogy is explicitly concerned with the intersection of power/knowledge, asking how power works within discourses to produce knowledge and how knowledge involves the exercise of power. Genealogy asks 'how did series of discourses come to be formed, across the grain of, in spite of, or with the aid of these systems of constraints; what was the specific norm of each one, and what were their conditions of appearance, growth, variation[?]' (Foucault, 1981, p. 70).

An example: Researching sexuality and social welfare

Foucault's work on sexuality ranges across a number of important texts (Foucault, 1980a, 1987, 1990a, b). He argued that any investigation of sexuality should treat it as discursive, to 'account for the fact that it is spoken about, to discover who does the speaking, the positions and viewpoints from which they speak, the institutions which prompt people to speak about it and which store and distribute the things that are said' (Foucault, 1990a, p. 11). In relation to homosexuality, Foucault examined how notions of 'perversion' were incorporated and transformed into 'a new *specification of individuals*' (Foucault, 1990a, pp. 42–43) , so that the nineteenth century witnessed the birth of 'the homosexual' as a new type, as a bio-psycho-social character: 'The sodomite had been a temporary aberration; the homosexual was now a species' (Foucault, 1990a, p. 43).

He also investigated the productive nature of power relations, how sexual 'types' were produced through medical or psychological work, but also looked at resistances to power: 'Where there is power, there is resistance' (Foucault, 1990a, p. 95), which also implies that no-one is powerless. He used the example of reverse discourses to show that homosexual people began speaking about their own lives asserting their own versions of homosexuality. As Ian Hacking notes, a homosexual life 'was no simple product of the labelling [and] the labelling did not occur in a social vacuum, in which those identified as homosexual people passively accepted the format' (Hacking, 1986, p. 233).

Foucault's point here was that relations of power, exerted through knowledge-making activities, established 'sexuality' as a 'possible object' (Foucault, 1990a, p. 98). That is, sexologists or psychiatrists did not study and uncover an existing 'thing', but rather they produced the notion of a field called 'sexuality'. Foucault wrote: '[s]exuality must not be thought of as a kind of natural given which power tries to hold in check, or as an obscure domain which knowledge tries gradually to uncover. It is the name that can be given to a historical construct' (Foucault, 1990a, p. 105).

Foucault's work on sexuality inspired an approach to research that requires us to examine power relations and to avoid entering into 'the evidence game' (Smith, 1994, p. 191). Within the 'evidence game', past 'myths' about sexuality are replaced with current 'truths', so – for example – within health or social welfare research, ideas about lesbians and gay men deemed 'homophobic' are countered with new 'facts'. As Smith notes, this 'game' of truth claiming does little to challenge the terms of debate in the first place. Inspired by Foucault's work on sexuality, David Halperin commented in relation to homophobic discourses:

> The discourses of homophobia, moreover, cannot be refuted by means of rational argument (although many of the individual propositions that constitute them are easily falsifiable); they can only be resisted. That is because homophobic discourses are not reducible to a set of statements with a specific truth-content that can be rationally tested. Rather, homophobic discourses function as part of more general and systematic strategies of delegitimation. (Halperin, 1995, p. 32)

Instead, research inspired by Foucault would ask how 'sexuality' itself is produced and put to use within various fields of practice see Bell (1993), Carabine (2001). How, for example, is sexuality made into an object of professional knowledge (Hicks, 2008). This, of course, also creates problems for researching into the lived experiences of lesbians and gay men, for example, since, if 'lived experiences of "the social" are always constituted by systems of discourse, then to study such experiences as *experiences* rather than narratives, or to report on them autobiographically as though reporting were a direct translation of reality, is hopelessly distorted' (Gamson, 2000, p. 357).

Nevertheless, reported experiences will always form an important part of the archive (Foucault, 1980a); it is just that they should not be treated as 'authentic' and unquestionable accounts.

For researchers, terms, such as 'lesbian', 'gay', 'bisexual', 'heterosexual', and similar such, should not be treated as descriptive; they are 'socially achieved ideas that are part of a wider set of sexual discourses that regulate what can and cannot be known or said' (Hicks, 2005, p. 142). This means, too, that discourse analytic work must ask questions that extend beyond 'how are lesbians or gay men treated?' or 'how can we work fairly with bisexuals and transgendered people?' Instead, it needs to ask how such notions are arrived at and used within fields of practice such as health care, social welfare, and education (Hepburn, 1997). For example, what versions of 'sexuality' are dominant within your field of study/practice? (Hicks, 2008).

An example of research that draws upon Foucault's work is Carol-Anne O'Brien's study of sexuality and social work (O'Brien, 1999). In this work O'Brien analyses published articles – social work texts dealing with young people and sexuality published between 1983 and 1995, and interviews with young lesbian, gay, and bisexual clients of residential youth services in Canada because 'academic social work discourse about youth sexuality ... contributes to the development of social work discussions about sexuality and helps to constitute the paradigms of social work knowledge on the topic' (O'Brien, 1999, p. 132). She is interested in how an expert version of social work knowledge is formulated and used.

O'Brien (1999, pp. 133–144) found that the articles she analysed presented 'sexuality' as an object of professional concern (often citing 'factual' statistics), and proposed aetiological explanations for young people's sexual behaviour, such as 'rebelliousness' or 'low self-esteem'. Their behaviour was described in ways suggesting something dangerous or endangered; early childbearing was seen as morally negative and generally, authors proposed the reduction of sexual activity amongst young people as a way forward. These ideas were racialized (in that there was a focus on black young people as particularly problematic), and homosexuality was presented as pathological in the texts published in the early 1980s (it was seen as a 'non-mature' phase, as something with negative 'causes', and as a result of 'predatory' older homosexuals). In later texts, 'sexuality' itself was treated as synonymous with heterosexuality, with minor or token references to homosexuality. O'Brien notes that discussions of lesbian, gay, and bisexual youth migrate into specialist texts which remain marginalized and rarely cited in other publications, a process by which they 'are constituted as a subordinate form of knowledge' (O'Brien, 1999, p. 146).

O'Brien highlights an absence of 'discourses of desire' in relation to young people and sexuality (O'Brien, 1999, p. 138). That is, references to sexual pleasure, agency, or knowledge amongst young people are absent. This 'diverse sexual knowledge of young people' constitutes 'subjugated knowledge' (O'Brien, 1999, p. 139), a term which O'Brien derives from Foucault, who described it as a 'whole set of knowledges that have been disqualified as inadequate to their task or insufficiently elaborated: naïve knowledges, located low down on the hierarchy, beneath the required level of cognition or scientificity' (Foucault, 1980b, p. 82). This is not to say that accounts by young people should not be subject to critique – a discourse approach ought never to treat any part of 'the archive' as innocent/straightforward knowledge – but, within the wider discursive field of social welfare/sexuality, it is important to ask which versions of knowledge are present/absent and dominant/subordinate, cited/ignored.

Discourse analysis: A critical assessment

Discourse Analysis challenges positivst research as a 'fact-finding mission'; instead preferring to explore how facts are constructed in descriptions and accounts in interactional business. It is not our contention that DA should supplant all other forms of research; rather it should be accepted as providing an important and hitherto neglected approach to the study of institutional discourse. Interviews between professionals and patients/ users, collegial talk, reports and case records, memos, policy documents and even visual materials can all be subjected to DA. However, this approach raises numerous challenges as well as strengths.

'The geography of the discourse terrain is complex' (Antaki et al., 2002) because it comprises some quite different approaches. We have outlined just two (see, for example, Wetherell et al., 2001a, b; Wooffitt, 2005). Practitioners of DA will need to familiarize themselves with the differences between the various strands of thought and decide where to locate themselves. Researchers new to DA will also find that it is an approach that needs practice. It should also be emphasized that 'any-thing does not go': DA is not an excuse to conduct research that lacks rigour and systematic analysis. In particular, summary and repetition should not take the place of illuminating critique (Antaki et al., 2002). In DA, it is not enough to simply repeat or paraphrase the argument of the original text/narrative, rather it is important to focus on how the account is constructed, what is *included*, and what is omitted. A key question for DA is what does the speaker/writer achieve by producing their account in this way? DA aspires to provide a well-conducted and serious set of methods for analysis (van Dijk, 1990, p. 14). In a corpus of data, this would necessitate analysing anomalous and disconfirming cases, something that space has prevented us doing here.

However, this close focus on textual analysis can also lead to fur-ther problems with DA, the disappearance of the researcher and/or social context. For example, it is possible within DA (of all types) to focus on what is in the text only (in fact, some people insist on this) at the expense of the researcher's prior theoretical and/or political concerns. Others employ discourse techniques as a 'new objectivity', leaving little sense of a theorizing (and even feeling) person doing the research. However, there are discourse analysts who deal with this (e.g., analyses of gender, femininity and sexuality in Smith, 1990;

Speer, 2005) and we recommend their work to readers interested in such debates.

Another potential problem with close analysis of text or narrative can be a tendency to elide social, political, and historical contexts and concerns. Whilst Foucault's work is clearly concerned with the material practices of discourse, *some* discourse analysis is curiously quiet about effect, context, subjectivity, or power. Representation is not everything! Both these concerns – the analytical position of the researcher and the wider context and social location of the data – are addressed in discourse analytic work that maintains a reflexive practice.

Discourse analysis also offers a number of strengths as a research approach. First, it focuses on texts as topics for inquiry rather than resources to be mined for information. The problem with a great deal of social inquiry is that it focuses on amassing propositional knowledge. Child death inquiries, for example, often look to establish facts about 'what went wrong' and make recommendations for improvements to the social welfare system. They rarely ask questions about the work that evidence does to establish particular versions of events (Taylor and White, 2000).

Second, DA often demonstrates or makes use of accessible or retrievable data: that is, data are reproduced in a form that comes close to the original. Returning to our earlier point about context, this is an important concern in relation to interview data. Much qualitative research simply reproduces shorter quotations from interviews, but tends to overlook the context within which things are said and the dialogic nature of statements. Accessible or retrievable data enables other researchers to make their own analyses, rather than rely on the researcher's, a point that has also been made in feminist arguments for 'analytical reflexivity' (Wise and Stanley, 2006, p. 449).

Third, DA maintains a scepticism about 'factual' claims, monocausal explanations, 'second order judgements' (Kendall and Wickham, 1999, p. 13). Research that simply replaces past 'myths' with present 'facts'; or that explains complex social phenomena according to a single cause (such as 'capitalism' or 'gender' or 'poverty'); or that relies on judgements made by others is problematic, DA tries to avoid these pitfalls, questioning where explanations and judgements come from.

For applied social researchers working in fields such as nursing, medicine, social work, DA offers a powerful means of making sense of professional practice through exploring the communicative practices through which the business of agencies and institutions is enacted. It permits scrutiny of worker-user interactions, collegial interactions in formal and informal settings, and the production and consumption of documentary sources within organizations. Instead of focusing on what staff say they do in *post hoc* interviews, using DA makes it possible to examine the minutiae of practice in specific local situations (Taylor and White, 2000).

Finally, it is possible to argue that analysing need not only be an academic enterprise but also one that has the potential to contribute to social change. Fine-grained analyses of how practitioners transform people and problems into 'cases', for example, could be used to effect a reassessment of the practitioner–client relationship and might ultimately be more successful than pious exhortations to 'anti-discriminatory' practice.

Conclusion

The discursive turn has had considerable impact since the 1960s. It has challenged grand narratives and absolutist statements about the capacities of scientific knowledge to achieve change, arguing instead that knowledge claims are 'partial, situated and contingent' (Speer, 2005, p. 178). Rejecting absolutism, it embraces relativism, multivocality, and a plurality of versions of the world.

Critics argue that this weakens the grounds for an emancipatory politics. If there are no certain truths about injustice and oppression, how can we set common goals to engage in collective political struggle? Have we not simply disappeared into a swirl of texts and versions whose authenticity can never be definitively stated? Without the possibility of establishing bottom lines about what is 'really real' and what 'ought to be' in a fair and just world, how can we act in the world to achieve social change? Feminists have been exercised by these issues, with critics of the discursive turn asserting that feminism is 'politically dis-membered by relativism' (Ramazanoglu with Holland, 2002, p. 57), since it undermines the grounds upon which claims of sexism and oppression can be made. Lacking 'a vocabulary of value' (Gill, 1995), relativism offers no grounds for choosing between competing versions; between sexist and racist views on the one hand and those that endorse justice and equality on the other, with 'political paralysis' being the result (Wilkinson, 1997, p. 186). Foucault, is described as one of a band of 'pessimistic and shamefaced libertarians' by Eagleton (2003, p. 14) because he is not properly committed to a 'new social order' (p. 37). The demand therefore is for some independent, foundational criteria by which to judge the validity of political claims.

Interested readers might wish to pursue these debates in greater detail than is possible here (e.g., Edwards et al., 1995; Megill, 1994; Nightingale and Cromby, 1999; Taylor and White, 2000; Velody and Williams, 1998). However, we make the following points in response to these criticisms: first, we have tried to show how DP and Foucault address issues relevant to social change. The construction of 'difference' and 'Otherness' is central to Foucault's concerns with the categorization of normality and abnormality in modern society; DP, CA, and discourse studies have given us new ways of exploring topics such as race and gender. In conventional studies 'gender', race', and 'class' are taken for granted as independent variables with the power to explain actions and behaviour. In DA 'gender' or 'race' are not treated as stable and invariant categories that do not require scrutiny within an inquiry; rather they are treated as topics in their own right. In relation to investigations of sexuality, Speer and Potter argue,

> heterosexist talk is not a straightforward emptying out of preformed, stable, homophobic attitudes by the heterosexist *person*, nor something one can easily identify prior to analysis... [I]f one were to divide the world into those individuals with heterosexist attitudes and those who are (apparently) more liberal, one would overlook the point that the complicated contours of prejudice need to be understood in their interactional particulars (Speer & Potter, 2000, pp. 562–563).

While Foucault concentrated on the discursive regimes that produce 'the homosexual' (and others) in modern society, discursive psychology explores 'reality-constructing' work as participants engage in everyday social interactions, that is 'the rhetorical and discursive resources that participants use to construct sex and gender, *as* real (i.e., as factual, timeless, objective and *beyond construction*)' (Speer, 2005, p. 188, italics in original). By the very act of problematizing what had been taken as natural facts, DA has enriched our understanding of these subjects.

Second, it is possible to refute accusations of political quietism that are often associated with DA. Literary critic and theorist Barbara Herrnstein Smith argues that acknowledging the contingency of values does not render it impossible to make value judgements and act morally and responsibly:

> There is nothing in the non-objectivist's epistemology that obliges her to endure passively what she sees as peril or injustice to herself or to other people. How a non-objectivist *acts* under such conditions will depend, as always, on specific features of the situation as she

perceives and evaluates them, and thus also on her general values and tendencies as shaped by her prior personal history within a particular culture.

(Herrnstein Smith, 1994, p. 301)

This leads us to our final point, namely that for DA the idea of 'social change' is one that should not simply be taken for granted. How it is defined and by whom in what particular circumstances warrant enquiry. Discourse Analysis does not assume that there is an underlying truth that makes a particular form of emancipatory politics inevitable. Rather it seeks to question the processes by which something is constructed as 'true' and 'right' (or 'false' and 'wrong'). It does so because it argues that all truth claims should be treated in the same way; none should be privileged as being above scrutiny. This inevitably introduces a sceptical and reflexive stance towards all knowledges and truths, including one's own. As Foucault argued, 'everything is dangerous' (2000b, p. 256). But arguably this is no bad thing in a world where absolutist certainties have done so much harm.

Notes

1. Interview talk is common in this area of discourse analytic research, presumably because the gathering of 'naturally occurring' data poses more difficulties for researchers, both practically and ethically. Speeches and written texts may provide alternative sources of naturally occurring material (Augoustinos et al., 2002). For a spirited debate on 'natural' versus 'contrived' data see *Discourse Studies* 4 (4) 2002, 511–548.
2. Readers will no doubt wish to refer to the original article for fuller discussion which cannot be replicated here.

Part II

Welfare Issues and Community Development

4
Bringing about Social Change: The Role of Community Research

Roger Green

Introduction

As a university academic researcher and community activist, I have been researching, writing about, and working with marginalized and excluded groups and communities for over twelve years on the Kingsmead Housing Estate in Hackney, East London, the most deprived local authority in England (London Borough of Hackney, 2004). During this time my aim has been to listen to residents of this housing estate and to help 'give people a voice' to their needs, issues, and concerns by involving them in a participatory action research project. I have attempted to be what Ledwith (2005, p. 24) has termed, 'a tool for liberation rather than a product which is owned by the academic establishment'. In a community which has historically experienced poverty, disadvantage, and social exclusion over many years the research project aims to break what Freire (1972, p. 19) has termed the 'culture of silence', with its oppressive and passive acceptance of the status quo.

In this chapter, I will argue that only by listening to the concerns and needs of those experiencing poverty and acting with them to tackle their daily realities will (we) effectively eradicate this enduring social phenomenon. In using a participatory action research project, in working with a NGO based on the estate, local residents of the estate, and other key stakeholder community organizations and agencies providing services on and to the estate, it is supporting collective community action to tackle residents poverty, marginalization, social exclusion, and the general disenfranchisement residents experience on a daily basis. The research project is ongoing and has been influential in providing evidence of the community's needs thereby supporting community initiatives such as obtaining funding for a legal advice service; the establishment of an employment, training, and education service; programmes and projects for youth, and several community development projects. The chapter concludes by discussing the lessons learnt from this research project for the European Union and National Governments in how they might usefully tackle issues of poverty and social exclusion at the local community level.

Background to the project

The research is giving what Hardcastle et al. (1997, p. 48) have called a 'hearing' to the community by listening to them, recording their needs and working with them to initiate a 'bottom up' community development processes for social change and re-empowerment. It is a Community–University Partnership, between the Centre for Community Research (CCR), University of Hertfordshire, and the Hackney Marsh Partnership (HMP), an NGO based on the estate. The project has a research project office in the offices of the NGO.

The HMP is a community development NGO based on the estate at two venues, the Kingsmead Kabin Project and the Concorde Centre for Young People. Established in 1995 HMP is committed to locally based, long-term work with all sections of the community to support them in finding solutions to the challenges of unemployment, poverty, and powerlessness. The priority is to encourage the potential, imagination, and creativity in people and to work to promote social inclusion, sustainability, and social change (Hackney Marsh Partnership, 2005). The CCR is a nationally known applied social research centre based in the University of Hertfordshire's Health and Human Sciences Research Institute.

The Centre brings together a wide range of contemporary community, social work and social care, probation and criminal justice, and related themes that are grounded in the needs of professionals, users, community-based agencies, and the communities they serve. Applied social research undertaken by CCR aims to be of direct relevance to users of services, communities, policy-makers, practitioners, and statutory and voluntary sector organizations (NGOs). Research conducted is committed to involving participants in the research process with the aim of supporting an understanding and communicating the relationships between research, policy, practice, and outcomes. Research project steering groups that oversee the research activity comprised of funders, key stakeholders, users/community representatives/research participants, and researchers is a key feature of this work.

The major impact from this research project has been working with the NGO and the estates residents in providing research evidence (for example, Green, 1997; Green et al., 2007) of residents needs which has supported funding of over £1 million Sterling (EUR 1,324,125) from the UK's Big Lottery and other key UK grant-giving organizations. Several community projects have been started including: a free Legal Advice Service (East Hackney Law); the reopening of a much needed youth project (Concorde Centre for Young People); an Education, Training and Advice project for unemployed people; and ESOL classes for residents wishing to learn English. In addition, there are a number of community projects aimed at marginalized groups, such as older people and women.

Unusually for such collaborative projects dissemination of the project's research activities have been at international, European, UK national and community levels (for example, Green, 2000, 2003, 2006a; Green and Dicks, 2008, in press; Green and Hammond, 2005; Green and Turner, 1999). The project has also gained UK national reputation, for example, the community history project is highlighted as a 'best practice' case study for the UK National Archives, Community Access to Archives Project (CAAP) (Green, 2006b)

Contextualizing the research

> The King and Queen in visiting the King's Mead Housing Estate at Hackney Marsh yesterday, saw some of the most up-to-date features of any flats in the country. (North London Record, 1939, p. 10)

The Kingsmead Housing Estate:
A brief history

The Kingsmead Estate was built in the mid-1930s by the London County Council (LCC) for people affected by slum clearance and it is situated in the London Borough of Hackney. The estate consists of 16 five-storey blocks of flats, with a population in excess of 3000 people (Kingsmead Community Trust, 1995). By the 1970s, it was being labelled a 'dump' estate, a community which had lost its traditional East End community spirit. This was blamed on the Greater London Council's (the new landlord) policy of housing people onto the estate from all over London, many with existing problems:

> If this is your address, you will probably find it more difficult to get goods on hire purchase or to get a job, because of the reputation of

being filled with 'problem families'... there are many one parent families... have history of rent arrears... there are families with low income and many children.(*The Guardian*, 1973, p. 4)

The term 'island' also began to be used by some writers to describe the estate and its decline and physical isolation from other neighbouring Hackney communities (Murphy and Fearon, 1985, p. 8). This continued from the mid-1980s through to the 1990s and Barwick's description of the estate at the time graphically highlights its image:

> There is no other word than slum for the Kingsmead Estate in Hackney, North East London. Here they all are, the visual clichés of the genre: the blocks of grimy brick, five stories high, with urine-soaked stairways and bleak passages running along their backs; the shattered windows; the empty flats blinded and gagged by steel shutters; the sordid yards with their rusted discarded fridges and washing machines; and cars with shattered windscreens and flat tyres. (Barwick, 1991 p. 26)

The fear of crime increasingly began to haunt the estate which suffered from high levels of crime, particularly domestic burglaries, and street robberies, what the local authority Housing Department called, 'gangs of youths "steaming" on Kingsmead Estate i.e. committing robberies in gangs' (Crime Concern, 1993, p. 14). From the 1980s onwards, the estate began to be seen by sections of the media as a manifestation of the breakdown of civil society and law and order (Pearce, 1993, p. 15). It was not until 1993 that the London Borough of Hackney in a joint strategy with the police used civil rather than criminal law in obtaining civil injunctions against a number of young residents and their families involved in criminal activities on the estate (Parry-Davies, 1993, p. 4; Tendler, 1993). Repossession orders were used to evict 'persistent troublemakers' including one family which had threatened violence against anyone on the estate reporting their criminal activities (Duce, 1993, p. 11). As a result the number of burglaries on the estate, which had made up for a quarter of all burglaries dealt with by Hackney Police, fell dramatically (Osborn and Shaftoe, 1995). These initiatives coupled with the setting up of an estate community trust, the Kingsmead Community Trust, in 1993, began to attract resources on to the estate (London Borough of Hackney, 1994).

The estate, still, continued to be labelled by the local press as a 'problem estate' (Hackney Gazette, 1994, p. 10) and journalists continued to use the estate as a benchmark to illustrate inner city urban decay particularly council estates in decline, so-called 'sink' estates (Bowcott, 1997, p. 6) In 1998, in a close vote, residents voted to transfer their tenancies to Kingsmead Homes, a Housing Association, rather than remain with the London Borough of Hackney as their landlord. This new landlord promised to invest £39 million over the next five years in modernizing flats on the estate and promoting social and economic regeneration.

The estate was then managed by Kingsmead Homes, a Registered Social Landlord and part of the Shaftesbury Housing Group, established in 1997 to manage the stock transfer of the estate's flats from the London Borough of Hackney. The housing association recently completed its multimillion pound regeneration of the estate and 99 per cent of homes on the estate now meet the Decent Homes Standard (Kingsmead Homes, 2005); for example, all the flats have been extensively refurbished, and lifts have been installed in each block of flats.

For many residents, despite a number of estate-based community regeneration initiatives, the issues of poverty and social exclusion have not gone away. Additionally the influx of asylum seekers, refugees, and economic migrants from the new EU countries onto the estate in recent years, many with young families, who become socially isolated through language, cultural, and religious differences, and through barriers to accessing, for example, health and welfare services, has further heightened this situation.

The physical refurbishment of the flats by the estate's landlord disrupted residents lives on a daily basis for a number of years, and the social and economic regeneration programmes which continually flood the estate would appear to have had only a limited impact on some residents' quality of life. Crime flourishes as does crack cocaine dealing. A 'drop in' sub-police station has recently been installed on the estate. Occasional bullets whistle around the estate at night. The unemployed and the 'mad' still walk the streets. Many of the estates' children and young people rarely have holidays away from the estate and rely instead on subsidized community trips to London Zoo and the seaside.

Anti-social behaviour and a youth gang culture, which is rife in Hackney generally, is an ongoing problem despite heroic and innovatory initiatives by youth workers at the Concorde Centre for Young People, local residents, and other agencies such as the Police, and Community Safety Officers from the London Borough of Hackney (Green and Sender, 2005).

In 2007, the estate yet again experienced another change in its land-lord by becoming part of the Sanctuary Housing Group. However, as Durston (1997) noted some ten years previously:

> Physical regeneration alone will not solve the problems on this estate ... poverty is one such problem. (p. 7)

Researching with the community:
The contribution of Paulo Freire's writings

> Washing one's hands of the conflict between the powerful and the powerless means to side with the powerful, not to be neutral. (Freire, 1972, p. 24)

Talking with Bob Holman many years ago when he had resigned from his post as a Professor of Social Policy at the University of Bath and was working as a community worker on an estate in the West of England, his 'world view' was at the forefront of his work. Theory went hand in hand with practice at the community level on the streets of the estate where he was working. His writings and research on working with communities (for example, Holman, 1981, 1993, 1997, 2000) have challenged the dominant way of seeing how communities are not trusted to organize themselves by governments and their agencies, and how they are continually being disempowered rather than empowered despite the rhetoric of the latter. As May (2001), in a useful discussion on the relationship between social theory and social research, highlights, for the researcher concerned with power structures at the communal and societal levels: 'the production of theory and research then become "critical projects" which go hand in hand in challenging oppression in society' (p. 36).

Such a challenge has for me been informed greatly by the ideas of Paulo Freire, whose thinking underpins my research and community work on the Kingsmead Estate. Freire's work has provided the framework in which my research, and empowerment and social action for change addresses the issues of oppression, marginalization, and deprivation which are rife in the community. His richness of writings on individualization and social transformation had, in my view, a far broader application in relation to my own work in Hackney with the re-creating and re-writing of his ideas being a constant challenge for me.

Freire's approach was concerned with the development of a 'just society' (Taylor, 1993, p. 92) and his view that the majority of the population were living in circumstances of poverty and deprivation alongside pockets of wealth and opportunity. This gave him the basis for his theories and my rationale for undertaking a participatory community-based research which supported community change. His theme of consciousness raising, conscientization, for example, a process that encourages the individual to analyse and examine their reality to become fully aware of constraints on their lives, has had an ongoing resonance with me in my research with residents.

Listening to residents talk about their daily lives it became clear to me that conscientization might help them to begin to understand, challenge, and pose alternatives to the oppressive and exclusionary socio-economic forces at the microlevel they experienced within their own lives and in their community. I shared Freire's conviction that social reform and the politicization of the individual was also education. Researching and writing about the 'marginalised' on the estate demonstrated to me that oppression, social exclusion, and poverty dehumanizes the individual, taking away their ability to critically examine their life and situation. What Freire saw as the identification with the oppressor, seen on the estate as 'top down' local authority departments, 'the council', distorts the individual's understanding of the true nature of the oppression and, for example, what their needs are. This 'effect' is evident in my work with residents. It paralleled Freire's 'culture of silence' (1970b, p. 37). Not only do residents internalize the values and norms of the powerful, which he called the 'myths' (Freire, 1970b, p. 72), but they also become dependent on so-called 'experts' such as health and welfare professionals who whizz around the estate eager to dispense their wares and quickly depart (Fritz, 1982; Green and Turner, 1999). This is continually reinforced by the countless reports about the estate and its residents which 'hoover up' data by the bucket full using quantitative methodologies and which exclude residents in the process (see, for example, CAG, 1997; NACRO, 1996).

Freire described the oppressed as experiencing a 'magical consciousness' (p. 62), being totally accepting of their situation, lacking autonomy and believing in the supernatural forces of God, destiny, and fate. This 'effect' is seen in lone parents on the estate living on state welfare benefits and expressing the view that their poverty was somehow inevitable. Where some residents, for example, Billy, a white male resident in his late forties, who had a long history of schizophrenic episodes, viewing the lack of community mental health service provision to meet his needs as being 'normal'. Freire's view that education should be relevant to each individual person, honour and respect a person's cultural identity, and lead to insight and desire for growth and change paralleled my view of undertaking community-based research which emphasized a two-way educative process.

Whilst he passionately believed that the genuine desire for liberation, freedom from oppression, could only be born out of education that offered respect for the student's culture, I similarly take the position that the construction of a piece of research should take cognizance of where residents were at in their lives, and who they were, for example, their ethnicity, gender, and age, rather than who I am as the researcher.

I have continually encouraged the participation of residents in the research design and management of research activity from the beginning by developing the trust of residents and staff at HMP. By, for example, becoming known to residents over the years, through undertaking the role of a volunteer in the Kingsmead Kabin, a local community project, and part of HMP; becoming a Trustee with the HMP; being invited and participating in numerous community events and meetings, and giving the eulogy at residents' funerals.

Equally, the research language I use, as Freire argued with education, is contextualized to be familiar to residents. 'University research speak' is often not appropriate at the community level. Terms such as 'what's the issue?'; 'how do you think we should look at this?'; 'what information do we need?' became new forms of expression for research, methodology, and data collection. This community research approach mirrored Freire's view of education based on using cultural and community identity as a building block for raising consciousness, awareness, and self-esteem, and identifying needs.

My view of research as a learning process for all involved similarly developed out of Freire's antagonism towards what he termed the 'banking' system of education where the teacher is the 'expert' filling students with knowledge in a static, unengaged way. For me residents are the 'experts'.

The issues around 'research exclusion', for example, where non-disabled people set the research agenda in disability research excludes disabled people as Oliver (1992), amongst others, has highlighted, was still predominantly the norm within residents' experiences of researchers on the estate when I began working there. Encouraging people where possible to begin to learn to become their own researchers (Green, 2007) has been part of the participatory action/community development approach I have adopted. Indeed 'going beyond' the traditional scientific orthodoxy of positivist research with what Robson (1993) has called its five sequential steps centred on hypothesis testing (p. 71), I have encompassed Freire's view that people need the opportunity to learn through their own experiences rather than be 'objects', without knowledge of their needs, shaped by the 'subjects', the researcher. This is a method of learning that encourages active participation and relies upon the examination of personal and community experiences.

In using such a 'bottom up' approach it has actively sought to get residents to, what Freire called 'name their world' (p. 50), to identify and analyse their concerns, hopes, problems, and needs within the wider context of their lives. The research process therefore becomes the start of this awareness-raising process which allows individuals to gain some insight into their situation whether it be their low-income and poverty, being a 'newcomer' to the area such as an asylum seeker, or dealing with anti-social behaviour. However, as Freire recognized, at this stage, although participants may identify problems they do not necessarily make connections and often see others as being responsible or to blame for their problems. Freire called this phenomenon 'naive consciousness'.

Achieving these links I made extensive use of what Freire (p. 28) called the 'circulo de cultura' (culture circle) to promote dialogue, to encourage groups of residents to identify emerging themes, through informal meetings and discussion, and to help them move to a clearer understanding of what was going on. An example of this was discussing the lack of facilities on the estate for children to play and for young people to meet up in a safe environment – Freire called this reaching a state of 'critical consciousness' (Freire, 1973, p. 49). Such an understanding has helped move residents involved in research projects towards a commitment for community development and action: 'its okay to think about it and change it', as one resident remarked. Freire called this process praxis; action preceded, accompanied, and followed by reflection. Although somewhat problematic to operationalize as a researcher on occasions, it was possible, for example, to reach a consensus on the multiplicity of issues highlighted across competing groups on the estate.

This notion of liberatory education that I have used closely resembles the principles of social action theory that underpins self-directed group work (Mullender and Ward, 1991). This theory supports Freire's ideas in embracing the continuous process of identifying themes, reflection, and re-evaluation allowing participants to move from recognition to action. Through dialogue and the exploration of experiences, both confidence and consciousness are raised. By these means, it is possible for residents to recognize that community issues and needs are complex and often involve multiple themes, such as local council politics, service and resource allocation, social policy development and implementation, and economic and environmental factors. However, it is evident, as Lovett et al. (1983) have noted, that communities often carry with them a broad range of focus, which reflects the diverse nature of local needs and interests.

This was particularly noticeable in interviewing residents and taking part in informal group discussions with residents at the Kingsmead Kabin Project drop-in, the 'front room' as it was named, a sifting of data, summarizing and re-presenting the gathered information was often found to be a required part of the research process (see Green et al., 2007). This was a process by which residents identified emerging themes and helped to name significant situations and needs within the community, often in conflict with my perceptions and in a sense very similar to what Plummer (1983), noted in another context, whereby the researcher can be forced into the position of 'forcing the data' (p. 69) by restricting issues of interest which fit the researchers agenda. Using a participatory action research approach in helping people to make connections between their world and the socio-economic conditions in which they are living is the very 'liberatory' force to which Freire refers and a chance for people to begin to take charge of their lives.

The cultural oppression in Brazil that concerned Freire can be likened to the alienation and powerlessness of many marginalized minority groups and communities in inner city communities in the United Kingdom. There can be little doubt that the application of his ideas to researching the voices of marginalized communities offers the potential for empowerment, creates change within communities, and potentially encourages personal growth and liberation through the identification of people's needs. As Blackburn (2000 p. 10) has stated in relation to Freire's work: 'His message is as relevant to the poor as it is to those who seek to work with the poor.'

Taking sides: A community-based research approach

> The one who rides the donkey does not know the ground is hot. (Dogbe, 1998, p. 97)

A community research approach, using a participatory action research methodology, attempts to give a voice to people, to make visible their lives, and their experiences. If an essential ingredient of this venture is to empower people, their communities and promote social change at the micro level, then as community researchers, two questions arise. First, who brings about this change, and in which direction should it go? Second, if we are in the business of consciousness raising, do we include ourselves in this process?

My research in this context has aimed to involve residents across the community through interactive and collaborative listening, what Humphries (2000, p. 31), has called 'traditional positivist-influenced approaches' to research have been no more than a useful backdrop. I have used valuing people and the community's understanding and experiences of their concerns, needs, expressed as felt needs, as the basis for my research, and in doing so, as Beresford and Evans (1999, p. 672) argue, I have not supported the so-called 'scientific' research with its monolithic values of neutrality, objectivity, and distance. The key to this successful research and community development approach has been its cyclical process of in-depth listening, information processing and reflection, and feedback with more listening and reformulation of ideas. This process has drawn heavily on Freire's model of the cycle of action and reflection.

An important element of this approach has also been the acknowledgement of Arnstein's (1971) typology of community participation, and Brager's and Specht's (1973) model of the degrees of such participation. Through the involvement of professionals from the community's health and social care agencies, when appropriate, I have aimed to ensure that their collaboration, participation, or involvement in the research supports empowerment, not further disempowerment. Of paramount concern in this process has been the community development role in such activity and to avoid what Barr (1991, p. 140) has called 'token consultation' with the community. A key question for me throughout my research has been who, or from where, has the community research been initiated? This is at the heart of the 'top down' and 'bottom up' research debate in researching marginalized groups and communities.

The participatory research action approach is by definition a way of challenging who sets the research agenda, as Shortall (2003) has noted, which is important because of the tendency of much 'officially' sponsored research to use a methodology which is primarily quantitative in approach. In doing so the latter seek data and information with only limited or no involvement with the community they are attempting to research. This has resulted in so-called experts coming on to the estate, asking questions and then simply vanishing, to be replaced later by new professionals colonizing the estate and pursuing their own agendas based on these research findings. This is a positivist paradigm which historically has tended not to involve or listen to the 'researched', nor feed back the research findings in a form which potentially empowers them.

To counter this, the contribution of 'new paradigm research' (Reason, 1988; Reason and Rowan, 1981), which Reason (1988, p. 1) calls: 'research that was *with* and *for* people rather than *on* people' has proved useful in this process This model of research, which emerged along with feminist research and critical theory as a result of criticisms of positivist research, has moved away from the researched as passive subjects and offers a shared research agenda. By using the cycle of cooperative inquiry model of 'new paradigm' research (Reason, 1988) with the 'essentially anti-discriminatory, reciprocal and empowering essence of this approach' (Ledwith, 1997, p. 103), I have attempted to avoid the pitfalls of alienating and exploiting the researched through avoiding what Heron (1981) sees as assuming the researcher is intelligent, open and self-directing, but then applying different assumptions to the research subjects. This model challenges the worldly academic researcher who may wish to act as an empowering agent as long as the empowered do not encroach on his or her 'expert' privileged and powerful position. The ideological contradictions are obvious. Equally Packham's view (1998, p. 249) which supports this 'new paradigm' model, that some 'research methods are exploitative and deskilling of their subjects, and are therefore inappropriate to use as part of community development' was a prime consideration.

This community research approach has been distinct in their connected differences. They have included interviews and observations, but repackaged as talking with people, informal group discussions, and community observations. The aim has been to maximize the number of sources and applying 'method triangulation' and 'data triangulation' (Denzin, 1978) to a community context by obtaining data/information from a number of different locations, for example, in residents' homes, in the pub, over a cup of tea, or on the street, during the day and evening and at weekends. Gathering information has often used a combination of these approaches and largely been determined by the nature of the research question. An example of this is my first study of poverty on the estate (Green, 1997) where it was imperative to formulate a community view of how poverty was experienced on a daily basis and not as a narrow theoretical construct.

Talking with people

Research language or professional jargon used by academic researchers has the power to exclude and certainly to confuse people on the receiving end of research. As Dockery (2000) quite rightly states, it very rarely, if ever, equates with the daily language of non-researchers and their communities. 'Could I interview you?', for example, was therefore not an appropriate method of entering residents' social worlds. Instead, talking and listening to residents, in a number of different locations, provided a home territory context for residents in sharing their lives with me. In undertaking interviews the nature of selecting residents as respondents is primarily determined through purposive sampling, in which, in conjunction with residents and professionals working on the estate, a sample is chosen on the basis of known characteristics or experiences, and 'snowball sampling' where one respondent is identified and then introduced to me by another resident. Using such qualitative non-random sampling techniques for interviews allows me to collect and analyse, manually, non-numerical data on the meanings people gave to their everyday lives. These 'interviews' are what Burgess (1984, p. 49) refers to as 'conversations with a purpose' and Robson (1993, p. 62) as 'the potential for providing rich and highly illuminating material'.

The advantages of using this approach are its usefulness as a method of discovery and exploration in helping to define residents' views, ideas or needs, a new and complicated area to most of them. Indeed as Silverman (1993) has noted such interviews have the potential to empower people by allowing respondents to articulate their own views and raise their own issues. For many residents somebody listening to their stories was a new creative experience which, for example, was captured in the research involved in producing the first community history of the estate (Green, 2005a). Applying Fielding's (1994) analysis of research interviews, to such issues as that of respondent truthfulness, the influence of the researcher, and directed answers, and other potentially problematic areas, ensured I was continually checking the nature of the data being collected and the purpose to which is was to be put. Equally I was clear I had no wish to follow the traditional positivist interview paradigm, which feminist researchers such as Oakley (1981) and Finch (1984) amongst others have long criticized as being essentially a one-way process primarily controlled by the interviewer, with its power differential towards interviewees, and the objectified function of data collected.

Informal group discussions

To avoid the formality of focus groups, with their particular emphasis of specific issues, group discussions with residents proved to be a productive alternative approach. This approach aims to catch the voice of the 'community at large' with a balance of community leaders, interest groups, such as a pensioners group, and locations where individual residents came together informally (Cohen et al., 2000; Payne, 1999). It allows, as Janesick (1996) has argued, an exploratory approach in identifying preliminary research questions particularly in a new area of inquiry; for example, in the sensitive discussions on the arrival and needs of refugees and asylum seekers arriving into the estate. Similarly group discussions with residents who knew each other as neighbours and friends, allows them to talk, in a safe environment, for example, their home turf (territory), their experiences and views on a number of different topics which results in useful ongoing data collection and additionally opens up other new avenues of research inquiry; for example, the social isolation of older residents and lone parents with limited support networks. To encourage groups of residents to discuss, to clarify situations, to identify issues and concerns, and 'futures', the culture circle approach helped to promote this dialogue. By meeting spontaneously and informally, talking opportunities were provided to help residents move to a clearer understanding of what was going on; for example, why a change of housing landlord on the estate does not necessarily result in the greater involvement and voice for residents, nor indeed additional resources and services on to the estate.

This as Freire (Freire and Macedo, 1998) has argued helps people make connections between themselves as the individual, their group's situation, their community, and the socio-economic conditions in which they were daily living in. This awareness encourages, in my view, the analysis of their reality, thereby highlighting contradictions and inequalities, and indeed, why their individual and the community's needs often remained unmet despite, for example, many residents being excluded from mainstream banking opportunities because of their postal address.

Community observations

In applying both participant observation and non-participant observation, my involvement in community-based groups, and 'informal' community gathering points, such as local shops, has allowed me to observe daily street life. This has been very similar to the 'community walk' (Payne, 1999, p. 17), it has enabled me to study various aspects of the estate's life and in conjunction with other approaches has given me a more holistic view of the community. This is often undertaken with a resident. This use of observation is also aimed at elucidating a 'world view' of residents, to build up a picture of the way their experiences are structured in the community and how this might relate to wider aspects of their lives such as the 'non-participatory politics' of the London Borough of Hackney in which they live.

In undertaking observation, a major concern for me is to remain self-critical of the data I am collecting and the need continually to evaluate the quality of observation in terms of possible error and bias. The work of Loftland and Loftland (1984) is particularly useful in achieving this, for example, being aware of the spatial location of the observer in relation to participants, the dangers of describing events and observations through my own analytical framework, and the consistency of data. The use of research diaries to write up my observations is invaluable in this situation. Drawing on Bruyn's (1966) criteria for writing up fieldnotes and Grbich's work (1999), the diary allows me to be aware in both my observations and the other qualitative aspects of my research such as recording group discussions. It is also helpful in considering such issues as whether my research approach of involving people is both trustworthy and credible and the importance of reflexive subjectivity for me as the researcher.

Taking sides

By using such a range of methods in gathering data by talking and listening to residents, I observe and record, at first hand, over many years the ebb and flow of the social life of the community and in particular their diversity and differences, and indeed the different perspectives held on the estate. Whilst the concept of community might often convey images of social cohesion, cooperation, solidarity, and indeed even sameness (Payne, 1999) it is not always the case. Often the reality, or norm, in my experience, has been a community with overlapping membership, disagreement, and conflict, for example, communities within a community. As Ledwith (1997, 2005) has noted, within communities the complex interaction between 'race', class, gender, ethnicity, sexual preference, and disability has to be seen as a whole in understanding any community and the forms of, for example, oppression, invisibility, and marginalization within it.

In wishing to involve residents in the research agenda I am acutely aware of Hardiman's (1986) and Midgley's (1986) observations that not everybody wishes to be involved or participate in an activity which might affect their lives. Indeed, as Peter Berger (1977) once famously remarked that if everybody were to participate, it would be too overwhelming for the researcher. Equally, the researcher must not lose sight of the fact that they are still an outsider seeking to change things

(Chambers, 1983). The 'genuine philanthropic intervener' in Dudley's (1993, p. 72) words has to be aware of this and to act accordingly. This continuously raises the question for me as Carter (1960) has noted, that a social change agenda places a heavy responsibility on the researcher in taking sides and not remaining somehow distanced (Becker, 1970). It is a question which I have continually asked myself and in doing so the danger of adopting a neutral perspective, as Filkin and Naish (1982) have highlighted, in relation to community workers, led me to Freire's position, that so-called 'objective research' means siding with the powerful (Freire, 1970a).

Researching with residents has had to take cognizance of their concerns, needs, and problems as defined by them with the object of enabling residents to express themselves and to promote programmes addressed to issues defined by them (Freire, 1972). I have therefore at times acted as a facilitator, in doing so challenging mainstream positivist models of research that are committed to the discovery of the truth by means of reliable research instruments which presuppose one knows what the research questions are and the questions to frame. Becoming part of a community and undertaking community-based research with its potential as a positive change element for the intended beneficiaries necessitates getting off the fence!

'Local Solutions to Local Needs'

This most recent collaborative research project undertaken on the estate was between May 2005 and June 2006 which aimed to update and expand on the 'Community Action against Poverty' survey undertaken on the estate in 1996 (Green, 1997). It also examined in far greater depth a number of themes that went beyond the issues of poverty on which the first study had focused: for example, issues of social exclusion and marginalization; and to examine issues the estate experiences such as criminality and the perception of crime; anti-social behaviour; community safety; service provision and unmet needs.

The research again used a participatory action research approach to involve a variety of people at the local level, particularly residents, in the research process. It aimed to facilitate a partnership between the researchers and the researched, and the direct involvement and empowerment of the people taking part, leading to positive action and change (Lindsey et al., 1998; Seymour-Rolls et al., 2000).

The project included all key stakeholders, particularly residents, community representatives, and professionals working on the estate and their agencies. This process was facilitated by a Research Project Steering Group, consisting of residents living on the estate, NGO community representatives, professionals and others who worked for agencies on the estate, and the research team. The group met on a monthly basis to enable discussion and feedback from the various members of the group and to monitor and progress the research. It also 'grounded' the researchers in the realities of the community's experiences.

The principal approach used in gathering information was the undertaking of a community needs profile (Hawtin et al., 1994) that aimed to gather a wide range of information that will provide general baseline and specific information such as unmet community needs, gaps in current service provision, and the need for new or expanded services. The research team from the Centre for Community Research worked from the base at the Kabin Project so that they could engage and network more easily with the residents and other agencies involved in the estate, thus 'grounding' the research.

Conclusion: Bringing about social change: community research as part of the community development process)

Whilst the work of Holman (1998) and Beresford et al. (1999), for example, provide first-hand accounts of the daily life experiences of marginalized groups and communities, traditionally this debate has been underpinned by 'top-down' non-qualitative research. Such research has attempted to statistically measure poverty and social exclusion, and determine, for example, the percentage of people who have incomes below the national average. There are numerous examples of this approach, including, for example, research undertaken by Tennant et al. (1996) which, in providing an analysis of poverty in two areas of Glasgow in Scotland where residents experienced multiple deprivations, relied extensively on 'hard' statistical data to the exclusion of local people's views of poverty. Griffiths' study of poverty in some London boroughs is another such example (Griffiths, 1996, 1997).

At the UK national level, the UK government's 'flagship' New Deal for Communities (NDC) is another more recent example of this approach. A nationwide community-based regeneration the NDC programme is an example of a 'top down' government funded, intensive, and innovative community involvement programmes that attempt to bridge the gap between poor deprived neighbourhoods and the rest of the country. Launched in 1998 with 17 pathfinder partnerships, followed by 22 further partnerships in 1999, over £2 billion pounds has been committed to these partnerships (Department for Communities, and Local Government, 2008). Such research also tends to reinforce the marginalization of multiply deprived communities further by suggesting researchers' and practitioners' attempt to involve them in identifying poverty, but to a large extent either ignoring them or 'controlling' their involvement in any proposed action to alleviate it, instead viewing the role of the 'expert' as paramount and with residents and the community lost in the rhetoric of partnership and promised involvement.

Community research on the Kingsmead Estate has challenged this approach by listening to the voices of those experiencing social exclusion, poverty, and marginalization on a daily basis, and so finding out what their concerns were and what ideas people had to tackle them. It also emphasizes the community development approach that is absent in much of the previous literature (for example, BMRB, 1994; London Research Centre, 1996). Developing this theme further, I have argued the case for using the participatory action approach in undertaking community research as a methodological tool for addressing poverty, which could be used as a first stage in any anti-poverty strategy (Green, 1998), such as locally based community action, for example, establishing a credit union. Such an approach poses an alternative model to existing paradigms, which rely predominantly on measuring poverty and its distribution and causes, and which is underpinned by 'top down' agendas concerned with planning and strategies for tackling poverty and social exclusion. This approach also challenges the mainstream body of literature in this area in the United Kingdom and the United States such as the work of Soriano (1995), Percy-Smith (1996), Reviere et al. (1996), and Baldwin (1998) all of which have to a large extent focused on the mechanics of 'experts' undertaking community research only.

A key aim of my research has therefore been to shift away from seeing people in communities as passive victims of forces beyond their control. By challenging central government, local council, or professional policies and practice which have placed residents on the Kingsmead estate in what Williams et al. (1999), call 'fixed single social categories of "poor", "old", "single parent" or as one-dimensional, objective socio-economic classifications' (p. 2). This model of undertaking community research using a participatory action research approach is, however, not without its problems. There is undeniably a political and ideological content to this type of research, which I freely admit; its research outcomes are difficult to generalize or replicate; the idea for the research is no doubt already in the head of the academic researcher rather than the 'community'; and it could be said to completely ignore the broader macro social and economic structures and processes which are a constant, yet changing feature, of post-capitalist societies. To counteract some of these criticisms, I have actively sought to emphasize an approach which has aimed to enable residents to participate in discussing their lives, their realities, and the way they are affected at the local community level, where they live, by the contemporary social, economic, and political landscape.

Change in communities is, however, in my experience often painfully slow, as Gramsci (1971) noted in a different context, change is a process not an immediate event, and supported by Forgacs (1988), was a continual reminder to me to keep to the pace of the community and not my agenda. Moving from research to social change and community development necessitated avoiding the hegemonic trap (Gramsci, 1971) of framing recommendations for the few rather than the many. Research reports and commentaries disseminated at the community level was one way of circumventing and facilitating the community who participated to be at the forefront of the dissemination of the research findings. The research activity on the estate continues to influence social policy development and social change as a localized case study, but also importantly is disseminated both nationally and internationally.

In conclusion, the project is perhaps in a unique position as probably only one of a small number of UK university research centres actively involved in taking the university out into the community and applying social research methods to the needs of a community. This dual community research and community development approach is now an accepted part of 'community life' on the estate as a 'bottom up' approach to poverty reduction, and demonstrates to the UK national government the need to take into account such community-based initiatives in planning sustainable 'top down' poverty strategies. The social change and community development potential of the research remains ongoing based on the premise that residents continue to be involved in looking at their concerns, ideas, problems and seeking sustainable solutions. Any lasting change will come from themselves and their community.

5
Forum Theatre as a Participatory Tool for Social Research and Development: A Reflection on 'Nobody is perfect' – A Project with Homeless People

Dr Michael Wrentschur

Introduction

The chapter begins with some background of research practice, followed by a review of theatre and drama in social research. The focus of the chapter is 'Nobody is perfect': a Forum Theatre project with homeless people, which includes discussion of Forum Theatre as an emancipatory research method; bodies and communities; Forum Theatre in the making; outcomes of 'Nobody is perfect' and further reflection.

Background

Qualitative methods of social research have contributed much to empirical research in the social and educational sciences. As a rule, qualitative methods of research are realized only in contact, in dialogue, within a given field of action, and engaging with the real lives and worlds of stakeholders; such methods aim to understand the people directly affected and their actions against the background of social structures; to take their subjective views and perspectives seriously. In this way, qualitative methods aim to do better justice to the many different meanings and the complexity of social processes and conditions than seems possible using quantitative methods of research (Heinze, 1987; Hopf and Weingarten, 1979; Strauss and Corbin, 1996).

With qualitative methods, however, a number of problematic aspects remain unsolved, in my view. The subjective perspectives of people who are 'being researched' constitute the chief basis for the empirical material in question; however, as a rule (with Action Research being one of the few exceptions), interpretations and insights developed from those positions, remain a matter for researchers to dispose of as they think fit. Some danger persists, then, of degrading research participants to mere 'objects of research', particularly as there is rarely any feedback of knowledge generated in this way, to be reintegrated in the very lives that were the 'objects of research' in the first place. Moreover, many of the qualitative methods of research are addressed to single individuals, for instance the much-used qualitative interview. In evaluating and interpreting results, it is themes and aspects that connect, which are collective and of social relevance, that will often be sought and ana-lysed; however, generating the empirical material itself is no part of that process. Finally, the body as a source of knowledge and insight rarely plays a role in qualitative research, although it has gained more impor-tance in various analyses based on social theory over recent decades (Elias, 1976; Foucault, 1977; Kamper and Wulf, 1982).

In this chapter, I hope to show how research processes can be designed using methods of the theatre and of drama activity in ways that give an active role to real-life stakeholders (that is, to people who find themselves in a certain problematic situation). Participation and cooperation charac-terize the research process – *their* research process – which comes into play in group and community contexts; it is geared to everyday matters in par-ticipants' real lives. Such research affords space for individual and social processes that are educational and developmental; it includes the body with its pre-linguistic, non-verbal possibilities of perception and expres-sion. Results of such research processes are presented in dramatic perform-ances – as feedback not only to the scientific community – but beyond, to the social groups directly involved. These performances are themselves an integral part of a type of research bent on intervention and social change.

First, I offer some general thoughts and review a number of projects that have used dramatic play as a medium for procedural social research. I shall then present a project called 'Nobody is perfect'; here, with the help of Forum Theatre, people directly affected by homelessness received support in their own active (re)search on how to recognize, reflect on, and (if possible) change, their real social lives and make possible sugges-tions and demands addressed to the relevant institutions and politi-cians in the city of Graz, Austria,[1] on how Graz might improve its assistance to the homeless, and its homelessness policy.

Theatre and drama in social research: A review

The development of research methods in the social sciences includes well-known examples of the use (at least the implicit use) of drama methods: one may think of ethno-methodologists' 'breaching experiments' (Garfinkel, 1985), in which everyday rules and norms were broken in irritating ways; where people's reactions helped researchers understand the everyday social meaning of rules and reasons why those rules were established in the first place. Some classic experiments in psychology may also be interpreted as 'hidden drama'; for instance, in the well-known Milgram experiment (Milgram, 1974) probands did not know what roles were 'played' to them (in the proper sense of the word) – they moved, behaved, and acted as though they found themselves in real-life conditions while, in fact, they were in the hypothetical, 'as if' conditions of the laboratory. Further, as we know from various areas of ethnological research, scientists with field research in social space or other community projects behind them, have communicated the results of their labours by way of dramatic performances, to trigger reflection and provide impetus for communication (Marcus, 1997).

In the context of drama work, a number of approaches that see themselves as research methods may be a lot less well known, such as the *Lehrstückspiel* (a short play that provides learning opportunities) following Steinweg (1995); *Szenisches Spiel* (drama activity/dramatic play) following Nitsch/Scheller (1997); and the *Theatre of the Oppressed*, after Boal (1992). Each of those concepts uses a different approach; yet their common denominator is the idea that the medium of dramatic play can be a useful tool for learning processes, insights, and research. What happens in dramatic activity and play is a complex, many-layered process that creates a hypothetical reality ('as if...'), in which space, bodies, movement, rhythm, gestures, expression, emotion, language, roles, figures, action, the stage, and symbols are some of the basic points of reference and elements of design. Boal (1995, pp. 18–29) speaks of an 'aesthetic space', which is characterized by plasticity and ease of management and change, where the past, and scenes or things from the past, may come alive and be part of the present. Moreover, it is 'dichotomous', that is, there is space within a given space – a phenomenon that may also be called 'telemicroscopic'; as things that are far away can be looked at from a very close distance (as under a magnifying glass): whatever is small may be seen enlarged. Aesthetic practice using dramatic play may be understood to be a special form of seeing, of perceiving and observing, which corresponds to the 'theatron' as a place of action. In this process, the 'theoreticians' perceive real life (as presented and acted out) and evaluate it (Koch, 1997). To illustrate these claims and to provide some more distinguishing characteristics, I will now refer to a few projects as examples.

The study *Weil wir ohne Waffen sind* ('Because we are without weapons') was an 'educational drama activity and research project'. Young people of various social groups were engaged to play scenes from *Lehrstücke*, by Bertolt Brecht, in order to reflect together on ways of coping and coming to terms with violence (Steinweg and Petsch, 1986). This project belonged to the type of 'social research in communication' (ibid., p. 94); the main idea was to deal with the texts of these *Lehrstücke* in a playfully experimental and reflective way, to activate and elicit correspondences with the everyday lives and biographies of the young participants.

This *reference to everyday life and to participants' real lives*, as well as participants' own experiences and perceptions, are essential parts of social research processes using drama activity. *Action knowledge* is stimulated in dramas 'as if' action, in an artificial situation comparable to a laboratory. In this framework, social reality is reconstructed as a coming-together of actions and their interpretations. In 'aesthetic space', everyday experiences gain a pointedness, are given a creative working-over; they are compressed and defamiliarized. In research processes using drama activities, great potential is accorded to participants' oscillating between aesthetic space and the world of real life; positions and ways of action that were experienced as effective, as 'the right thing to do', can be tried out in social practice, and be put to the test by 'pragmatic validation'.

The body is seen as an essential source of knowledge and insight; hence, it is revalued, that is, physical perceptions, meanings, positions, attitudes, and valuations are made part of the process of research. That is particularly true if body memory is stimulated making people aware of body positions and norms in everyday life, and of opportunities for pre-linguistic, non-verbal possibilities of expression and dimensions of a theme. One example of this was a research project called *Lehrkörper: Haltungen von Männern in der Lehre – erkundet mit Mitteln des szenischen Spiels* ('Attitudes/positions of men who are university teachers, explored with the help of dramatic play'). The German 'Lehrkörper' can be read as a pun on 'members of faculty' and 'bodies of (male) teachers'. This was a study conducted by Nitsch and Scheller (1998): the point of departure was the question whether, and (if yes) in what ways, male university teachers' behaviour and attitudes generate, or reproduce, 'male' structures in the university (as an institutional setting). Following the principle of triangulation, various different methods of dramatic play (e.g., theatrical images, interpretation through drama activity) were supplemented by qualitative methods (participatory observation, interviews). Nitsch and Scheller (1997, p. 709) argue for the recognition of drama as an 'activating type of enquiry in its own right', which is also suited to accompanying other kinds of qualitative processes through reflection: since dramatic play – via body memory – 'revives latent, in part rejected and hidden, inner attitudes and feelings, and expresses them through the senses and in concrete, sensory ways' (ibid.).

Research using dramatic play has *a playfully experimental character*: scenes represented are made unfamiliar ('alienated'), interrupted; new variations are played; immediate participation as an actor, observer, and reflector alternate in quick succession. The aims, framework conditions, rules, and processes are clear for all concerned unlike conditions in classic psychological experiments. In *research using theatre and drama activity, participants or stakeholders are not the objects of research, but subjects, that is, responsible free agents.* That is also the result of a study called *Gewalt in der Stadt* ('Violence in the city'), in which a working group, including members of various city institutions and authorities in the city of Graz, worked on different forms of violence experienced by participants (either in the role of victims or as perpetrators), with the help of dramatic play. The study saw itself in one tradition of Action Research; during the research process, attempts were made 'to influence the position of city institutions vis-à-vis violence, and to be active in the prevention of violence' (Steinweg, 1994, p. 17). Selecting and interpreting materials were not the responsibility of the study's author alone; the text could only be cleared for further use with the agreement of the group, whose members 'were not to be made the *object* of a scientific enquiry, but should be, and remain, *subjects*, with free hands and minds' (Steinweg, 1994, p. 19).

This process of gaining insight and understanding, and of doing research, is characterized by *participation and sharing*, and by *tying-up research with action*. Knowledge, generated through communication between participants and contact with each other, as well as through diverse types of experimentation and reflection (the mirroring of social reality, in dramatic play), remains accessible – in a large part – to all participants; this may also refer to documentation, interpretation, and text production. *As a basic requirement*, research using dramatic play needs *a group that plays, that researches through dramatic play, and* group leaders who are competent and well-versed in drama pedagogy; such research will only come into its own in medium- to long-term projects, together with a correspondingly long period of time in which the presence of all participants is assured.

Through *theatrical productions and performances, results can be presented* that may be put to good use for social research processes themselves. In these ways, emphases can be placed, substantial findings can be high-lighted and made communicable – as was the case with the university study project *Brüchiger Habitus* ('Brittle/fragile *habitus*'). This was empir-ical research undertaken over several years, into possible cooperative action between students and university teachers (Bülow-Schramm and Gipser, 1991, 1997; Gipser, 1996). Drama sessions and performances were explicitly understood to be an alternative form of mediating results and insights, and – at the same time – as interventions regarding every-day matters at university (Bülow-Schramm and Gipser, 1997). In the course of that study, Forum Theatre was used as a method of action-related and emancipatory research, to analyse power relations and power structures in everyday university affairs; to try out alternative ways of action in scenic play; and to see how much of this might become part of ordinary university dealings through potential transfer.

In the following section, I will focus on another project with home-less people where Forum Theatre was put to good use, as a principal method of research. Methods and approaches employed will be pre-sented in combination with a description of the project's progress, together with project results, and reflections on aspects that are rele-vant to research.

'Nobody is perfect': A Forum Theatre project with homeless people

This Forum Theatre project was realized in the framework of *wohnungs/ LOS/theatern* ('home/LESS/theatricals'), between May 2002 and April 2004 (Ruckerbauer und Wrentschur, 2004; Wrentschur et al., 2005; Wrentschur, 2006)[2]. It involved a number of homeless people of the city of Graz who had named their group (and the project) 'Nobody is per-fect'. Through using theatre work methods, the project aimed at giving support to people affected by homelessness; at encouraging them to become active in developing and properly articulating their own requests and demands for improving assistance given to the homeless, and how to improve the relevant policy in Graz. Subjective experiences derived from real life; views and perspectives; requests or demands for change – all with reference to homelessness – underwent a creative, cooperative, and participatory process, to be condensed into a series of theatrical *tableaux* and scenes, which were considered and discussed. From all those elements a series of scenes resulted that was publicly presented in interactive performances. 'Nobody is perfect' was meant to be a socio-cultural and political theatre project, in the first place; a sort of the so-called Legislative Theatre (Boal, 1998; Wrentschur et al., 2005) leading to formulating a number of suggestions and demands addressed to politicians on how to improve the situation of homeless people. The project's importance as a research undertaking lay, largely, in the basic choice of Forum Theatre as a theatrical method.

Forum Theatre as an emancipatory research method

Forum Theatre as a method of the Theatre of the Oppressed (Boal, 1992; Mazzini and Wrentschur, 2004; Wrentschur, 2003), is understood (in one reading) to be an interactive form of theatrical performance in which the public is invited to take part in what happens on stage, to try out ideas for solutions or changes in a conflict, or problem shown on stage. Results of this process may serve as impulses for many different forms of action outside the 'aesthetic space'. In another reading, Forum Theatre denotes a group dynamic triggered by drama performance methods; a dynamic that is characterized by a collective search for ways of acting and changing stressful, oppressive situations or structures. Turning individual subjective experiences into theatre and reflecting on them through theatrical methods of learning and research leads to condensing the shape of scenes and images that can be worked up creatively in multiple ways. Forum Theatre claims to be an emancipatory method of research that combines processes such as gaining understanding and awareness raising with the search for change in one's individual, social, and political real life. In these ways, Forum Theatre is in the tradition of emancipatory theories of education along the lines proposed by Freire (1982); it focuses first and foremost on (re)presenting, analysing, and changing power relations, from the point of view of people who are 'powerless'. With reference to Bourdieu's habitus and capitalia (1993, 1999, 2001), Forum Theatre on the one hand examines spaces for action within habitual constraints; on the other hand, it puts the question about what capital resources can be activated to provide more opportunities for social participation, above all, for socially disadvantaged groups.

Examining research methods in Forum Theatre activities, Gipser (1996, pp. 28–30) sees 'biographical self-reflection' as an important point of departure (meaning the appropriation of one's own biography against the background of social conditions, through updating and reflecting on one's own past experience); particularly where the activation of body memory is at issue. Connections are established with 'sociological experimentation', in the sense of people dealing productively with matters and actions of everyday life, as advocated by Brecht:

> It is the critical stance and behaviour during experimentation, experience-oriented and bent on change, that Brecht wishes to make use of; it is human action, human activity in an ongoing process that Brecht stresses as being a source of human insight and understanding of the world, and of changing the world – in other words, of human *praxis*. (Koch, 1988, p. 45)

Processes of teaching and learning may in this sense be understood as 'action- and subject-orientated processes of social research' (Gipser, 1996, p. 29): biographical self-reflection and sociological experimenting are tied up with each other as regards changing real-life experience.

Forum Theatre as an emancipatory process of research and of consciousness raising is based on tying-up research and action; understanding and insight are led by practical and political interests, and are intimately connected with people's practical lives. From similar positions, based on similar interests, participants intervene in social reality to change it – or to change their own attitude to it. In this way, they are immediately drawn into the process of research; all parties concerned learn and do research together. Gipser is convinced that this creates opportunities 'to implement the postulated demands of emancipatory Action Research, in practice' (ibid., p. 30). Just like Forum Theatre, some forms of Action Research follow a participatory paradigm (Reason and Bradbury, 2001) which may be understood as a reflective process of problem solving undertaken by individuals and groups working with others in teams, or as part of a 'community of practice', to get a clearer focus on issues. Another point of reference for Forum Theatre can be seen in those approaches of Participatory Action Research that effectively intervene in social and political space (Hale, 2007).

What did all that look like, in the concrete process of developing 'Nobody is perfect'? It is the research aspects of 'doing' our project that interests me here, as opposed to educational drama aspects, which are discussed elsewhere (Vieregg, 2005; Wrentschur et al., 2005).

Bodies and communities: Forum Theatre in the making

'Nobody is perfect', the project properly speaking, extended over a number of stages, and was developed in close cooperation and dialogue with participants. After a kick-off workshop in October 2002, the 'Nobody is perfect' group met once a week for two to three hours, over a period of more than twelve months. In these sessions, a lot of time and space were devoted to confidence building and cooperation training; physical exercises, movement, and improvisation were to stimulate and improve the group's love of play, love of life, and creativity. These activities provided a realistic base for gradually allowing unwelcome and difficult topics to be articulated and for these to be expressed in images and scenes. To do this, an atmosphere of appreciation and respect was needed that made participants feel accepted in this project, with all and any of their idiosyncrasies. This necessitated building up a culture of group relations (including conflicts) and space away from theatre work, where stressful situations could be addressed, worked off, and clarified (Ruckerbauer and Wrentschur, 2004). At this stage, a lot of mistrust, isolation, and feelings of shame could be observed in the group; only in due course were certain openness and the building of cooperative group relations achieved.

Once the group had successfully formed, members' individual requests and situations were taken as starting-points to find out about common, shared problems and participants' wishes for change as far as they related to homelessness; these wishes or problems were then given expression. At this stage of the research process, the body played an essential role – less as the object of research than as a tool, an aid to perception, cognition, and expression. In live acting, experience and knowledge are based on the body, as 'one reflects on a situation, on a figure, on a problem' by means of the body (Renk, 1997, p. 44). Participants' bodies perceived and experienced what social roles, situations, and interactions feel like when being represented in dramatic play; they therefore found gestures and body positions derived from their everyday lives, for improvisation, and to reflect on their meaning in social situations. Playful 'status exercises' (Johnstone, 1993) helped to express differences of status and power through physical (body) positions, to be analysed subsequently.

Methods relating to the body start from socially induced awareness and knowledge of the body; that is, from the social rules and patterns that we digest and appropriate (as it were) through our physical socialization. The

Forum Theatre process and methods, however, also meant 'allowing the body to speak'; giving space to bodies' spontaneous ways of expression – particularly when talking about thorny topics proved to be difficult. In this way, scenes and situations from their past lives arose in participants' minds and memories: scenes and events to do with powerlessness and discrimination. With the help of Statue Theatre, 'living sculptures' were then developed and presented: which had project participants express social situations and problems relevant to them by means of body positions, gestures, and facial expressions. This enabled them to perceive and feel various different levels and structures and, in this way, body-related and non-verbal images and their shared analysis became an important impulse, leading to intense discussions about situations of, and issues for, homeless people. Here the point was not to get participants to talk: they were to decide for themselves what they wanted to communicate – as opposed to feeling forced to 'confess', as criticized by Foucault (1978). At this stage, a first loop for feedback from the 'community of homeless people' was formed: group members undertook to interview other homeless people, to find out what they thought were the most pressing problems and wishes of homeless men and women.

Based on this work, the next stage of the 'Nobody is perfect' project consisted in improvising short scenes and scenic images about the most important problems and requests, and reflecting on how they referred to the world of participants' everyday lives. Generally, a scene improvised on a particular topic was followed by shared group reflection about how consistent, how true to life the scene had been; what the relevance of its content was; its presentation of *habitus*, of social roles, and of status and power relations. This made concurrent research activities necessary while scenes were being developed; for instance, checking the current situation in institutions for the homeless in the city of Graz; or finding out what relevant rules and regulations were. This research process was undertaken with a high degree of cooperation and participation from everyone concerned. It gave support to participants, helping them to recognize ties and common traits in their experiences, perspectives, and concerns (which had at first been subjective, often problematic); to 'condense' these and express them in a series of scenes. Producing scenes and related efforts and insights in a shared process was the result of everyone's commitment, everyone's participation. At this stage, the group decided which scenes (the compressed, foreshortened results of their research processes) were to reach a public; and in what contexts knowledge might be gained by addressees, or where implementation might take place.

In 'Nobody is perfect', the piece of Forum Theatre developed in this way; authenticity and closeness to real life were writ large. The series of scenes begins with the protagonist being 'chucked out' of his flat. After a night under the stars, he looks for help, turning to family, friends, the authorities, institutions. A difficult search, involving the experience of being rejected, of being up against bureaucratic barriers, stigmatization, discrimination, particularly when trying to reintegrate into the housing and labour markets. The succession of scenes is shaped like a spiral – a downward spiral: into poverty, social, and economic exclusion, and finally, being obliged to accept precarious and inhuman types of employment. (For more details about the text and the play's content, see Vieregg, 2005). 'Nobody is perfect', the provisional result of a shared scenic research process, ends at this point.

From then on (between December 2002 and March 2004), the research process was continued through 12 interactive performances, as *collective research forums,* which may be seen as an action-oriented, consciousness-raising process of research in a social field. Another form of dialogical feedback, to the communities concerned, was also part of these Forum Theatre performances, addressing the question whether the scenes shown recognizably referred audiences to authentic life experiences. Audiences consisted of homeless people; people active in social institutions; and other persons with an interest in the subject matter. Following Forum Theatre tradition, audiences were invited to participate in what happens on stage; for people to replace the homeless protagonist, and to try out ideas for change. Insight and understanding focused mainly on the question of how it might be possible to step out of the downward spiral of events and conditions and how to react to practices leading to discrimination and exclusion. All contributions were documented – approaches, suggested solutions, any other interventions: this was what Brecht had meant by 'sociological experimenting'. Interventions during Forum Theatre scenes of 'Nobody is perfect' probed the depths of participants' roles and scope for action; made them and audiences aware of oft-repeated restrictions and high-handed practices of which homeless people are victims, or with which they are confronted. Considering what small amounts of social, economic, cultural, and symbolic capital homeless persons dispose of – and how unequally power is shared – might the homeless not at least be taken seriously (it was suggested), as partners in dialogue, in situations that to them are charged with existential meaning? Another effect of this stage of procedures was that performances facilitated thoughts and discussions about what institutional or regulatory changes would be needed to facilitate the reintegration and participation of homeless people.

After the end of the series of performances of 'Nobody is perfect', the minutes recording all interventions and contributions were reread for audience ideas and suggestions that might lead to solutions: the most important results were summed up, to be considered and discussed in the group. Part of this process was the question whether general 'desires' could be found in these suggestions; which of those ideas might be thought helpful in the real everyday lives of homeless persons; and where there was a need for change on the part of politics, institutions, and authorities. On this basis, a host of suggestions and demands aimed at improving the situation of the homeless were articulated by the group; these were then arranged in order of priority. Those suggestions were vetted in talks held with legal experts; additional information was given on what legal matters or which political level might be affected by the relevant proposals. In this way, the list of demands grew into a volu-minous, complex document, which was consulted and made part of expert discussions in various contexts. Finally, in late March 2004, the results, suggestions, and demands of the (now truly) Legislative Theatre process were presented at Graz City Hall. The Forum Theatre perform-ance of 'Nobody is perfect' at this prominent venue, and the 'proclama-tion' of the most important demands, drew attention to the problem of homelessness in an unusual way; it made a lasting impression. As a result, a dialogue between people directly concerned and decision mak-ers was created.

Results of 'Nobody is perfect'

As a Forum Theatre project with homeless people, 'Nobody is perfect ' was an example of how socially disadvantaged people are able to make a substantial contribution to a participatory, cooperative research project and to the production of insight and knowledge. In various ways they took advantage of their role as (re)searchers, through expressing their own experience of homelessness by way of dramatic play and 'sce-nic' methods; by reflecting on these experiences; conducting interviews with colleagues; doing research. Through interactive performances, they provided input and impetus for a shared production of under-standing, and formulated suggestions and demands resulting from this process. In numerous other ways too, the project produced remarkable results.

Can the Forum Theatre piece be generalized, as a product?

The text and action sequence of the piece under discussion, the outcome of the group's joint process of scenic and dramatic research, underwent a sequential analysis (Vieregg, 2005). It turned out that the piece which had been developed by stakeholders could be generalized (in a sociological sense): it presents homelessness as a multi-causal problem; it renders the concomitant socio-psychological crises, the (often less than 'constructive') patterns of coping, the deficits and problems of homelessness assistance, and the barriers and lack of concepts and perspectives regarding reintegration, apparent. Fear of social stigmatization leads people in this emergency to wait much too long before taking advantage of professional help. As 'Nobody is perfect' makes clear, the other cardinal problem is how to cope with a crisis. Usually no constructive solutions can be found: instead, there is illness such as addiction or depression; silence (the 'loss of language'); inability to act. Loss of self-confidence combines with failures experienced in everyday life situations; very often, social networks collapse followed by social isolation.

Individual solutions vs structural deficits

Forum Theatre performances took their key from those problems and created a socio-aesthetic space to allow participants to try and test individual ways of action: it could be seen that homeless people, when faced with a situation that – from their point of view – was a difficult one, do have ways and means successfully to come to terms with it and are able to obtain important information and supporting services. For these purposes, a number of attitudes and activities were needed: a self-reliant or persistent approach; friendliness and humour; making clear that theirs is an emergency; bartering and negotiating solutions; reinterpreting situations. However, most of these qualities and behaviours contrast strongly with the fact that homeless persons, as a rule, experience feelings of shame and failure and have little self-worth and self-confidence. To demand that they should change their individual attitudes misses the point; seeing that social systems of support and authorities (on their part) erect barriers and commit practices of exclusion that run counter to legal provisions that give homeless persons rights to information and assistance. Indeed, the play revealed that there are many deficits and problems in the field of homelessness assistance and that in the political area no concepts or policies exist that might reintegrate homeless people (Vieregg, 2005).

Suggestions for structural improvements, in homeless people's view

In this sense, a number of ideas first thought of in the performances found direct expression in the declaration and in the list of suggestions and demands regarding the rights of homeless people and how to improve their lot. These included wide-ranging extensive advice; specific information; quick support through establishing an information centre; having trained advisors at the Labour Market Service (Vieregg, 2005). The subsequent production of this Catalogue was the result of a collective process of discussions and clarifications, which demonstrated the importance of taking seriously the experiences and perspectives of people with first-hand knowledge; people who, over time, had become much clearer about their own issues in a research process that involved their minds and consciousness completely. That much became particularly clear when 'Nobody is perfect', the Forum Theatre project described above, was compared and contrasted with an empirical study on homelessness assistance in the city of Graz (Ohmacht, 2004), which was conducted concurrently[3]. The political commitment of the Forum Theatre group was based on the results of the longer-term scenic and social process of research: it supported suggestions and demands to improve the situation of the homeless; a fact that was confirmed by political representatives present (Vieregg, 2005). In their view, the dramatic representation by stakeholders had provided an important impetus to establishing a *Beratungsstelle für Wohnungssicherung* (an Advisory Centre to Safeguard Housing and Homes) which – it was stated – had been in the planning stage for years; a centre that would 'network' with authorities, building companies, and relevant institutions.[4]

Joint production of embodied knowledge: Joint development of competences

This research procedure – a very demanding, expensive procedure – left its mark on the minds and bodies of the participants themselves; it turned out to be an educational, awareness-raising process, which had a demonstrable effect on the production of knowledge, and on the development of various competences in everyone taking part – as can be seen from individual and group interviews held with actors, spectators, and professional helpers (Vieregg, 2005). Apart from the fact that participants' creative faculties, their skills of expression, and their self-confidence were strengthened, there was an increase in their will to live and enjoy life. Playing a role, and the changes of perspective that go with dramatic play, allowed 'Nobody is perfect' participants to take a more distant view of their current situation, which made for a positive change and helped them come to terms with their conditions of life. A critical consciousness of their own social situation and its power relations was generated, together with the ability to name and react to practices tending to discrimination or exclusion:

> Holding one's ground, being self-confident, and standing up for one's own opinion. Showing no fear of institutions and authorities. Demonstrating strength – that I, too, am a human being; I, too, have an opinion ... not allowing anyone to treat you like dirt. ... not letting them get rid of you quickly ... not letting them get the better of you and oppress you. (A woman participant: Vieregg, 2005, p. 189)

Increase in social and symbolic capital

Participants' range of possible ways of action in conflict-laden situations involving powerlessness and discrimination was enlarged; their cooperative and conflictual skills received support. That increase in social capital could be seen in participants' successful building of networks both within and outside the Forum Theatre project group. Homelessness was no longer considered as a merely individual problem; the desire for structural change had been awakened. In the course of these experiences, stakeholders' self-assurance had grown, along with a feeling that they were no longer in a situation of dependency vis-à-vis institutional providers. Since that time, all the participants from the 'Nobody is perfect' group have been able to move into housing of their own (Vieregg, 2005). Beyond the individual level, influence was exerted on social developments, thanks to the project group's readiness to go public and counteract their stigmatization and marginalization with artistic and communicative means and to participate in social-political processes. This also entailed an increase in symbolic capital for the 'Nobody is perfect' group (Vieregg, 2005).

The author's role as a researcher and as a participant: A few reflections

To conclude this chapter, here are a few thoughts about how the persons heading this project – my colleague A. Ruckerbauer and myself – saw their role as researchers, and how I see it today – though in fact everyone concerned with this project did active research, as emphasized. Our role differed greatly from that of the others, however, in that the two of us had no experience of homelessness; we did share the project participants' desire for improved homelessness assistance and better homelessness policies, but the focus was on stakeholders' expertise, that is, the experience, views and perspectives of people directly affected by homelessness. We thought our role consisted above all in putting scenic/theatrical tools and methods at participants' disposal; accompanying them while they tried out and made practical use of these; reflecting upon results together; and making and keeping records. Again and again, that meant structuring the process along the lines of the group's wishes and interests, fine-tuning decisions with the people concerned, asking new questions and developing and applying relevant settings in which everyone could participate, or in which as many people as possible could be actively involved.

The experimental sweep of this open dialogical process led – in the course of time – to a very intense, shared, coming-to-terms with the issues concerned: after feelings of strangeness, of being strangers (as we were when we started), the joint efforts of work helped to create real closeness, almost intimacy, between all participants. Beyond the various different social positions and perspectives, interests could thus be articulated and formulated together; moreover, relationships and some friendships developed beyond the confines of this project, which – in the greater part – have continued to this day.

Conclusion

Theatre and drama as methods of social research enlarge the range of research possibilities, bringing perspectives and viewpoints of participating stakeholders into the picture: it is the people directly concerned that create or shape a collective process that leaves no-one cold. Such research methods take their clue from embodiments of everyday situations, from the everyday lives of stakeholders; their use in theatrical performance; and relevant reflection. These processes of research, being both aesthetic and social, oscillate between real-life social relations, and those of the theatre: it is Forum Theatre, together with *Lehrstückspiel*, that have proved to be methods of research which support emancipatory moves and promote awareness and insight. Participants in this process dispose of the perceptions and knowledge generated in this way in a large measure, which may be used directly in coming to terms with real-life struggles and which are ongoing. In this process, the body is an important tool for research procedures, and for the 'incorporation' of action-oriented insights based on those. Over and above these elements, participants have a strong voice in deciding about whether, and (if yes) how, results will reach the public domain, in the shape of acted-out scenes and texts; thereby creating loops that refer back to real life and social spaces.

In this way, research is tied up with social development that raises 'social awareness': such consciousness activates social competences and stimulates processes of individual as well as political empowerment. The use of research procedures and processes that avail themselves of Forum Theatre methods is motivated by an interest in participants' insights, understanding, concerns – and in questions put by participants, rather than academic questions. In this way, stakeholders in a problematic social situation become participants who are themselves experts in, and of, their situation. Through dramatic presentation that projects results back into participants' lives and into political structures, manifold social forces may be launched that might well be examined further. While individual experiences of the process may have been particular, one-sided, subjective ones, results do allow for a degree of generalization. Their validity was seen in the relevant feedback and opportunities for transfer, with performances playing an important role. In connection with ethnological research, Marcus (1997, p. 16) speaks of 'performances' that disseminate research results as having more potential than written texts such as research papers or reports, to stimulate complex, interesting discussions, as this Forum Theatre project has demonstrated. This leads to one last question: in what framework of conditions can other Forum Theatre performances be used to show and reflect on results in scholarly and scientific contexts; contexts that are simultaneously interfaces of social and political real-life moves and conditions?

Translated by Volker Horn, M. A. (Cantab.), Mag. phil (Graz): vhorn@ kphgraz.at

Notes

1. Graz is Austria's second largest city, in the south-east of the country, with a quarter of a million inhabitants. With seasonal variations, about 1,000 to 1,500 people are homeless.
2. The project was directed by Armin Ruckerbauer and myself; concomitant scholarly research was done by Martin Vieregg (2005), who wrote a *Diplomarbeit* on it as part fulfilment of academic degree requirements.
3. That study arrived at similar results, mainly with regard to the barriers to reintegrating homeless people; however, the weighting of recommendations was different at first. Only when a dialogue had been established with the members of the 'Nobody is perfect' Forum Theatre group and once the results of the 'scenic' process of research were included, was the weighting of recommendations changed. The following example illustrates this: in the play is a

scene in which the protagonist – now homeless – is sent away by the labour exchange as he cannot produce a certificate of registration (which specifies a person's permanent place to live, complete with an address). In this situation – more than any other – unemployment benefit would make an existential difference to him: however, he has lost his claim to such a benefit. In the course of performances, it turned out that at the time, two Graz institutions for the homeless were in fact able to furnish such registration certificates – a fact known to very few of the people directly affected. The demands developed from here – that all institutions for the homeless should issue such certificates of registration; that the labour exchange should be told expressly, if needed; and that social assistance should be granted, regardless of a permanent abode or home – were much more important, indeed essential, to people directly concerned in the precarious financial situation they were in, than the importance first attributed to such demands by the social workers (in the last-mentioned concurrent study).

4. This office works in the tradition of eviction prevention; its aim is to prevent homelessness in the long term; to safeguard housing for households in danger of losing their homes; and to give advice to people who find themselves in the acute situation of being on the streets.

6
Psycho-social Perspectives in Policy and Professional Practice Research

Chris Miller, Paul Hoggett, and Marjorie Mayo

Introduction

In this chapter we explore the use of a psycho-social perspective in a two-year research project[1] on how public service urban regeneration professionals negotiate ethical dilemmas and the coping strategies and resources they draw upon in doing so. We examine some of the dilemmas and challenges to emerge from the adopted research methodology. We suggest that a psycho-social perspective adds a valuable dimension to the field of qualitative research when using in-depth narrative interviewing. Further, it heightens awareness of the researcher–researched dynamic and its relationship to both data production and analysis. In contrast to other psycho-social researchers, we argue for more of a dialogical relationship between researcher and research participants. This provided additional insights and enabled us to share our understandings with the research participants throughout the process. The research outcomes were intended to have an impact on professional training, practice and development, and the method gave due recognition to the participants' value-base and provided a reflective space for participants to develop new insights and change behaviour. We begin by outlining the development of a psycho-social perspective to research. We identify its core components developed to date and explain how we modified a number of them before exploring some of the dilemmas in using a psycho-social approach.

A psycho-social perspective

A psycho-social approach draws upon both critical theory and psycho-analysis. Alvesson and Sköldberg (2000) suggest that both traditions express a 'hermeneutics of suspicion' (p. 95) seeking to probe beyond the discursive consciousness of actors; for example, as expressed in interview narratives, to understand more about its unconscious and ideological underpinnings. While it remains an emergent perspective with indeterminate contours (Clarke, 2006) there is a growing body of policy-related literature (Cooper and Lousada, 2005; Froggett, 2002; Hoggett, 2000). Nevertheless, Frosh concluded in his review of the field: 'the idea of the psycho-social *subject* as a meeting point of inner and outer forces, something construct*ed* and yet construct*ing*, a power-using subject which is also subject to power, is a difficult subject to theorize, and no one has yet worked it out.' (original emphasis, Frosh, 2003, p. 1564).

A psycho-social approach seeks to understand the interaction between the psyche and society, that is, their mutual influencing, while eschewing both psychological and sociological reductionism. It recognizes that both psyche and society have their own rules of structure formation. For the psyche, we call this 'psycho-logic' and include the mechanisms of splitting, projection, repression, denial, integration, and reparation producing dynamic patterns of internal relations between different parts of the personality. For society, such rules of structure formation generate relations of class, gender, and race, as well as relations between status groups and those between economy, state, and civil society. Psycho-social approaches are concerned to understand how such power relations shape and are shaped by 'internal relations' (that is, social relations and object relations). It recognizes that, rather than being unitary, the psyche is the site of powerful feelings that are often in conflict. As passionate beings, we do not always know why we are doing, what we are doing as we do it. In other words, there are limits to our capacity for reflexivity. We are 'meaning seeking' beings but the meanings we generate are subject to distortion and forgetting. A psycho-social approach is hermeneutic with a focus on lived experience but this is 'depth hermeneutics', what needs to be understood is not necessarily immediately present.

The research

We adopted Konig's (1996) concept of a 'dilemmatic space' to describe this area of public service work located on the boundary between state and civil society. The research involved 30 professionals engaged with the 'regeneration' of contested and fragmented UK neighbourhoods. Participants included equal numbers of men and women, a significant number of minority ethnic members and with variable lengths of time as public service professionals. The majority occupied 'frontline' positions and worked with considerable role discretion, authority, and autonomy. Most were employed within local public bodies, and also private non-profit and for-profit organizations. The majority worked directly with community organizations and individual citizens; the 'socially excluded' in UK policy rhetoric, as well as statutory bodies, elected members, and local policy makers. A minority combined management and practice roles. For the majority, social development was their primary task while for others it was becoming a significant part of the role.[2]

The academic leading the multidisciplinary research team was also a qualified psychotherapist. Others included a therapist and two experts in development work. Those responsible for the data gathering were paired (male and female) with each allocated to one of the two research sites. Pilot interviews were preceded by the team trialling the interview process using taped interviews of each other, followed by discussions of interviewer interventions and interviewee reactions.

The research was divided into three stages. The first stage involved six in-depth interviews over one year approximately. These included a biographical narrative, an exploration of the participant's professional role and context, and the identification of current dilemmas and coping strategies. The interviews were undertaken in two equal but distinct parts. The first three concentrated on the subject's life story, current role and context, while the three subsequent interviews, each approximately two months apart, tracked the ethical challenges as they arose and identified in the subject's monthly log or diary. While each interview had a primary focus and was undertaken sequentially, the interviewer role was to make links to related themes raised previously or seek clarification where necessary. All six interviews were transcribed and coded using Nvivo software. Stage two involved four inquiry groups, two in each research site, each meeting on three occasions over six months. These added depth in our understanding of the data; emergent findings related to training and professional development could be considered. Our participants could explore the implications of working within dilemmatic spaces and common themes, issues, and good practice from their collective experiences. The final stage involved a 'findings workshop' for participants and researchers to consider the findings and implications for professional practice, training, and support.

The application of a psycho-social perspective in qualitative research

Interest in the field of psycho-social studies has been matched by attempts to apply this perspective in qualitative research (Hollway and Jefferson, 2000; Walkerdine, 1997). Psycho-social research appeared as qualitative researchers sought a more reflexive interpretative position, especially in relation to the researcher role in data production (Alvesson and Sköldberg, 2000) and one that accorded due recognition to the research subject by focusing on narrative and biographical methods (Hollway, 2001). Previously, research provided new insights into interpretative methods, engaging critically with epistemological concerns around the research interview, the positioning and subjectivities of interviewer and participant, and constructing and representing respondent meanings (Gubrium and Holstein, 2003). Knowledge was recognized as situational and conditional, the interview an interactive encounter in which the researcher is actively engaged in its co-production yet focused on giving voice to the respondent's interpretations and meanings of the world.

Chamberlayne et al. (2002) reflect such methodological developments. In exploring 'life journeys', they note the richness and variety of experience, the importance of individual particularities, and the potential for making connections between the detail of the individual lived experience, social structures, contexts, and processes. Building on the work of Rosenthal and Bar-On (1992) they employed a socio-biographical method (2002, p. 4) in which subjects are considered 'active, self-reflective agents in their own lives'. The subject is given voice by being invited to tell his/her life history, that combination of narrative and story, in his/her own words. Using inductive analysis familiar to the practices of grounded theory this 'told story' is then linked to the subject's 'lived life' (Rosenthal, 1993). The 'lived life' is to be found in data derived from social structures and processes or the 'collection of objective relations' (Bourdieu, 2000, p. 302), in which the individual actor finds himself/herself, between specific social contexts and the response of social actors (Wengraf, 2002). These changing life-story biographical texts can be understood as the 'production of self' (Bourdieu, 2000, p. 301) or 'part of the strategies people have developed to get along with their lives, their experiences and the sense they make of them in the context of their biographies' (Brecker and Rupp, 2002, p. 292).

A psycho-social perspective takes these insights as its starting point but extends the scope of interpretation using psychoanalytic concepts, with particular reference to the work of Melanie Klein. The psycho-social subject is always in a state of incipient disequilibrium (Frosh, 2003). The accompanying anxieties give rise to attempts to restore equilibrium and contribute to a 'defended subject', forged in infancy when totally dependent (Lucey et al., 2003) and applicable to both researcher and respondent. The defended subject does have the capacity for reflexivity and agency within structural constraints, but seeks to protect himself/herself against anxiety and does so largely at an *unconscious* level and in relationship to others (Klein, 1988). Consequently, subjects may not be able to fully explain or understand reactions to particular circumstances. Thus, as in all research, subject voices need to be heard but they should not be adopted uncritically (Hunt, 1989, p. 28–29).

Hollway's and Jefferson's work (2000) remains the benchmark of psycho-social research. They question the assumption of the transparency of the interviewee's awareness and account within the biographical interview, insisting that both are problematic rather than faithful reflections of reality and should be treated as such. To do otherwise would, 'fly in the face of what is known about people's less clear-cut, more confused and contradictory relationship to knowing and telling about themselves' (2000, p. 3). All accounts, including the role played by the researcher in the co-production of knowledge, need an interpretation. The respondent must be allowed to tell the life story free from intrusive interviewer questioning and to develop the narrative in whatever way they choose. However, this cannot be understood without relating the experience to how the subject's inner world shapes an understanding of the outer world and conversely how the inner world is shaped by the experience of the outer.

This approach addresses the so-called, 'individual-social paradox' in which individual reactions or understandings do not follow predictable patterns derived from an understanding of their social position. Rather, to understand individual positions we need to explore the relationship between biography and individual investment in a particular discourse. In other words, what is it about the discourse that protects them against anxiety or supports an identity? In the interview, such unconscious defences will help shape what is provided and how it is provided. Critically, Hollway and Jefferson stress the relationship between the psychic and the social lives of the defended subject. It is psychic, because, 'it is the product of a unique biography of anxiety provoking events and the manner in which they have been unconsciously defended against'

(2000, p. 240). It is social because (1) acting defensively affects and is affected by socially created discourses; (2) as an intersubjective process our defences are affected by and affect others; and (3) it is both real and imagined events against which individuals react.

Thus a number of core elements have emerged that begin to shape a psycho-social approach, some of which were developed further in our research. Narrative inquiry has been identified as the most effective way to elicit subject meanings that are both unique to the subject and to the research encounter, and enable an understanding of how external reality has impinged upon the self. In particular the 'free association' interview using few open-ended questions specifically structured to elicit stories can allow the interviewee to construct the story's 'pattern', however incoherent (Hollway and Jefferson, 2000). Interviews should be free from interpretation, judgement, or interviewer preference but structured to maximize trust. The interviewer's role is to give recognition to the subject and act as a container for the subject's emotional pain. Recognition of the intersubjective nature of the interview and the co-production of data is essential (Kvale, 1999, p. 101) and the positioning of interviewer and interviewee in the unfolding space of the interview encounter critical (Frosh and Emerson, 2005).

The dynamic of the research encounter is characterized by the operation of 'unconscious inter-subjectivity' (Hollway, 2001, p. 21), a complex process involving fantasy, transferences, and the projection and introjection of ideas and feelings between the researcher and the respondent (Hunt, 1989). Interviewer reflexivity should therefore include an exploration of unconscious and conflictual processes, as well as conscious dynamics, as interviewer defences can undermine their capacity to contain the anxieties generated by the interview (Gadd, 2004). Further, the researcher's experience and understanding can be a supplement to theory in understanding the complex and contradictory lives as presented by the respondent (Lucey et al., 2003). The complexity of the interview dynamic is such that it requires an opportunity for clarification and further exploration once the narrative is represented to the interviewer. The use of a second interview, with a suitable time period between interviews allows for data to be processed in conjunction with someone other than the interviewer, provides a reflective space for both interviewer and respondent, and an opportunity to explore emerging hypotheses before returning to the life story. To understand the specific in context (Clarke, 2002) a process of data immersion is required in the life of the subject, moving between the detail and the whole picture, or *Gestalt*. However, Hollway and Jefferson argue that data interpretation, being designed for a different audience, should be separated from the process of data production (2000, p. 77).

Questioning methodical assumptions and developing new practice

The psycho-social model of the subject lurking behind the persons assigned the roles of interviewer and respondent (Holstein and Gubrium, 2003, p. 12) is of someone who is neither active nor passive, acting consciously or unconsciously, but is all simultaneously. Yet too much emphasis accorded to the 'defended subject' can neglect those parts of the personality that seek greater self-understanding and the internal and external forces that impinge upon self and are prepared to risk the anxiety attendant upon such understanding. Melanie Klein was aware that alongside love and hate there existed a third formative impulse that fuels subjective longings. This epistemic impulse, the desire to understand, was explored in greater depth by one of Klein's followers, Wilfred Bion who, in examining the mind, utilized the metaphor of the digestive system, the corporeal foundation of mental life, the body in the mind (Meltzer, 1978). Just as the body grows by taking in life-giving sustenance, so the psyche grows by taking in life-giving 'food for thought', that is, good sense. Good sense emerges from the digestion of experience and is rich in meaning; it is generative and open to becoming. Deploying concepts from a different discourse, we can say that it is reflexive and it is critical. It follows that just as we assume that there are two *defended* subjects present in the interview encounter so there will be two *inquiring* subjects interested in making sense of their experiences, but also anxious/cautious about any disturbance of their psychic equilibrium. The challenge is to construct an epistemic researcher–participant alliance that hinges upon the kinds of connections made between the inquiring parts of their subjectivities.

Our inclination to recognize both the inquiring and defended aspects of researcher and participant subjectivities was reinforced by the nature of the research. Our research subjects, professional welfare practitioners committed to a participative and inclusive developmental philosophy and anxious to reflect upon the findings and the practice implications, sought an active role in the research process. First, we continued with the qualitative research practice of not separating the processes of data analysis and data generation. Second, we utilized a wider range of research methods beyond the biographical interview, including inquiry groups and participant diaries kept over a six-month period; conducted more interviews, six as compared with the more standard two; and our data analysis involved participants in a number of ways that was then used to help shape each subsequent phase in the research.

Participant verification was an essential part of the process, particularly because the participants then had an opportunity to apply any insights gained from the research. We shared our analysis in various ways. First, respondents were given the transcript of each interview and an opportunity to discuss these at the subsequent interview. Second, we shared our coding scheme, and the basis of analysis, that had emerged from the data. Third, the 'inquiry groups' engaged respondents more directly in thinking about some of the emerging issues. Fourth, after completing the interviews we disseminated 'research briefing notes', each designed to capture aspects of our analysis in an accessible way. For some the impact was immediate, confirming or surfacing a previous thought, for example, that it was time to make a work-related change. For others it began a process of reflection on the value of different strategies in relation to specific issues (Squire, 2000).

From the outset, we began the process of collective 'sense-making' with full-day team meetings every three weeks, 26 in all. After the first interviews tapes were listened to, transcripts were read, interpretations and ideas discussed, and views shared on interview dynamics and interviewer interventions. Transcripts were analysed together until their numbers meant this was no longer practical and we devised a different strategy in which the principal researcher continued to read transcripts as they were produced and provided interviewer feedback that focused on the content of the material, the interview dynamic, emotions, interviewer role, and the nature and timing of interventions. Themes began to emerge from the data that became the basis for coding transcripts and for further exploration with interviewees. Additionally, each researcher-participant dyad was 'buddied' with another researcher who read the associated transcripts prior to the third interview to identify gaps or omissions or themes worthy of exploration. To ensure that the research team shared similar understandings about the meaning of the research codes, a number of early interview transcripts were discussed and coded collectively. To retain the holistic nature of the interview process, and capture non-verbal communication and the emotions within the interview (whilst also using a computer-based software package that privileged the interviewee's spoken words transcribed into text), we regularly listened to the tapes alongside reading the text, paying attention to emotion in the voice as well as the content of the language. Throughout, there remained some anxiety that in applying psychoanalytically inspired approaches to data analysis we had to guard against a situation in which subjective speculation was left unbalanced by reality testing.

Thus the participants' value base together with our own predispositions, pre-existing theories, and the opportunity to establish an ongoing relationship with the participants, led us towards what we came to think of as a 'dialogical stance'. Although the biographical interviews began with the free association narrative approach, we modified it in various ways. For example, while the interviewer followed the interviewee's lead, they had to ensure the subject had the opportunity to reflect on what were assumed to be critical areas such as early family background and the subject's place within it, the identification and role of significant others, friendships, community or neighbourhood life, schooling and adolescence, post-schooling and employment. Whilst adhering to the view that the 'told story' would depart in many ways from the 'lived life', where possible we shared our thoughts regarding the latter with our respondents. With interviews spread over one year this seemed appropriate as the later ones would be influenced by the experience of the earlier ones.

For some participants this was either the first time of telling or a long time since having told their story to a relative 'stranger'. Invariably, participants chose to explore their journey from a variety of starting points and some hesitated in taking up the invitation, being uncertain about what they felt might be relevant or interesting to the researcher or unsure about how to 'explain' everything or provide sufficient coherence. Thus while one participant started with, *'I will begin with the family I was born into ...'* another launched straight into an account of their adult career trajectory. Uncertainty and hesitation often characterizes this phase and it was not unusual for participants to say, *'I don't like talking about myself ...'*, to skip quickly over whole periods of their lives or make only glancing references to key events or influences. However, we more frequently experienced that at the end of the interview participants were surprised about how much they had shared *'I've probably said far more than I thought I would ...'*, how interesting they found their own stories and how useful, even cathartic, it was to have the space to begin to make some connections between their different selves (Squire, 2000, p. 202).

When further clarification is needed, where the participant glides over critical areas or seems reluctant to discuss some aspect, the interviewer must judge whether it is appropriate to invite further exploration. Similarly, if a recurring theme either in the interview content or in process is identified, they must judge whether to reflect this back and invite comment. In other words, the interviewer role is one of selective probing, either directly or indirectly reflecting back, clarifying, connecting or linking, and seeking further information. While the aim is to enable the interviewee to tell their own story by offering them full attention and active listening skills, and securing a secure and safe environment, the interviewer is proactive in teasing out critical aspects.

In qualitative research, there are two different forms of analysis. Themes emerge across individual cases and provide the basis for coding and theoretical generalization. Then there is the analysis of individual cases and as successive transcripts are read, an individual 'gestalt' emerges in which particular parts or extracts can be understood more thoroughly by considering their relationship to the whole (Hollway and Jefferson, 2000, pp. 68–72). A psycho-social approach seeks to combine both nomothetic and idiographic approaches because it is concerned to understand both social relations and the nature of individual investments in these relations. However, it is easier to share ideas with respondents about the social relations impinging upon their lives than it is to share thoughts about what they bring to these social relations that are personal to them. Yet such points of connection between individual lives and social relations are illuminating, casting a new light upon the individual life and the social relation.

But what of our capacity as researchers to share our thinking about the respondents themselves and what we are learning about their biography, values, passions, coping strategies, and defences? Kvale (1999, p. 107) cautions against interpretations that go beyond 'the self-understanding of the interviewee' as such disclosures are not usually part of the research contract and have not been explicitly sought by the research subject. Hollway and Jefferson seek but struggle to make a clear distinction between a clinical and a research interview. They remind us that researchers are not therapists but recognize that 'this distinction breaks down in the necessary exchanges of understanding that take place in the interview' (2000, p. 78). We suggest that a separation of data analysis and production is untenable. Researchers cannot but 'think into the encounter' and this necessarily assumes the form of interpretations. Our approach, whilst guarding against offering or imposing (Britton, 1977) unwanted, and possibly inappropriate, 'interpretations', was to provide opportunities to re-examine areas where there appeared to be inconsistencies or confusion and to offer our reflections when participants seemed ready to receive these. Researcher judgement is again critical and inevitable as are sensitivity, timing, and the stage of development in the interviewer–interviewee relationship (Faraday and Plummer, 1979).

A dialogic model of the interview process

The following examples from our research explore the nature and role of thinking, analysis, and interpretation as work performed both inside the here-and-now of the interview or outside the here-and-now but still inside the ongoing research relationship. The extracts demonstrate some of the ways in which we attempted to share our thinking with each other and with our respondents.

Observing the effects of interpretations in the interview process

In what follows an interviewer tests a hypothesis about a respondent's performance in their professional role. This man managed a team of youth workers on a neglected and stigmatized outer city housing estate. He had worked there for many years and he and his team had a reputation for working effectively with some very troubled young people. We begin with an extract from the feedback of the principal researcher who had been reading interview transcripts:

> *One of the things that began to come through for me...I'd just read his fourth transcript before re-reading his first...He is very principled. He doesn't take the easy way out or turn a blind eye to things...he adopts a clear line. He is quite tough but...also a doubter...it might be interesting to ask him to reflect on this...in the last interview – would he agree that he takes a 'principled approach'? Part of him seems to wish that he didn't...Does he have any reflections on this conflict going on inside him? Does he (or his colleagues) sometimes feel that he is a bit stubborn?*

We can see how the principal researcher's immersion in the transcripts leads to the formation of a gestalt in his mind. The transcript of the subsequent interview illustrates how the interviewer used some of these thoughts:

> *one of the things that has come up in looking back at the transcripts is your...quite highly principled approach, um, of wanting to do things in the way that you see as, um, proper, with quite clear principles, and clear boundaries, would you say?...might come across as, kind of, stubborn sometimes. Can you reflect on that for a little bit?*

The respondent replies first by clarifying how he understands clarity:

> *Well, in some ways...clarity is something you have to get towards. It's not something you can impose.*

He then uses as an example whether they should close the centre following a major incident. His team wants to impose a strict line but he insists that they must think it through, *'I've said each time there is a process that you go through and then you take the decision'*. In this particular case, two young people had stolen a staff member's car. Our respondent opposed calls that the centre be closed, as this was an unfair form of 'blanket punishment'. He continued:

> *people said they were feeling stressed, but ... professionally, you have to say, 'I'm upset because my colleague's car has got stolen, but actually I'm here to do this job' ... they've found that a bit stubborn ... then there was an argument that young people need to know the consequences. I said, 'Yes, but the right people ... not the wrong people' ... there's been quite a fierce argument ... we will have a staff meeting about this.*

Emerging from this extract and the ensuing conversation is something we had not understood before, that the essence of this man's approach hinges upon 'process' – bringing everyone together to argue an issue out before making a decision. Later he provides a number of examples of the dilemmas of practice, situations where there is no obvious right thing to do (Banks, 2004), and how he sees 'process' as the only way of proceeding. However, 'arguing things out' can be stressful for those already quite stressed, and so he is tough in his insistence that decisions are thought about and made collectively. He reflects upon *'how much to demand of people that is fair'*, the tension between firmness and compassion, the government's 'tough love' philosophy and the difference between being judgemental and solidarity.

Summarizing, in this example we tested an interpretation with our respondent and what emerged is that he was principled, and sometimes stubborn, but not in the way in which we had anticipated. He was stubborn about the value of a 'dialogic process', indeed for him it is impossible to do this kind of work effectively without it. By sharing our thinking, new thoughts were generated and some things became clearer, such as how this man performed his role and some of the emotional labour involved. Our hypothesis had a generative value, facilitating a stream of linkages and connections in his thinking, each new connection being like a door opening into a new room.

Exploring the past to understand an individual's investment in a discourse

This example, from an interview with a black female regeneration programme manager, illustrates our attempt to share not only our thinking but also how an understanding of someone's life history enabled us to see a person's present investment in a discourse in a different light. Unlike many of the participants, the respondent presented herself as upbeat and uncritical about the government's modernization agenda and the possibilities for change. The principal researcher, on reading the transcripts of the first two interviews, noted that:

> *Taking both transcripts together what really hits me is ... her 'positivism' ... Repeatedly she talks about the impact she is able to have ... so different to the ... views of many others. It's not that she's unaware of barriers and constraints ... try and find out where this comes from, to reflect it back to her in terms of what personal qualities, aspects of her personality and upbringing she connects it to.*

In the final interview, when the respondent's positive outlook is once more to the fore, the interviewer returned to these issues:

> *I was wondering ... I haven't quite still got a sense of, what is or has been the experience for you all these years in the sense of being a female, black person trying to do your best to get where you are?*

For the next 30 minutes, the respondent returns into her life history but in a deeper way than she had previously. She recounts the widely different paths taken by her siblings and their personal experiences of discrimination. She links how she was in the educational system as a child, *'I used to go around unseen, unheard and didn't create many ripples'*, with how she operates as a professional, *'I realised ... if I just go along my business quietly, I tend to be able to go through things without too much restriction, too much notice'*. A picture emerged of a strategy developed for using the system to struggle for greater equality. Her teenage daughter had encountered just as much discrimination at school as she did, *'things haven't really changed, they've just become more sophisticated'* and so, she argued, *'rather than me standing up and shouting, I have to be more sophisticated in my approach ... as a black person, I always have to be very conscious about what I am going to say ...'*. She developed multiple networks *'so you have lots of ways to get your message in'*, and used the language of targets, outcomes, and success stories to push forward the equalities agenda. She also talked from her own experience about the value of *'anything that will make your life a little better and more pleasant, a little easier, it has such an impact even though it may be a very, very small thing'*.

Many of our participants had been involved in political activism and expressed radical values. In contrast, at first sight, this woman appeared as someone who had a belief in the system, saw the value of making measurable small gains, and firmly believed that *'for every challenge there's an opportunity'*. Prompted in the final interview she again positioned herself as a black woman, *'I can focus on the negative but the negative is there in our eyes all the time'*. She continued:

> *It doesn't mean that because I'm a black single parent from parents who came in the 1950s from a colonial existence that I should be unemployed...but that's what statistics say I should be...So I tend to...buck against those systems...in this life there are opportunities...globalisation is a real opportunity for us as black people...there are more black people than white people in this world...we're a majority, it's just that where we live we're a minority.*

For this woman, whose family experience tells her *'it's much easier to go down and under than it is to kind of succeed'*, staying positive became an enduring strategy for survival and progress (Breckner and Rupp, 2002, p. 292). Now we can understand her investment in discourses of modernization in a new light, as a way in which it can be used to advance people like herself.

Reality, fiction, and interpretation

At its best, the research interview is a recognition-producing exercise in which the participant has the experience of 'being understood'. When it breaks down, perhaps because the interviewer cannot contain their own anxiety or because he/she imposes his/her own thinking in an intrusive way, then the narrative becomes concrete and descriptive, producing facts rather than generating meanings. However, when the epistemic alliance is working well, evidence for its recognition-producing qualities can be found in participant responses to researcher interventions. Here there is a precise parallel with psychoanalysis. A good interpretation produces new material, or enables new connections to be made within what is already known and spoken about. Judging the value of an interpretation in this way combines elements of pragmatism and realism. Pragmatism, to the extent that the 'truth value' of a formulation can be judged according to its capacity to generate new insights, is referred to by Lakatos as its 'heuristic power' (Lakatos, 1970, p. 175). Realism to the extent that by deploying perspectives from psychoanalysis and critical theory, we endeavour to highlight something rather personal and unique about who is the person telling us a story and how this particular person draws upon specific values and motivations to give further meaning and context to the lived aspects of the told story.

Ethical dilemmas in psycho-social research

Researcher influence and its uses

In our research, we refrained from making use of counter-transference based interpretations. For researchers who have not themselves been through intensive psychotherapy or psychoanalysis the use of counter-transference as data runs considerable risks (Lucey et al., 2003). Stopford argues that in the brief encounter provided by research, ways must be found to, 'facilitate our participants' involvement in construction of interpretation' (Stopford, 2004, p. 18). Like Stopford we introduced our own 'questions and perspectives during the interview' (p. 20), monitoring whether these facilitated a further elaboration of the respondent's subjectivity or 'a protective closing down/disconnection' (p. 22). Indeed, there are strong ethical grounds for arguing that in psychosocial methodologies that make use of transference, interpretations should necessarily adopt a dialogical and democratic stance, for this is the only basis upon which the efficacy of analysis and interpretation can be judged.

In all qualitative interviews respondent–researcher influencing is mutual and continuous and 'researcher effects' inevitable. What is important is that the interviewer tries to sustain what Bion, following Keats, calls 'negative capability' a capacity for 'being in uncertainties, mysteries, doubts, without any irritable reaching after fact and reason' (French and Simpson, 2001). Interviewers must learn to tolerate silences and provide the space within which issues can emerge. Nevertheless, from the outset the researcher is engaged in a sense-making process or, in Bion's terms, digesting the experience of the interview. The issue is not whether they *should* share their thinking, it is inevitable that they will, but *how* they share it, especially when the researcher's thoughts concern the respondent's character, identity, and values rather than the nature of the social relations in which they are immersed. Yet it is not always possible to share personalized reflections and judgements are required about the respondent's defensive organization. Having psychotherapists in the team or as mentors to the research can help make such judgements.

This has implications for many 'taken-for-granted' research concepts. For example, it suggests that in qualitative research the idea of 'data collection' is misleading, implying that the researcher's role is limited to some kind of 'collecting' activity occurring prior to data analysis and without interpretation (Alldred and Gillies, 2002, p. 159). Relational models of research assume that data is generated and overlaps with data analysis and interpretation. However, we question the assumption that the analytical work and theory building must be done outside of the research relationship. We distinguished between the thinking that occurs inside the here-and-now of the interview from that which goes on inside the interview relationship but outside the here-and-now. The latter occurs in team meetings, in individual reflections on listening to tapes, reading transcripts and through the work of the principal researcher. By having multiple interviews this second kind of thinking can be brought back into the here-and-now of subsequent interviews. This allows for 'hypothesis testing' and new perspectives, something akin to Klein's notion of 'thirdness'. While sharing drafts of articles with respondents can pose questions of confidentiality (Mauthner, 2000), if this can be overcome the practice becomes integral to democratic ethics of research. Like much participatory practice, it can be tokenistic but it is worth trying, not least because it opens to scrutiny researcher claims to knowledge.

Although we focused on the coping strategies adopted by a group of professionals negotiating ethical dilemmas, sometimes this produced a highly personalized response. Agreement had to be secured that an exploration of the relationship between personal biography and professional role was legitimate. Inappropriate probing can be recovered but it can damage irretrievably the research relationship and result in participant withdrawal. The question of when and if to probe for more information beyond that which subjects offer, that could be experienced as intrusive and potentially harmful, was a constant topic within the research team.

Confidentiality, anonymity, and a duty of care

Psycho-social research must grapple with a number of other recognizable ethical dilemmas. A critical concern is that of confidentiality, anonymity, and participant involvement in data analysis (BSA, 1996). Complete anonymity was not possible as the research included a conference and inquiry groups in which themes generated in the interviews were explored and participants could identify with their own interview material and make associations between their experience and that of other participants. As the research was conducted within relatively small geographical areas and a limited area of professional practice, many participants were already known to each other. Anyone determined to link quotations with individuals could do so either because of familiarity with the views expressed or by the subject's role designation, agency description, or involvement in specific initiatives. However, repeated opportunities to reaffirm participant consent were provided by the 'invitation' to join an inquiry group, a reminder that they could withdraw at any point, regular reviews at each project phase and outlines of what was still to come.

Additional steps to 'protect' subjects included allocating different interviewers to participants employed by the same agency. In such cases, data was not shared between researchers, thereby protecting it from interviewer corruption, although in all other cases it was made clear that data would be shared. Consideration was given to altering certain details in the biographic stories although traditional practises such as changes to gender, age, or role are inappropriate within a psycho-social framework (Hollway and Jefferson 2000, p. 96). Participant permission was always sought whenever writing for the public domain, especially for those papers that included a life story in a 'case-study' format. Further, we ensured that information gained about another participant was not disclosed.

Psycho-social research demands much of its subjects and the experience of a biographical interview can disrupt or disturb the participant's equilibrium. Some participant distress can be anticipated and an approach agreed as to how to respond and the extent to which participants are protected from it. We adopted the view that to be distressed is not to be equated with being 'harmed', although inappropriate responses to distress can generate a level of harm. At the outset we explained, verbally and in writing, our interest in the biographical journey and the values held. As participants were invited to tell their life story beginning at whatever point they wished it was impossible to predict what would follow, what they would choose to speak of, how painful or difficult that might be, and whether any subsequent probing would open up aspects that the participants had not anticipated or prepared themselves for their own response to the telling. For example, early in the initial interview one participant prefaced a reference to a traumatic event in her early teens *'without going into detail'*. In telling the sequential life story the subject returned to that moment and, prompted by a 'what then' question, went on to recount the event in some detail. In that moment, both interviewer and interviewee faced a choice. In anticipation that this could be distressing, the researcher could have accepted the initial statement as a clear signal that the person was not ready to go further, did not want to say more, or did not think it would be relevant. The interviewer judged that the participant could decide for herself (Gadd, 2004, p. 397). The interviewee, a reflective professional working with challenging issues, could have declined but chose to speak about it.

Researcher anxiety about being witness to or 'causing' distress can result in a more tentative, less confident self, less able to contain the anxiety of self or other, and a participant more reluctant to disclose what they feel might be difficult for the researcher. Although interviews are sometimes distressing, participants often find them valuable opportunities for reflection and occasionally decision-making. It is the researcher's responsibility to ensure an emotionally suitable environment, including the setting in which to conduct the interviews (Hunt, 1989). Our focus was with 'self' in relation to work and subjects were identified through the workplace. Interviews were often conducted in the workplace and in work time, taking responsibility for the setting away from the researcher. This sometimes presented difficulties in relation to accessing a quiet, comfortable, soundproof space protected against interruptions, in which participants felt secure to talk without feeling observed. As knowledge about the research spread, workplace interviewing also raised the participant's profile generating fantasies about the basis on which some were 'chosen' and others 'excluded' as well as what might be being revealed about the agency, work, or colleagues.

The co-production of data and inter-subjectivity

Much has been said on the co-production of data and the researcher's role in data creation as a product of the 'inter-view' although caution is needed so as not to over-exaggerate the 'researcher factor'. Researchers contribute to what is produced in various ways. They establish the research setting and climate, both social and psychological. The assumptions they bring, underpinning theories, and epistemological positions are all significant given the attendant danger of reproducing cultural norms and expectations (Alldred and Gillies, 2002, p. 151). Within the interview, researcher influence is evident in the framing of questions, verbal and non-verbal responses to interviewee answers, in the selection/rejection and amount of time given to particular lines of inquiry, researcher competency in facilitative practice, and critically through unconscious communications, derived from what their presence elicits within the interviewee, and researcher fantasies (Walkerdine, 1997, pp. 66–75).

When co-production is understood as a joint, collaborative, and unique endeavour, it can increase the potential significance afforded to accessing participant emotions through an exploration of researcher emotions. Lucey et al. (2003) suggest that these may mirror those of the interviewee while Walkerdine (1997) offers a robust defence of the inclusion of researcher subjectivity: 'Sometimes the feelings stirred up in the researcher...will be an indication of what is actually happening for the interviewee' (1997, p. 72) and insists that the researcher's material be made explicit as this may further our understanding the significance of what is communicated by the interviewee. Yet, too close attention to the researcher's emotional state or any automatic 'reading-off' of that experience to the interviewee can detract from the interviewee's ownership of the data and undermine their capacity to reproduce a sufficiently recognizable 'told account' (Wengraf, 2000, p. 145). Variations will be apparent, and explanations for these might be readily available, but there is likely to be sufficient continuity and consistency: the research subject is always closer than the researcher to the authenticity of his or her own story. Researchers can be seduced or enchanted by the subject's detailed life story or narcissistically engrossed in the researcher role (Chamberlayne and Spano, 2000). Gadd (2004) suggests a 'cooling-off' period and a return to the data when researcher emotional involvement has subsided. Achieving a better understanding of social processes, individual meanings, and researcher contribution are legitimate research goals but interpretations can become too process-focused at the expense of the substantive topic. We may end up knowing more about the researcher and the interview dynamic, at both conscious and unconscious levels, while neglecting the data's social utility that is often at the core of the research contract.

Finally, psycho-social research must grapple with the challenge of whether the quality of data produced is sufficient to make the claims implicit within the methodology. Hollway and Jefferson (2000) offered a psycho-social analysis based on two interviews while Clarke (2002) and Lucey et al. (2003) did so with one. We conducted six interviews yet it was difficult in a five-person research team and with 30 participants to ensure consistency and avoid variable data. We need also to guard against over speculative interpretations especially when offered by those trained in disciplines other than psychotherapy, yet the relative importance of a grounding in psychoanalysis, how this is acquired and whether it should extend to the whole research team remains unresolved. It was important for us that a practising psychotherapist led our research team while the contributions of other voices with different perspectives were equally critical.

Conclusion

We have argued that a psycho-social perspective adds a valuable dimension to qualitative research. Drawing upon psychoanalytic concepts, particularly the understanding of the subject as defended against anxieties, as well as the inquiring subject seeking insight and knowledge and whose anxieties are often experienced unconsciously and intersubjectively, we can move beyond the simple recognition of the research participant's voice. This requires the researcher to pay attention to a different dimension in the interview process. Similarly, it extends our understanding of the intersubjective nature of the research interview and the co-production of knowledge through recognition of the unconscious behaviour of the researcher and what is happening at that level between the researcher and the researched. Thus, a psycho-social perspective provides a means to get beneath the surface of the subject's told story, connecting the psychic and social dimensions underpinning the meanings and responses attached to experiences. We have also argued, somewhat against the grain of psycho-social research, that participant verification and collective sense-making remains a critical dimension, perhaps more so than in other qualitative research approaches and have argued for the development of a dialogical relationship throughout the research process. This created the potential for the interview to provide new insights and participant sense-making, as well as being experienced as a process of recognition. The inclusion of a number of interviews spread over a lengthy period meant that such 'findings' could be tested and then reflected upon further. This recognition-producing element was especially critical in the context of research into how people occupying professional roles operating on the state-civil society boundary negotiate ethical dilemmas. Conversely, we have warned against the use of over-speculative interpretations and cautioned against the elevation of researcher emotions as a way of understanding the research participant. We have also identified the need for some expertise in psychoanalysis, either within the research team or as consultant to it. In future research, we would want to include participant observation as an additional dimension, so as to consider participant behaviour in relation to participant understandings about behaviour.

Notes

1. Negotiating ethical dilemmas in contested communities, Economics and Social Research Council, reference.
2. For details about the research see Hoggett et al., 2006.

Part III
Issues in Research

7

Evaluating Risk Assessment: A Methodological Study of Mentally Disordered Offenders in the London Probation Area

Diana Wendy Fitzgibbon

Introduction

This chapter concerns the effectiveness in practice of the current pre-occupation with risk assessment in criminal justice and social services. It examines aspects of the new orientation towards risk and the effects this has had in the probation service and in social work, both of which have moved away from traditional casework methods towards various methodologies of risk assessment. The dynamics of this shift are now well-known (Kemshall, 2003; Oldfield, 2002; Robinson 2003b, 2005). Such change may form part of wider social and political changes, which have been much discussed in the social sciences (Garland, 2001; Lea, 2002; Young, 1999, 2003). The rise to predominance in the United Kingdom of the 'risk agenda'; the concern by government to protect the public against the risks posed by offenders and other high risk groups is, it can be argued, inextricably connected to 'the decline of the welfare state' (Hudson, 2003). In its widest sense, the welfare state is incompatible with the 'risk society', in that a commitment to welfare presupposes a desire by tax payers to invest in the reintegration of offenders for the good of society as a whole. The risk society is concerned with excluding those it deems a threat and ensuring that the worthy majority feel protected against such persons. The main aim in this chapter, however, is to identify, on the basis of a small study[1] of the implementation of The Offender Assessment System (E-OASys) risk-assessment tool currently in use in the English and Welsh Probation Service, some of the contradictions and problems inherent in the operation of such risk containment techniques by probation practitioners. After a review of the main themes in research in this area, methodological issues arising from an evaluation of the E-OASys used by the Probation Service in England and Wales are described and analysed. In the final section of the chapter, the strengths and weaknesses of the research methodology for yielding policy relevant knowledge concerning risk reduction and client support for mentally disordered offenders are assessed and implications for social change evaluated.

Background

The E-OASys is a joint Probation and Prison Services initiative which was designed primarily to replace previously existing instruments, which had failed to meet the requirements of the two Services (Home Office, 2002). E-OASys, an actuarial and dynamic assessment tool, consolidated the fundamental changes in values and professional practice that have occurred within the Probation Service. These concern the focus on the protection of the public, the punishment of offenders, and a decrease in crime and evidence-based practice (Bhui, 2002; Oldfield, 2002; Robinson, 2001). The two main principles it incorporates are adherence to evidence-based practice – the so-called 'What Works' agenda – (Robinson, 2005), and the necessity to bring about a reduction in risk.

The new culture of public sector management which dominates public services in Britain and other countries like Australia, America – and which may well feature increasingly in other European countries – involves performance targets, measures of efficiency and effectiveness and has made its way into all areas of criminal justice including probation (Cutler and Waine, 1997; James and Raine, 1998). The overriding concern has been to ensure 'best value' in public expenditure. The accountability of both welfare and criminal justice professionals moved from a focus on the 'client' to a focus centring on the agency and on the taxpayer as both source of funds and potential victim of crime and risk.

The second dimension is that of accountability to the public as actual or potential victim of harm, caused by the clients of social service and criminal justice agencies. In the criminal justice system as a whole, the shift from a focus on the rights of the accused, in favour of greater emphasis on the efficiency of the system in protecting the public and the victim has been noted with concern by civil libertarians (Belloni and Hodgson, 1999; Kennedy, 2004).

The shift, both in probation and wider areas of welfare provision (including social work), away from traditional client-based casework approaches, has been widely noted (Froggett, 2002; Goodman, 2003; Hudson 2001, 2003; Kemshall, 2003; Nellis, 2004; Oldfield, 2002; Robinson 2003a, b, 2005). Traditional relations of trust and accountability between client and practitioner involved work with the client as a whole person – who was a citizen with rights and needs – in terms of their own biographies and experiences (Froggett, 2002). Thus, in probation, various therapeutic or work-related strategies of rehabilitation aimed to help clients understand their life in non-offending terms (Burnett and McNeill, 2005; Smith and Vanstone, 2002; Vanstone, 2004). The logic behind the old casework strategy of 'advise, assist and befriend' was precisely the need to develop a one-to-one therapeutic relationship of mutual trust and suspended judgement between practitioner and client, on the basis of which the totality of the client's life trajectory could be problematized and reoriented (Burnett, 2004). Rehabilitation could be grasped as a life-change, and one that involved a complex reworking of the relationship between the individual offender and their community and environment (Smith and Vanstone, 2002).

The shift to a risk orientation involves two components. First, the status of the client as citizen in need of reclamation and rehabilitation tends to be replaced by the concept of risk to the public. While such risks might seem amenable to careful calibration, in the extreme case they can be elaborated into notions of the threatening 'other', taking the form either of an *underclass* with alleged distinct cultural traits of fecklessness and criminality (Murray, 1990, 1994) or of the rationally calculating 'welfare scrounger' and criminal entrepreneur (Van Dijk, 1994). Either way, the client is a risk to be encountered and managed and, as welfare scrounger or criminal offender, is in direct competition for resources with the honest taxpayer.

Second, once established as alien 'other' – and with the therapeutic and biographical approaches pushed to the background – effectively the client can then be deconstructed into manifestations of the various actuarially established indicators of risk. The contextual knowledge of the client is gradually replaced by the collection of disembodied data derived from various standardized indicators of risk (Castel, 1991; Franko Aas, 2004).

The categorization and classification of client types becomes coterminus with the classification of risks. What were previously indicators of citizens in need of assistance and rehabilitation, the young unemployed, those with mental health problems, young offenders, become indicators of risk and danger (Fitzgibbon, 2004). The most important shift is that the social situation of the offender is pushed to the background in favour of a set of *characteristics of the offender* described as 'criminogenic needs' which are to be established by a 'tick box' approach rather than by an in-depth knowledge of the client, their biography, and their interaction with the environment with which they have to cope. The precise criminogenic needs, in terms of which the individual client is constructed, are identified from a complex of factors including previous and current offence(s) and the potential for harm to self or members of the public which such offences indicate. A number of background factors are included, such as accommodation, education, employment, financial situation, relationships, lifestyle and associates, drug and alcohol misuse, emotional well-being, thinking and behaviour, attitudes, health, and other considerations. The E-OASys system then allocates a score between 0 and 2 (2 being a serious problem) and guides the practitioner to the level and type of intervention required by the offender's profile (Home Office, 2002).

The offender as a complex of criminogenic needs then requires training in cognitive skills to enable those needs to be managed. This is quite distinct from previous welfare-oriented strategies of rehabilitation. The emphasis is primarily in training offenders to adjust to their circumstances and keep quiet (that is, cease to engage in criminality or risky behaviour) (Hannah-Moffat, 2005, p. 42). Offending is here portrayed in terms of *failure* to make rational choice, rather than as the *outcome* of rational choice or, yet alone as a revolt against the very rationality of the social system which appears to have put the offender in his/ her initial predicament (Young, 2003). Thus in the currently deployed E-OASys template, criminogenic need scores will be enhanced if the client exhibits 'a great deal of antipathy towards legal system and agencies'; 'justifies own behaviour by comparisons with misdemeanours of others'; 'favours or excuses criminal behaviour regularly and with conviction'; or, 'expresses views supportive of offending at any time in interview' (Home Office, 2002, p. 109).

However, it could be argued that sophisticated and easily administered risk-assessment tools as criminogenic needs analysis (Aubrey and Hough, 1997) exhibit a marked failure to contextualize adequately the offender's relationship to their social situation. Here, offending is purely a characteristic of the offender's failure to make prudent decisions. There is no longer a social context to criminality (Goodman, 2003). Thus, the job of both the welfare and criminal justice systems is increasingly that of managing a social stratum identified and categorized in terms of various indicators of risk to the public. The role of the practitioner is transformed as part of this process. This research examined a purposive sample of 24 cases from the London area in order to evaluate whether practitioners were aided by the E-OASys assessments to make more accurate assessments – and therefore enabled to make better interventions and risk management. The study specifically explored whether E-OASys had identified those offenders with mental health problems, those at most risk and whether it had led to effective case management to (1) reduce risk and (2) provide support to clients.

Introduction to choice of research study

There has been considerable rhetoric about working with offenders with mental health difficulties since the introduction of Home Office Circular 66/90: Provision for Mentally Disordered Offenders (Home Office, 1990) later supplemented with Circular 12/95, Mentally Disordered Offenders: Inter-agency Working (Home Office, 1995). Both these circulars outlined government policy aimed at achieving care and treatment for mentally disordered offenders, rather than punishment through the criminal justice system and emphasized a need for partnership working and the full and timely sharing of information across criminal justice, health agencies, and others involved in the care and management of mentally disordered offenders. Whilst the emphasis has moved away from diversion to offenders being *'properly punished for their crime'*; government policy has retained the importance of the need to 'make sure that people with mental disorders who offend get the treatment they need' and continues to place importance on information exchange (Home Office, 2006, p. 28).

'The National Action Plan for Reducing Re-offending' through greater strategic direction and joined up working (Home Office, 2004) would obviously disproportionately affect those with mentally ill and/ or people socially excluded, as mental illness is correlated with social exclusion (see Lea, 2002; Young, 1999). The National Action Plan, whilst not addressing the issues of mental disorder directly, acknowledged that offenders are not a homogeneous group and that they are differentiated by age, gender, ethnicity, family background, and geographic location, and by the nature, circumstances, and frequency of the crimes they commit (Home Office, 2004).

The National Action Plan summarized three areas that needed to be successfully addressed both at strategic development level and at the point of service delivery, so that the plan could attain its maximum impact (Home Office, 2004). These areas were

- communication,
- information sharing,
- risk assessment.

Thus, the key aim of the plan was to identify and target offenders, particularly those most at risk of reoffending and/or causing harm to themselves and others. The report stated clearly that achievement in these areas is dependent on up-to-date offender assessments being carried out by prison and probation staff. E-OASys is seen as central to effective risk assessment and a major factor determining how the offender is managed.

Effective work with offenders with mental health problems can only happen if offender managers have the ability to identify the problem in the first place. Much has been written about the need for training in this area (Kemshall, 2003; Prins, 2005) but less focus has been given to the use of E-OASys, which has designed into the tool the capacity to identify problems related to mental health and personality disorder. For this reason, the author decided to undertake research in this area to look at two broad areas. First, whether E-OASys was improving the situation for mentally vulnerable offenders and second to look at its accuracy as an assessment tool to predict risk of serious harm to others or themselves, and enable offenders with mental disorders to receive the treatment they require.

Exploration of research methodology

My research is rooted in a critical theoretical approach as the aim of my research was to analyse how shifts in probation and wider agencies reflected political and ideological concerns with security, risk, and predicting future behaviours (Noaks and Wincup, 2004). The purpose of these changes of emphasis is not, I argue, to enable offenders to be reintegrated more effectively, but to manage and contain certain vulnerable and 'risky' groups such as those with mental health problems.

I decided to conduct a small-scale exploratory research project, using a purposive sample of ten cases with mental health problems, in a large metropolitan probation area over a period of three months between December 2004 and February 2005. Permission was obtained for access to data from the area's probation research unit and ethical approval for the research was given by the University of Hertfordshire and the probation service in question.

Due to the nature of the questions arising out of the use of E-OASys with mentally vulnerable offenders, I decided to apply a qualitative research methodology. Qualitative research can be utilized to explore the way social reality can be constructed through examining social phenomena and their meanings and how these are continually being produced and altered in relation to their cultural and historical context (Gubrium and Holstein, 1997). My research utilized a qualitative approach as this enabled me to gain a deeper knowledge of the offenders subject to my study, the social phenomena surrounding their situations and to appreciate the social world from the point of view of the offender, victim, and criminal justice professional. I aimed to explore the context of the offending and the meanings attached to the behaviours of both staff and offenders. Qualitative data can flesh out the context in which crime – and thus criminal justice – is administered, by adding detail to skeletal quantitative statistics. Thus, my research focuses particularly on examination of approaches to risk assessment by practitioners. As has been illustrated in the discussion above, the prevalence of risk assessment as opposed to more traditional means of assisting offenders to prevent criminal behaviour is emphasized by the introduction of a centralized unified approach to working with offenders, in this case the use of a formal risk-assessment tool namely E-OASys.

This general research question led to the consideration of data collection. It was decided to examine a small purposive sample of cases where the E-OASys had been undertaken and that these assessments and the relevant online case records would be analysed to explore whether mental health concerns had been appropriately identified and how this had influenced the management of the case. Documentary contextual analysis is of benefit in that it is a way of ascertaining information in a non-reactive environment. Therefore, it is not susceptible to possible distortion from the interaction between the researcher and the subject (Corbetta, 2003). The other advantage is that institutional documents are produced in large numbers, which means samples can be obtained and examined at low cost. Thus when considering the enormous pressures on staff in the Probation area studied, it was decided that documentary research would be undertaken as it could be conducted solely by the researcher and not impose any resource implications on probation staff. It was therefore approved readily by the Probation area as a method of investigation.

I was aware of the disadvantages of using institutional documents. The information provided could be incomplete and could primarily represent the official position in relation to offenders and their situations. However, despite these disadvantages, I felt that the institutional dimension might in fact throw more light on the pressures on staff completing the E-OASys assessments. Thus, live cases were accessed as a way to understand their substantive content and reveal the usefulness of the E-OASys tool, not only to the practitioner, but also as a method of communication and information sharing as part of the 'National Action Plan for Reducing Re-offending' (Home Office, 2004).

To ensure confidentiality a research number was allocated to all cases to protect their anonymity. Initially 24 cases that had had an E-OASys assessment undertaken were considered. All these cases were managed in the Probation area studied. This purposive sample was examined to reveal

(a) Those offenders with mental health problems identified by the assessor; usually, but not exclusively, a probation officer;
(b) Those offenders with mental health problems whose assessment was incomplete or inaccurate on basis of examination of follow-up materials in the case file;
(c) Other trends not particular or exclusive to those offenders with mental health problems, but which were significant to this research.

A factor which had to be considered was that within E-OASys, 18 questions in 6 domains are currently used to indicate the possible existence of a mental health or personality disorder issue. At the time of the research, there was no flag system within the E-OASys to identify offenders assessed in these areas and there were difficulties in accessing the data manually. This issue was a cause of some concern and influenced research design, particularly the design of the forms used to collect data.

After the initial screening the data was interpreted and it was decided that further data collection with a smaller purposive sample of ten cases with clear signs of mental health problems, personality disorder (PD) or both, would be undertaken at the probation offices where the case file was held. Also, those whose E-OASys assessment seemed to be incomplete or scored extremely low were identified for review in this research, to check if information had been overlooked which could be ascertained from case files. The documents were expected to be a reflection of the lived reality of the offenders and practitioners, through the examination of which their social and organizational contexts might be discovered.

Findings

Following the initial screening of 24 E-OASys assessments and their case records, ten cases were selected using the probation area's Criminal Record and Management System (CRAMs) record database. This purposive sample comprised two offenders who were black, three white offenders, and five offenders whose race/ethnicity were unknown. This was due to incomplete E-OASys data. As Bhui (1999) has noted, Black and Minority Ethnic groups' needs in terms of the importance of not assessing or addressing factors such as mental disorder are often highlighted by research as an area of concern (also see Fitzgibbon, 2007a). Three of the samples were women offenders and all were over eighteen years.

Analysis of the selected cases focused on three areas. These addressed the issue of whether practitioners using this tool were able to identify those offenders who may potentially have mental health needs. If these needs were highlighted, were they taken into account in future needs and risk assessments? Finally, did this then lead to more effective and sensitive management of their criminogenic needs and therefore more appropriate risk containment? The thoroughness and effectiveness of the E-OASys forms were evaluated throughout this process in terms of the quality of the completed documents and the level of details used. Here are some of the key findings from the research.

Issues concerning the quality and detail of E-OASys completion

There was evidence in some cases, particularly those with transient officers, that no full E-OASys risk assessment had been undertaken, nor had any other form of risk assessment pre-dating the introduction of E-OASys. This was despite mental health concerns being noted in the initial screening, where key factors like dual diagnosis, self-harm or inability to conform to psychiatric treatment, indicated that a full risk assessment should be completed. To compound this finding, the majority of the sample had little supplementary information to reinforce or expand on the 'tick boxes'. Whilst E-OASys allows for building in of 'evidence' (in script form) into the tool, the lack of this additional data on the form would support other research findings that when tick boxes are presented, assessors question their ability to clinically expand on the assessment and resort to 'just getting the job done' (Maynard-Moody et al., 1990).

Many of the E-OASys assessments failed to incorporate or expand on significant issues contained within the case file. For example, issues such as previous suicide attempts, psychiatric treatment, and domestic violence were often highly significant to deterioration of mental health and risk levels but not mentioned or only procedurally included with little analysis. Often assessments made previously in pre-sentence reports (PSRs) were not included, particularly if risk issues were regarding self-harm (also see Morgan, 2000). This was unfortunate as some of the most detailed casework in the files pre-dated the introduction of E-OASys and perhaps should have been included for a more complete assessment.

E-OASys could potentially be a significant aid to the transfer of information between officers but only if time is allocated to summarizing information present in the file and following up queries rigorously (Canton, 2004; Prins, 1999). One case had a Crown Court judge repeatedly requesting a psychiatric report which was never produced. The offence for which the offender was sentenced was of a less serious nature than the original charge. Neither of these occurrences was taken into account in the E-OASys assessment of the offender. Additionally, no account was taken of the suspected mental disorder and the case was managed with no reference to mental health agencies and with a number of internal transfers of supervisor. It appears to have been somewhat of a surprise to the offender's supervisor when a local mental health professional approached the probation service to inform them that the offender had spent some time as an in-patient in a local psychiatric facility during the period of supervision.

Examples of harassment and obsessional behaviours, and being the victim of rape were also factors which were not followed through in the E-OASys assessment and not therefore incorporated into the overall assessment or supervision planning concerning the case.

Many of the gaps in the case files occurred during transfer of cases between team members, and lack of thorough reading of case file materials before the E-OASys assessment was completed was revealed through obvious gaps in the transfer of information or level of detail in the assessment. This was particularly significant in cases where as many as five probation officers had supervised one case over a six-month period.

Although procedurally the E-OASys was completed in the majority of cases examined, there were significant gaps in transfer of data from the case files. As Prins (1999) states information regarding cases and risk is often present but the time to assimilate and collate this information is often a low priority. Transfer of the data to the E-OASys presumably is required if the risk assessment is going to be accurate and meaningful.

Evidence of the level of professional standards in management of the cases

Reading of case files revealed that far better risk assessments were undertaken when there was a consistent and sustained relationship built up with one probation officer/case manager. Additionally, Breach and focusing on practical issues, as opposed to the whole context of the mentally vulnerable offender's behaviour also significantly increased when very short-term work was done by varied staff. Much of the work undertaken with offenders with mental health issues was sensitive and focused when there was time to build up a rapport with the officer involved. However, where cases were quickly passed over to other team members, procedural concerns, particularly regarding practical considerations and enforcement, appear to have become the sole focus of the work with those offenders with mental disorder. Regular reviews were also required in these cases; however, there was rarely any evidence of these having been undertaken in the majority of case files examined. Again, reviews were more likely to have been undertaken when a consistent and sustained relationship existed with the offender and practitioner.

Another significant factor was the quality of the liaison with other agencies and the family, highlighted in other studies as key to risk reduction and containment in mentally disordered offenders (Moore, 1996; Rumgay, 2003). This was also lacking in these cases. Few of the sample examined had any evidence of consistent and sustained interventions by case managers, or other agents. This is of particular concern if the probation service is to discharge its role in achieving the government's overall priority to reduce crime and protect the public.

Special areas of concern

A significant number (n. six) of the sample had alcohol and/or drugs related problems. This would support other research in this area of the heightened risk/vulnerability of those with mental health problems and substance misuse problems (for example, Applin and Ward, 1998; Hills, 1993). The significance of dual diagnosis in this sample with mental health problems was highlighted. Often the focus of the work was on the drug problem rather than on a holistic treatment of both issues. This is borne out by other research, such as that by Applin and Ward (1998), and may be due to inexperienced staff, and/or the presence of a drugs partnership locally and their approach to dual diagnosis. It could also be the existence of a 'target driven funding regime' which does not reward dual interventions (Mc Sweeney et al., 2004) or could even be fear of engagement with the mental disorder and its complexities.

Whilst reading the case files I found that there was repeated over-looking and ignoring of insignificant mental health issues. Some clients then degenerated into the 'revolving door' syndrome of short custo-dial sentences leading to loss of family ties, employment, and housing (Revolving Doors Agency, 2002). The consequences escalated with the numerous petty offences leading one woman from a secure job, home, and family to eventual homelessness, her children taken into care and an inability to cooperate with even the smallest request such as keeping a probation appointment. The only option then remaining was short, repeated custodial sentences.

Although inconclusive about issues of race, due to omissions in data as noted above, there was evidence in reading the files of stereotyp-ing regarding mentally disordered offenders and those of minority eth-nic origin, in particular the case of a Asian Muslim offender, which affected the focus of the work undertaken. This supports findings by Hudson and Bramhall (2005) which state that Asian 'otherness' is viewed negatively by some probation assessors. Supervision case records and E-OASys information concentrated on possibilities of engagement, family details, and superficial assessments of practical issues such as housing were common in this example. There was no evidence of using the strong family ties as a resource or positive aspect of the case and no concentration on the offender's mental health needs, findings echoed by Hudson and Bramhall (2005).

Overall findings

What became apparent was that often E-OASys assessments were inaccurate and defensive in that they erred on the side of caution to protect the case worker rather than exploring the material thoroughly for an accurate detailed picture. This was possibly due to lack of experi-ence and exploration of the case files which did supply the materials required for a more informed assessment. As other research examining risk and mental disorder has indicated, the gender of the assessor (Ryan, 1998) was found to be significant. Female assessors are more likely to rate patients more 'risky' than their male counterparts. This is of inter-est when one recognizes the predominance of women in the probation service and other caring/social services dealing with those with mental health problems. The majority of these assessments were undertaken by women. In addition, differences in ethnicity and race have been shown to influence risk assessment, heightening perceptions of risk in black, mentally ill people (Bhui, 1999; Prins, 1999). Thus, mental disorder could have been wrongly identified or over-concentrated on as an indicator of risk concerns due to stereotypes which have previously been exposed as prejudicial or detrimental to the offenders being supervised (Peay, 2002).

Overall the findings of this research supported previous research findings on mentally disordered offenders, for example, Gray et al. (2002). Thus, those cases with incomplete E-OASys assessments were also the cases with little supplementary information and lacked the detailed analysis of past information contained in case records. Often omissions regarding ethnicity, family relationships, and liaison with other agencies accompanied those cases with incomplete or inaccurate E-OASys. This is illustrated by reflection on one case in particular (first cited in Fitzgibbon, 2007b, pp. 92–93).

> The offender had a chronic addiction to heroin and crack cocaine, the origins of which appear to have been following the break up of her violent marriage and a spiralling series of losses involving work, her house, and latterly the care of first her younger son and then her daughter. The offence she had committed most recently was one of deception for which she was placed on a drugs treatment and testing order which she subsequently breached. She had a long history of depression and self-harm with psychiatric treatment.

This case was an example of what occurs when there is a lack consistency and regular review or follow-up when the offender was transferred quickly between inexperienced practitioners…She had a series of five probation officers who had supervised her over a 6 month period. As a result of this inconsistency, highly important information on file was ignored and never incorporated into the OASys documentation…It was evident on examining the case file that there had been a long period where this woman had been offence free and this was when the offender had had a close one-one relationship with her probation officer. The escalation of missed appointments and breaches did appear to coincide with the changes in probation practice. This offender did end up with numerous short term custodial sentence.

The more detailed E-OASys assessments coincided with those cases with consistent and sustained relationship between offender and probation officer. These cases were more likely to have had regular case reviews completed, inter-agency working, and a more holistic focus on the mental health issues of the offender in relation to their other problems. Again, this is clearly demonstrated by the following case study.

> This offender had committed a number of shoplifting and credit card offences in the past, mainly as means of gaining money to acquire drugs, i.e. cannabis and tranquillisers. There had been a history of depression... The current offence was again related to drugs usage and depression and involved fraudulently using a credit card to buy whisky in order to obtain cash for cannabis.
>
> This mentally disordered offender was assessed and a thorough, accurate, and extensive OASys assessment was completed and there was evidence of regular follow-up with reviews being completed as required, on time. The assessment and supervision of the case was carried out by probation officer with previous one-one relationship with that same offender. The practitioner referred to previous reports, assessments, and case file records... Interestingly some of the most detailed casework in the file pre-dated the introduction of OASys... There was also evidence of a close and ongoing working relationship and liaison with the local mental health services. (Fitzgibbon, 2007b, p. 89)

Strengths and weaknesses of research methodology

As with any research study, the methodology adopted can be scrutinized in terms of its strengths and weaknesses. May (2001) uses Scott's (1990) typology for assessing the quality of evidence available from institutional documentary sources. There are four criteria with which to analyse the quality of the research.

Authenticity is the first criteria. By using documents that are produced by professionals working in the probation service, the evidence is genuine and of unquestionable origin. When looking at the second quality measurement, credibility of the evidence provided by the E-OASys assessments, Scott stated that 'evidence had to be undistorted and sincere, free from error, and evasion' (1990, p. 7). In reflecting on these criteria, one could argue that practitioners produce E-OASys assessments not only to assess the risks posed by their offenders but also to justify and to defend their own practice decisions (Kemshall, 2003). Thus, one could argue the credibility of the documents used for this research would need to be tested by further investigation, such as a semi-structured interview conducted with the author of the assessment.

However, the research has benefited in some ways from interpretation of the errors or omissions which have occurred in the E-OASys assessments as this has informed some of the findings. As Brookman et al. (1999, p. 55) stated when using court reports as evidence for her research, the reports are 'not neutral documents'.

The other two important areas that Scott identified were representativeness and meaning. These two criteria are hard to test by the research undertaken in this study. Obviously, a small sample taken from one probation area can hardly be claimed as representative of all probation areas, particularly when the particular large metropolitan area is unique in terms of its demographic makeup and size. Second, some of the E-OASys assessments provided information that was unclear and, because no follow-up interviews were undertaken with the staff producing the documents, some of the errors or judgments made within the documents could not be explored or questioned.

Although the E-OASys documents do provide a rich source of genuine material, the production of these documents needs to be placed within the organizational context and resource pressures exerted on staff, obviously influencing the priority given to their completion, and the emphasis placed on risk as opposed to other factors such as mental healthcare.

A more in-depth, extended exploration of E-OASys documents with follow-up semi-structured interviews with the staff undertaking the assessments would be advantageous. Not only would the findings be more representative of the work undertaken by probation practitioners, the meaning and interpretation of offenders' behaviour/risk could be more thoroughly investigated. However, as Silverman (2001), emphasizes it is important that data collection is limited to that which is manageable. He emphasizes the need for clarity of analytic approach which is explicit and defendable.

Conclusions

The research findings show that if used well, completed properly, and analysed in full, E-OASys assessments have the potential to highlight mental health and/or personality disorder (PD) issues. However, accessing the data collected by E-OASys in the Mental Health /PD areas is complex, as disorders are contained in a number of domains throughout the tool and not in discrete sections easily referenced. Craissati et al. also refer to this information being dispersed throughout the tool and the need for this 'to be collated and triggered' (2005, p. 41).

Fitzgibbon and Cameron (2005) comment that,

In order to enable the E-OASys assessor to take full account of the assessment made the development of a flag system (on E-OASys) for key areas is essential... A flag system would alert the assessor automatically to the presence of a number of factors which individually would not necessarily indicate mental health or PD concerns, but collectively would indicate there were significant characteristics in this case which would warrant further specialist assessment to examine whether there were mental health needs in the offender(s) which require consideration. (2005, p. 7)

Despite the emphasis given to assessment and to E-OASys by the government policies relating to Offender Management and crime reduction, this research reinforces that it is remarkable that The National Offender Management Service (NOMS), previously called the Probation Service, has not prioritized devising E-OASys to assist offenders managers in identifying mental health difficulties in offenders (Hough et al., 2006). E-OASys was introduced in an attempt to construct a common set of concepts, a shared vocabulary in which practitioners from a variety of differently trained professionals can discuss risk (Canton, 2004). However, as these findings illustrate, such a risk-assessment tool will only be effective if it leads to appropriate and sensitive support for mentally disordered offenders (Grounds, 1995). The failure to identify mental health issues could skew risk and needs assessments and limit the effectiveness of interventions aimed at tackling the factors linked to offending. This study highlights the increasing importance for professionals and other practitioners within Criminal Justice agencies to be trained and experienced with regard to the effective use of these assessments if they are going to avoid averse risk assessments based on prejudicial views about those with mental health problems and others (Hannah-Moffat, 2005) and start to bring about changes in attitudes and practice. Mental health, as the then Home Secretary (Clarke, 2005) reminds us, is one of the significant health problems which may have a considerable impact on a person's criminal behaviour. However, as Hershel Prins recently concluded:

This climate is much preoccupied with public protection, the assessment of risk and the resulting over-hasty implementation of more and more criminal justice measures... Professionals have a responsibility to keep their heads above these turbulent waters... Indeed they have a responsibility to promote better public understanding.

However , they can only do this if they have informed knowledge. (2005, p. 354)

Kemshall (2003) maintains that there are limitations and failures of risk analyses as predictors of individual behaviour and potential sources of injustice if people are treated purely on the basis of membership of risk groups whose boundaries are necessarily socially constructed. She also believes that risk-based analyses are in practice modified and mediated by more traditional professional casework skills of probation officers. How then are practitioners going to be assisted to utilize the E-OASys tool, given that it appears that standardized assessment tools will ultimately replace the last residues of the 'advise assist and befriend' tradition? There seems little doubt that the strategies of risk-analysis and the orientation to public protection have transformed the work and character of the Probation Service (Kemshall, 2003).

This qualitative research study has examined the implementation of risk-assessment techniques such as E-OASys and their effectiveness for working with mentally disordered offenders. It suggests that if such techniques are implemented under conditions of increasing resource and staffing constraints in probation, then they will be badly implemented. However, if they are utilized as a supplement to traditional casework skills, rather than their replacement or another part of the process of de-skilling of practitioners, they could assist in social change and positively influence policy development with mentally disordered offenders. This obviously not only has resource implications but also requires the English and Welsh Probation Service to revisit its underlying principles. Risk assessment if implemented in a climate of resource constraint and de-skilling will be more likely to lead to over-prediction of risk and dangerousness and the increasing consignment of wide sections of the poor to the category of the dangerous and risky 'other' on the social periphery. Social exclusion and criminality will be most likely reinforced rather than reduced.

By contrast, in my research it was clear that experienced practitioners who skilfully read case files could effectively utilize risk assessments and these were enhanced when there was a consistent and sustained relationship built up with one probation officer/case manager. This qualitative research has been able to expose the myth that traditional one-to-one relations between practitioners and clients led to subjectivity and unreliability (Burnett, 2004). On the contrary, by examining cases in detail and not just as statistical inputs my research has illustrated that it is precisely the persistence of such relationships which underpins what semblance of objectivity such assessment schemes may possess. A qualitative approach has suggested ways forward for practitioners and policy makers and these developments could lead to positive and effective interventions for mentally disordered offenders and the possibility of changes in policy, attitudes, and practice.

Note

1. This research was undertaken by the author during her PhD study.

8
Educational Research Need Not Be Irrelevant

Zvi Bekerman

Introduction

Do not let anyone fool you. In spite of the linguistic turn (Rorty, 1967), the diversity of epistemological and ontological assumptions, and the plethora of post-modern jargon, the bad news is that the social sciences – especially those associated with education – are still engaged in traditional quantitative research. What is surprising is that they have been involved in educational research for over fifty years now and that, in spite of their productivity regarding evaluation reports, enquiries into students', teachers', and parents' attitudes and research-proven ways to improve school achievement or increase students' performance, we all still worry about educational systems which are not doing well (Apple, 1999; Berliner, 2006; Cohen, 1995; Gordon and Rebell, 2007; Hirschland and Steinmo, 2003). Horace Mann's promise, well over a century old, that education (understood as schooling) will be the great equalizer goes, as yet, unfulfilled.

It is of course better to believe that the promise can be fulfilled than to question the promise itself given its institutionalized embodiment, but that is exactly one of the main points I invite the reader to consider. Though not wanting to bring this note to an abrupt end, I wish the reader to ask herself how her considerations would change if for a moment she would acknowledge that schooling in fact does work well but that education through schooling was not universalized in order to achieve equality/equity but precisely to prevent it from becoming a reality; that in reaching its unbelievable success it has been aided by traditional quantitative research methods which in their development were tightly connected to the political aims of that body which implemented universal schooling – the nation state. The nation state was the one that developed the powerful schooling machinery mostly in the shape of massive educational efforts which market universal (anonymous) literacy and the adoption of individualized perspectives together with the development of cultural/identity categories (Gellner, 1983; Smith, 1998). Regarding this point, it is worth recalling that recently historian, sociologists, culturalists, and even psychologists have expounded on the radical influence on conceptions of 'identity' becoming primordial and essential of the slow but steady development of the most universal of modern structure and ideology: 'nationalism' (Billig, 1995; Elias, 1991, 1998). Clearly other than mentioning this *en passant*, not much can be added in this short note.

I write this note out of a commitment to empirical research in the social sciences. I offer a short critique of traditional positivist educational research and contrast it to empirical perspectives which emphasize the observed and experienced and thus offer recognition to the complexity which characterizes that which is human. I further position this critique in the wider context of the most successful of modern ideologies – the nation state – and consider how traditional educational research might serve its colonializing efforts. I last reflect on my experience as a teacher of anthropology and education, and consider the problems I encounter when trying to share with my students the paradigmatic perspectives which I believe might help overcome traditional empirical perspectives in the social sciences in general and in education in particular.

The quantitative approach

An empiricist I am, but a positivist I am not. Working as I do in the anthropology of learning or education, I have for long been convinced that the customary scales and graphics produced by the social sciences offer poor representations of that which I study, that is humans learning, which, by the mere fact of their being alive, is intermittent, always in flux and stubbornly refuses reification. I seem to stand alongside the biologists in the scientific wars of the old hard natural sciences who, when criticized by physicists for their 'soft' scientific approach, would answer: What else can we do? What we study moves (Mayr, 1988). While physicists have, by now, removed themselves and their science from simplistic positivist stands having uncovered that relativity, uncertainty, and chaos govern that which they research, social scientists seem, for the most part, unfortunately not be able to overcome the traditional positivist paradigm which governed the physics of old.

All research designs base themselves on certain assumptions which in the case of quantitative methods are reflected in the use to which they put variables (gender, socioeconomic status, attitudes, etc.). Quantitative researchers develop instruments such as surveys or scales to measure them and apply statistical procedures to relate them to each other. What is important to recognize is that variables are abstractions from social life: assumptions which, after being abstracted, stay hidden and ultimately receive an aura of naturality as if they were givens. Thus the problem is not the quantitative approach per se, which undoubtedly can and has contributed much to the natural and social sciences, but the fact that in the social sciences in general and in education in particular, the assumptions which underlie the variables go for the most part unrecognized and thus uncritiqued (Denzin and Lincoln, 2000; Maykut and Morehouse, 1994). When uncovered and critiqued it is these social assumptions which need to be confronted and revised. Variables are abstract constructs which presumably represent human performance, activity, experience, and the conditions which influence these, be they intrinsic or extrinsic. Abstractions by nature detach these activities and their influencing conditions from the immediate and wider context within which they are produced and enacted, and thus serve well the insatiable thirst for generalization which characterizes quantitative research and, consequently, the needs of modern bureaucracies. According to the dictates of a rather passé natural sciences paradigm, these variables are afforded a status of objectivity by which quantification is foregrounded for anything that is observable. Unfortunately, for the social sciences which adopt this view, not all human conditions or experiences which are rendered relevant are objective, and they thus need to be pushed into a new level of abstraction by which they are operationalized through the construction of inference relations, a path which is premised on a leap of faith which is difficult to rationalize on any account. Self-report instruments such as surveys are supposed to operationalize subjective values and beliefs, and the subjects' responses to these instruments are assumed to reveal a 'truth' which reflects the abstracted individual in his contextualized, historicized condition now decontextualized and ahistoric (Lincoln and Guba, 1985, 2000). This leap of faith, unsustainable as it may be, implies that language can transmit exact meanings to which subjects respond trustfully and in a disinterested manner. If any one of you readers are ready to buy into this simplistic understanding of that which is human, then so it be, but if for a moment you sit back and reflect on your own complex experience, I doubt whether you would be ready to direct your business, romantic, or political life according to such assumptions. The problem is not the numbers but the assumptions upon which they rest; assumptions which, as stated, go for the most part unreflected upon.

More space would allow for an explication of the development and adoption of these research techniques based on their intricate connections to historical developments strongly related to the new political/economic conditions in a Europe entering modernity. Just to give you a hint, please remember that the earliest known occurrence of the word 'statistics' seems to be in the title of the satirical work *Microscopium Statisticum*, by Helenus Politanus in 1672, probably bearing the sense of pertaining to statists or to statecraft. The earliest use of the adjective in anything resembling its present meaning is found in modern Latin *statisticum collegium*, said to have been used by Martin Schmeizel (died 1747) for a course of lectures on the constitutions, resources, and policies of the various States of the world (Oxford English Dictionary). When adding to this the rather sad connections already shown by historians to exist between the development of psychological (the main discipline behind educational research today) premises and centralist state powers and their economies, we need to start asking ourselves what exactly these connections might mean: that is, how might the social sciences supported by such assumptions serve particular political interests? Social positivism and nation state politics get along well.

Up to this point and again resting on gross generalizations, philosophers of sorts would agree with the critique. They might also believe that scales and graphics offer poor representations of that which is human, but still 'traditional' philosophy will not help us here since it too is guided by modern Western thought (which, in a nutshell, is said to be merely footnotes to Plato), and thus engages in the trajectory which directly connects Plato and Descartes while trying, through the efforts of an ahistoric, decontextualized, and solipsistic self (yet to be discovered by empirical science) to uncover metaphysics in the shadows. Yet, again biology comes to the rescue and I worry not about that which I have never seen, the individual mind/self, and rather align myself with the true empiricist of all times, Darwin, who in 1838 already knew: 'He who understands baboon would do more towards metaphysics than Locke' (Barrett et al., 1987, p. 539).

The qualitative challenge

I discovered anthropology as a discipline over thirty years ago when I was working as a young moderator at a voluntary organization offering seminars to high-school students. I do not remember exactly why, but I remember being curious about what the academy had to say about what my educational activity was, at that time. Reviewing traditional quantitative educational research, I had a sense that what was being offered in terms of results and interpretations did not at all reflect my own experience while working in the field. By chance, I picked up Geertz's book, *The Interpretation of Cultures* (Geertz, 1973), read it, and was seized in a dialogue with the complexity of understanding the living. When compared to cause and effect relationships, the manipulation of variables, and generalizations, which did not at all mirror my sense of what I was doing in class, Geertz's descriptions resonated with my complex experiences and offered a sense that there was a way of looking at what I was doing and of reflecting on my and my colleagues' activities. Since then I have been trying to train my senses to meet the world and think about what I encounter in it through what I understand to be the traditional tools and paradigmatic perspectives that anthropology has to offer.

So what is it that qualitative methods can offer in exchange? The anthropological roots which sustain these perspectives – though historically related to colonialism and as such as open to criticism as the positivist paradigms, for they too have cooperated with state violence – have for long now undergone a process of penitence and transformation, slowly becoming one of the most humane of the social sciences (Wolcott, 1992).

They suggest, while strongly grounded in the scientific 'empirical' tradition, that we can only appraise and interpret that which we have been able to experience, not a surprising position when considering that 'empirical' derives from the Greek $\dot{\epsilon}\mu\pi\epsilon\iota\rho\iota\kappa\_\acute{o}s$ – (empeirikos) which stands for experience (Oxford English Dictionary). The 'deep' sense of experiencing is the qualitative form of inquiry.

In this sense qualitative approaches are egalitarian, that concept so much feared by specialists in the academic and other bureaucracies. All humans are by definition qualitative inquirers and developing this power critically and systematically is in itself a contribution to a better understanding of the world. The main features of qualitative approaches are rather few. The researcher is the main instrument in the research effort, his/her (god/nature-given) sensory system is the instrument through which he/she experiences the qualities of and in the world he/she wants to better understand. Using our senses implies learning how to use them and understanding that we have been trained to use them in certain ways which limit our experience. We thus need to ensure that the training process sharpens our senses, so that we might appreciate wider perspectives than the ones in which we have been trained.

Qualitative researchers direct their inquiry to that which is 'out there'; not 'in' the mind but in between people working hard in the world while trying to make sense of what to do next. This outward inclination should not be confused with simple materialism/behaviourism. Much of what we are interested in relates to 'things' we create in our daily activity, the interpretations and meanings we negotiate to make sense of the complex set of activities we attend to in order to make sense of the world and allow it to move forward. These meaning-making and interpretative activities are reflected and become available for analysis in human interaction; even if they do exist (which I doubt) in the human mind, they are never available to us. They only become available to us in their outwardly implementations. Qualitative researchers believe that if they expect to be able to understand a world, any world, even the educational world, they would do well to get to know it closely, I dare say intimately. Thus detached reflection or experimentation seems to them anathema. The option is then to spend time *in situ*, what has come to be known as having a 'naturalistic' approach. While there, for the most part, they are not inclined to manipulate the situations which they observe but instead to be attentive, very attentive, to its evolution, and to record it with as many technologies as possible at hand, trying not to be intrusive in so doing. Recording in detail is not an easy task, especially when considering that ethnographers do not reach the field with too specific research questions which allow them in advance to define or specify the parameters of the research. All in all, still the best ethnographic question seems to be: 'what the hell is going on here?' a question which to be answered, if at all, implies not only the detailed recording of events as they unfold in real life, but also accounting for the multiple contexts within which they evolve as well as their historical trajectories.

Such paramount demands make all ethnographic studies partial in their fulfilment. All we can expect are partial representations which, when dealing with that which is human, might mean all which might be achieved. The central method used to achieve this partiality are observations, the gathering of documentation, and interviewing while inhabiting the research site as much as possible (yes, believe it or not, ethnographers know schools not just from their childhood experience). Ethnographers enter the field with their minds crowded with theories, accompanied by their own preconceptions and the many notions they share with their home environments. Though freeing themselves from all these is rather impossible, they try hard not to allow these categories to invade their appreciation/understanding of the spheres they research.

They know well that people and/or objects carry no clear identifiable tags in reality, and that for them to be identified as certain people or certain objects, the world that surrounds them has to get organized for them to make their appearance. It is exactly these rules of organization which enable categories to appear, as if they where pre-given or natural, that the qualitative mind is after.

Let me give you an example. For the past few years, I have been researching the bilingual integrated Palestinian-Jewish schools in Israel (Bekerman, 2003b, 2004, 2005). While doing this it has taken me a time, too long a time, to free myself from seeing Jews and Palestinians as if the children carry a sign which clearly identifies them as belonging to one or the other group. By now, I feel I'm doing a better job. Time has made these categories less salient, but their shadows are always present, just enough to remind me that in the society in which I/we live, much activity is organized so as to cause these identities to make their appearance. Finding out the complex and multiple activities that make these categories so easy to identify and attend to is my task. The more practices (verbal and physical) I can uncover, the better I'm doing my job and if by the end of the day I'll be able to share with others the paths I have discovered of the ways people in the world (in our case the school and its surrounding contexts) make these identities relevant, the better my work will be since it will allow participants (according to their ideological inclinations and educational aims) to try to overcome them or strengthen them. Unbelievably, identities are not qualities in the mind but qualities in the world.

Judging individual and societal boundaries

Gregory Bateson (1972) put succinctly the complexity of realizing individual/societal boundaries when he asked:

> Suppose I am a blind man, and I use a stick. I go tap, tap, tap. Where do I start? Is my mental system bounded at the handle of the stick? Is it bounded by my skin? Does it start halfway up the stick? Does it start at the tip of the stick? But these are nonsense questions... The way to delineate the system is to draw the limiting line in such a way that you do not cut any of these pathways in ways which leave things inexplicable. If what you are trying to explain is a given piece of behavior, such as the locomotion of the blind man, then, for this purpose, you will need the street, the stick, the man; the street, the stick and so on, round and round. (p. 434)

The outcome mentioned in the example rendered above brings me to the last feature I want to mention: the criteria for judging the ethnographic effort. I believe these criteria relate to the coherence to be found in the story told (the description rendered), the insights it has to offer, and the utility it affords. Moreover, good educational ethnography should allow readers, participants, and others to identify the world described as the world they inhabit and experience. It should also surprise them by presenting a richness of details which otherwise would go unnoticed, and should allow participants to learn about what needs to be done next if they want to continue or change their present situation. These realizations don't necessarily mean that the world can be easily changed on the basis of the knowledge acquired; it just means that if we get lucky we might know what to do to organize the conditions which might allow for change and try to work towards them or identify them when they appear by chance.

Qualitative, ethnographic, anthropology-based research has taught us much already. It has shown the modern mantra of individuality in its multiple expressions – individual development/achievement/intelligence – to be a powerful tool that not only sustains present elites, but also an unsustainable empty theoretical sack (Verenne and McDermott, 1998). It has also shown its inseparable twin, 'culture', to be a myth we engage with to keep certain individuals in their 'right' social/political position. More recently and with the liberal cry for cultural recognition through multicultural policies, ethnographies have shown 'culture recognition' to be a cheap exchange for that which is truly needed – structural change (Bekerman, 2003a). All in all it has shown children from all backgrounds always working hard, at times too hard, to achieve success (and at others to achieve failure) and, as a rule, it has shown that children do not exist all by themselves thus pointing at the fact we all seem to refuse to acknowledge, that is, that while children should be our unit of concern, they should never never be our unit of analysis. Instead it is we, the adults – those that work hard to build the settings in which we call them to develop – who are the ones which need to be analysed and evaluated (Verenne and McDermott, 1998). However, beware: these adults need not necessarily be teachers. Politicians, parents, teachers, administrators, counsellors, curriculum builders, and evaluators in varying combinations, need to have their relations with each other and with the wider world reorganized. If it is equality we want to enhance, the adults must undergo changes. No 'one' is smart enough, resourceful enough, or generous enough to change the world alone, not even well-educated children (McDermott and Raley, 2007).

True, some of these insights have been attained within other disciplines (Chaiklin and Lave, 1996; Churchman, 1968, 1979); what ethnographic studies add is the detailed description of how these goals are achieved. They show the amount of work it takes, the strategies adopted, the practices implemented to make an intelligent and/or dumb student materialize on the scene. They point at all those involved and the activities they carry out to make what is otherwise sold to us as a natural/genetic condition, the individual, to emerge to be identified, measured, and recorded (the favourite hobby of school systems supported by the nation's bureaucracy). In many ways the work ethnography does is dangerous: if converted into a pedagogy (a curriculum on literacies through which to read the world) it has the potential of becoming emancipatory. If they are to be blamed for something, anthropological accounts of education should be blamed for increasing rather than decreasing complexity; and it is this that makes them easy to ignore.

Education in the state is a political act always (dressed as an angel). The state's essentializing and homogenizing forces fear complexity: what they are in need of are fast, clear, implementable, and accountable recipes. The fact that education has gone unchanged in spite of the unlimited amount of research conducted through the years seems not to bother politicians at all. They find easy solace (as do many researchers) when blaming the research for not yet having been done properly; or, in the worst case, because its recommendations have not been properly implemented by the teachers, the curriculum writers, the principals, or any other low-ranking clerk at hand. They are in need of reports, not their implementation. Politicians and other 'men' of great vision find it difficult to cope with complexity; they need a social science of simplicity to serve them and their power-thirsty schemes.

Teaching complexity

Now that these issues have been somewhat cleared, I want to turn to my own practice as a teacher and ask: what can/should I do? Many (almost all) students of mine come to my Anthropology and Education course expecting to get, without much difficulty, the credits needed to receive their degrees so as to join the lucky ones who might enter the race to achieve positions of power in the state bureaucracy which will allow for more than a rather minimalist survival in our consumerist society. They expect their teacher to offer a clear course of action, some straightforward formula which, if followed, promises success in the examination. I cannot blame them for this; I did much the same when I was a student.

Nonetheless, I want them first to have an appreciation for theory. But they fear theory as if the word belongs only to those who can afford the time for reflective introspection. They react to theory as if they knew the word's historical roots (from Greek *theoros*), which designated the clerks who were licensed by the sovereign to determine whether something had indeed taken place, to bear witness. Today's students fear it as if they would have known the etymology throughout and realized that theory, thus understood, represents the power of the state.

I would like my students, instead, to take seriously that we all beget theories while our lives unfold in the manifold tasks the world relentlessly affords us. I want them to appreciate that there are multiple ways in which the world can be known, and a variety of languages through which reality can be described. Still as true heirs to years of shallow positivist thinking in the social sciences, they want to know how to uncover a 'true' reality; they hope to find ways to describe it exactly so as, in the best of cases, to change it for the better. Even when I am successful in showing that the realities they experience are far more intricate than any answer they can expect to uncover through positivist perspectives, their expectations from research efforts do not change much. They still believe that good research should be able to offer a secure and easy path to a change for the better. If they are successful enough to join those in power, they know they will need first to be able to offer a convincing and sound analysis of reality, and later some clear, sharp conclusions as to how to act in order to change the reality described. That education has gone unchanged in spite of the large amount of research conducted through the years seems not to bother them at all.

When teaching them about us humans as the central tool of research, they doubt their potential to be objective, as if numerical manipulations could offer objective perspectives (Lindley, 1998). When teaching them about using their senses to collect data through observing, interviewing, and gathering documentation, they fear their personal perspectives might contaminate an otherwise immune/sterilized research effort. But even when the tools are explained and adopted (for lack of any other option, while participating in a university course) they endlessly express insecurity regarding their understanding of what it is exactly that they should do and how to do it well. My continuing attempts to convince them that the human world of activity is complex and forever influenced by changing contexts and historical trajectories, only creates more tensions; they prefer rather to be allowed to look for 'facts' and 'truths' but now armed with ethnographic tools. They become now a living questionnaire or a travelling laboratory site in which to uncover causality.

When I insist on the complexities of human interaction, when I emphasize the multiple contextual levels of analysis that need to be accounted for (that is, micro-, mezzo-, macro-, exo-), they lose patience. They insist that, if at all valid, what I expect would make the research process irrelevant for it would be too time consuming or in a sense made frivolous for it denies the possibility of making any clear statements on what to do next. When I ask my students to suspend, for a moment, their search for what stands behind what they are looking at – the transcendent, the unconscious, the intentional, and the unintentional – and instead to pay attention to the richness of the material as this is expressed in the physical and the verbal realms, they are annoyed as if I would be denying their and their 'research subjects' humanity. They seem to believe it is much more human to judge, to interpret a situation according to the observer's perception of that which is totally unavailable to the observer – that which the subjects think. Like our worst enemies, they fancy more our intentions than our deeds. I fear they are the true (hopefully unintentional) heirs of a psychologized, essentialized worldview whose relations to the development of the nation state seem to be unknown to them (Foucault, 1969, 1973). Could this be different? Have not all been funnelled through that great schooling machinery we referred to above?

Constructing new means in critical dialogue

Engaging in a critical dialogue with these perspectives is no easy task. It mainly involves re-presenting science as relative and arbitrary, while trying to construct new means of seeing other aspects of constructed realities. Human understanding is not mere representation – linguistic, mathematical, visual, or auditory; understanding is the exercise of proficiency. We understand a thing when we know how to interact with it and use it well. Though we have classically been taught that science is driven by the formulation of hypotheses and by experiments designed to discredit them, Popper's formulation seems insufficient for that which is alive and thus unpredictably complex, be it a biologist's cell or a social event. Only my fear of reproducing the dichotomies that I blame the nation state for enacting prevents me from bringing Feyerbend's 'anything goes' into the picture.

Countering these perspectives we all need to appreciate that the first step to understanding is to first comprehend how best to interact with the information we have received and that to understand is a creative, pleasing, or useful interaction with the information in hand – such interaction is the creation of meaning.

As Conant (1951) posited, science is an interconnected series of concepts and conceptual schemes that have developed as the result of experimentation and observation and are fruitful for further experimentation and observation. Thus, the process also involves abandoning the hope of finding fast solutions or writing praiseworthy bureaucratic reports. It involves acknowledging the intricacies of human interaction and networks, the intermittent nature of meaning-making, and the necessary exuberance and deficiency of language. It involves using the revealed complexities as a lever to humble our perspectives when confronting multifaceted 'realities.' Finally, as we have already mentioned, it requires getting all to realize that the anthropological quest is one that to become acceptable is in need not only of an epistemological change but also of a political one. The political change required is one which prevents its own reduction to convenient dichotomies and essentializations. It is a change which pervades all active spheres while recognizing that the practices of research constitute the relations among the participants and also are constituted by them in turn.

Politics, unfortunately, is the frame the state's institutionalized educational system hides systematically so as to seize and hold my students and me in the positivistic paradigm for life. We, all, need to work hard to further uncover the banal practices which the sovereign national state context utilizes to trap us in its cultural/semiotic frames. The task is similar to the one described by Duro for the arts: 'The task of any discussion of frames and framing in the visual arts is first and foremost to counter the tendency of the frame to invisibility with respect to the artwork' (Duro, 1996, p. 1). This activity is not easy. Derrida, in one of his less obscure pieces, poetically points out the difficulty:

> The parergon [accessory or frame] stands out both from the ergon [the work] and from the milieu, it stands out first of all like a figure on a ground. But it does not stand out like the work. The latter also stands out against a ground. The parergonal frame stands out against two grounds, but with respect to each of these two grounds, it merges into the other. With respect to the work which can serve it as a ground, it merges into the wall, and then gradually, into general text. With respect to the ground, which is the general text, it merges into the work, which stands out against the general ground. There is always a form, on the ground, but the parergon is a form which has its traditional determination not that it stands out but that it disappears, buries itself, effaces itself, melt away at the moment it deploys its great energy. (Derrida, 1987, p. 57)

The sovereign is a parergon (or frame) to present paradigmatic perspectives in the social sciences. They constitute each other, being neither absolutely intrinsic nor extrinsic to each other. Untying the knot that connects them, overcoming the nation state's paradigm involves finding ways to offer our students literacies with which to read the world – ours as well as any other. In Burkean terms, I want to offer them 'dramatism' (Burke, 1969): the realization that the relationships between life and theatre are not metaphorical but real and that the understanding of symbolic systems holds the key to the understanding of social organization. This literacy requires abundant theory and rich descriptive faculties in order to uncover and cope with the complexity of the sites and social phenomena that we expect the students to interpret. Thus, they need familiarity with a variety of disciplines and discourses. They need an economic discourse for discussing commodities, supplies, and management; an aesthetic discourse, to discuss architecture, advertising, and display; a political discourse, to discuss bodies, policies, planning, and discipline; a historical discourse to talk about change in organization, consumption, and community. They also need interpretative discourses to articulate understandings of each of the texts and their necessary intertextuality in practice, which, in concert, create culture.

All of the above are needed to read the world and the politics that constructs it, not only in the world outside but also inside the classrooms. It might not be all that is needed, but it is a critical step before offering solutions or directions.

More frontal teaching of theory, even when accompanied by fieldwork, though good, might not be good enough. We are in urgent need of new pedagogies and educational strategies. We urgently need to take risks, cross boundaries, and renegotiate horizons within our own institutions. We are in urgent need of reshaping the academic, compartmentalized curriculum – the one that constitutes and is constituted by the present relations of academic power. To improve the central tool of research in anthropology, that is, the researcher, we need to reconnect students to themselves and to that which constitutes them in the ever-changing contexts of living. We the teachers need to do the same. Doing the same might be painful and at times risky, taking chances in the academic world by truly engaging in dialogue while uncovering for and with our students how our own positions of power are constructed and maintained is no easy task, but from any anti-transcendental scientific perspective there seems to be no other way. It is not our intentions that count, though when declared they become consequential in the world, but our deeds.

Conclusions in short

Reading the world, even in its most banal aspects, is complex for nothing is natural, and all gets organized through the concerted efforts of inter-actants working hard at making sense of larger circumstances. Gregory Bateson offers the following example of 'banal' complexity:

> A certain mother habitually rewards her young son with ice cream after he eats his spinach. What additional information would you need to be able to predict whether the child will: a. Come to love or hate spinach, b. Come to love or hate ice cream, or c. Come to love or hate mother? (1972, p. xvii)

Complexity involves acknowledging the intricacies of human inter-action and networks, the intermittent 'nature' of meaning-making, and the necessary exuberance and deficiency of all translation, and thus the need to abandon the hope of finding fast solutions or writing praisewor-thy bureaucratic reports. This does not mean that anthropology applied to education has no practical solutions to offer. It just means that the solutions it can suggest are neither easy nor simple and they involve using the revealed complexities as a lever to humble our perspectives when confronting multifaceted 'realities'. Finally, it requires getting all to realize that the anthropological quest is one that, to become accept-able, is in need not only of an epistemological change but also of a political one. Yet, here, the political does not point at the grandeur of revolutions but at the painful paying attention to the immediate details of everyday life. Slavoj Zizek puts this well: 'The lesson here is that the truly subversive thing is not to insist on "infinite" demands we know those in power cannot fulfill. Since they know that we know it, such an "infinitely demanding" attitude presents no problem for those in power: "So wonderful that, with your critical demands, you remind us what kind of world we would all like to live in. Unfortunately, we live in the real world, where we have to make do with what is possible." The thing to do is, on the contrary, to bombard those in power with strategi-cally well-selected, precise, finite demands, which can't be met with the same excuse' (Zizek, 2007).

This chapter is a revised and extended version, portions of which have been previously published in Beckerman, Z. (2006). It's we the researchers who are in need of renovation; Journal of Research Practice, 2, (1), Article P1; http://jrp.icaap.org/contentv2.1/bekerman.html

9
Policy Analysis in Education – Multiplicity as a Key Orientation for Research

Dr Katrin Kraus

Introduction

This chapter takes a reflective approach to the practice of policy analysis in education in the context of social change. It is informed by the research in the field of policy analysis that I have conducted over the past several years and aims to weave this experience into a general framework for research in this field. Three broad themes form the focus of my research in policy analysis: one is the relationship between national and international levels, with a special emphasis on international organizations, such as the OECD, the EU, the ILO, and UNESCO, as actors in education policy. Another is the integration of regional levels and cultural contexts into comparative research into (vocational) education. The final theme is the relationship between different fields and areas of society, especially between education and the work/labour market, social policy, and the connection to processes of social, economic, and political change. What is common to all three themes is the interest in the interrelatedness of different levels and areas, the question of transfer and the contextualization of policy process. Methods applied have mainly been discourse analysis, content analysis of diverse kinds of documents, and different types of interviews. The aim of this chapter is to draw out the consequences for a general research orientation and the principles of research into the complex and dynamic nature of education policy as a research subject.

In first section, I discuss the relationship between social change and education policy, focusing on the dual relations between education/educational reform and social change on the one hand, and the changing role of the nation state on the other. Both these aspects show the dynamics and complexity of education policy as a subject of research. The second section tackles the question of how to capture the process dimension of policy by criticizing linear policy models and introducing the policy circle as a more complex model. Finally, research practices are targeted more concretely by discussing multiplicity as a key principle of policy analysis in different regards, such as multiperspectivity, multilayered approaches, and the necessity for a plurality of sources. It is argued that multiplicity as a key principle of policy analysis is necessary because of the intense relation between social change and education policy on the one hand, and the non-linear nature of political processes on the other. Both can only be addressed adequately by research if multiplicity is taken as a key orientation.

Social change and education policy

Social change, education, and education reform

There is a strong relationship between social change and both education and education reform. The nature of this relationship is dual. First, *social change is a driving force for education reform* and times of change are very also likely eras of reform in education. We see this in the example of Germany: during the Cold War it was not only Coombs' diagnoses of 'world education crises' (1968) and Picht's version of this phenomenon for the former Federal Republic, the 'German catastrophe in education' (1964) – in other words, diagnosis of the education system as such – but also the 'Sputnik-shock' that created a social climate fostering education reform. Nevertheless, the reform era in education in the 1970s followed the big agenda of equality of opportunity, supported by social movements of students and other reform forces in society. School reforms were introduced, promotion of education was enhanced, mass universities were created, adult education was integrated as a pillar of the education system, and the value of vocational education was increased, even if all measures were not successful (Kraus, 2006a; Leschinsky, 2005).

Meanwhile, times changed from the Sputnik-shock to the 'PISA-shock', as the agitated public debate following the publication of the results of the first PISA study in 2001 is called. PISA (Programme for International Student Assessment) is an indicator-led and comparative competence survey of the competences of fifteen-year-olds conducted by the OECD to measure the quality of education systems. The results of this study came as a surprise to Germany: it found itself in the bottom third of over 30 countries, with fifteen-year-old competence levels significantly lower than the OECD average. This result has again initiated an intense discussion about the appropriateness of the existing education system in Germany (Tillmann, 2008), especially regarding the social exclusion inherent in the system (Roeder, 2003).

Discussion of the PISA results contributed to a climate of change that enabled reform and enhanced innovation in the education system, even though the direction of this change is not directly linked to the issue of a more inclusive educational system. Instead, a more competitive system is envisaged, with the expected contribution of education to national – and European – competitiveness in the background. The results of these reforms include intense discussion about and implementation of standards, the introduction of autonomy and accountability in education, especially at the institutional level of schools, and the integration of market-elements into the education system, such as vouchers and choice of school. The big agenda of this reform era in the late 1990s is driven by desires for competitiveness, performance, efficiency, and social cohesion at both national and European levels.

What is obvious in both these German examples is that it is not only the fact of social change that drives educational reform but also public awareness of change – either a shared vision, of being left behind or a collective fear of change, thanks to the sensationalizing of social problems, for which education can be presented as a solution. Both these situations create a breeding ground for education reform – the public plays an important role in initiating education reform (Oelkers, 2001).

The second aspect of the dual relationship between social change and education is that *education is seen as a driving force for social change*, or at least that is the hope feeding different education or political programmes. It can be seen in the period in which the foundations for the apprenticeship model of vocational education in Germany were laid, at the turn of the nineteenth century. The process of nation state building (1871), the nineteenth-century 'Social Question', and the restructuring of economy and society during industrialization led to a social climate in which vocational education could be presented as a solution to problems of political and social integration, especially for the working class (Greinert, 1998).

Another example of education being used explicitly as an agent of change for a socio-political programme was for the agenda of the Third Way in the United Kingdom during the 1990s. Then, education was assigned the role of educating the people so that they could follow the new rules of the Third Way and thus help Labour's programme become reality, especially regarding social policy and the (historically reinforced) role of the self-reliant individual (Kraus, 2004a). In this regard, it is illuminating that Tony Blair declared 'education, education, education' to be the focus of Third Way policies (Tomlinson, 2001). Only recently, the OECD presented in its 'Economic Survey of Germany' an urgent need for reform in education to strengthen Germany's economic progress (OECD, 2008).

Research can play a critical role in investigating this dual relationship between social change, education, and education reform. It can point out and criticize the 'pedagogization' of social problems. Pedagogization means that social problems, such as unemployment or the exclusion of migrants, are seen not as effects of structural conditions but as failures of the individuals affected. Once problems are defined as problems of the individual, then education can be presented as the means, even a panacea, by which to overcome them. The individualization of social problems paves the way for pedagogy to replace policy as the way to overcome social problems. Furthermore, research can examine the implicit and explicit expectations of education as a tool for social or political change, and in doing so, criticize the functional character of education, including its self-functionalization pedagogy presenting itself as a potent force for accomplishing social or political change via education. In this regard, it is important to analyse such expectations and confront them with the limited, albeit real, direct influence that education has on change in a society – regardless of the direction of the intended change – as, for instance, Aldrich (2006) and Wolf (2002) show in their work.

Another question for critical research in the field of social change and education is whether or not the intended effects are achieved, and what unintended effects appear. For this, it is important to look beyond education itself and consider the wider context of society. For instance, one of the aims of the 1970s' education reforms in Germany was to improve girls' chances for a good education. Thirty years later, if we consider only this aim, we can concede success: these days, in general, girls achieve better school-leaving certificates. But related aims included a change in the gender division of unpaid labour, improved labour market positions for women and, more generally, a society with more equal opportunity. The first two of these aims are still not fulfilled; regarding the latter, the effects of reforms were to create new problems of social inequality, since it has been young women from the white middle class who have profited most (Kraus, 2006a). To raise these kinds of critical questions, we need a perspective that takes into account different areas of society, in other words an intersectional perspective, and to reflect critically on the role that education is expected to play, can play, and really plays in the context of social change.

The changing role of the nation state and the rise of global players in education policy

Nation states still regard education as an important area falling within their sovereignty, as the principle of subsidiarity, introduced in the Maastricht treaty (1997) after debate about the influence of the EU in education, shows. Education is a crucial issue for European nation states, having been established in national systems at the time of the foundation of the nation state in the nineteenth century as part of the process of nation-building (Aldrich 1996; Green 1990). Education systems serve as a constituent agency of the new nation state in a field of direct relevance for the population, and the fostering of national identity, via, among other things, compulsory schooling and national curricula. Similarly, the EU aims to make use of education to foster a European identity, and to strengthen the position and power of the EU as a political institution (Kraus, 2004b). In accordance with its role in politics, the nation state has been the main point of reference for policy analysis in education. Since the nation state is losing its role as political agent *par excellence*, the analysis of the relationship between political actors on different levels has become more important than before.

International organizations are becoming increasingly influential in education. First, there is the EU as a supranational organization. The EU implemented the 'Open method of coordination' (OMC) as an intergovernmental method for policy coordination taking place in areas within the competence of the member states of, *inter alia* education. The OMC provides the EU with a 'soft' steering power, in which the agreement of the sovereign nation states forms the basis of the commitment of member states to jointly defined objectives to achieve and concrete indicators for the benchmarking of the member states' performance. At the core of this method is a comparative and competitive peer pressure, since member states are evaluated and benchmarked against the indicators. As a steering instrument, the OMC is applied without directly questioning – but in the longer run undermining – national sovereignty. The ongoing process of shifting political power from the nation state to the European level is also analysed as the 'Europeanisation of education policy' (Alexiadou, 2007). Similarly, the increase in influence of international agencies could be called the 'internationalization of education policy' since in addition to the EU, international organizations such as the OECD are also influencing national policies even without direct power. By setting a global agenda for education policy, they influence national ones, as shown above with the example of the PISA study conducted by the OECD and in the discourse of lifelong learning (Jakobi, 2007; Kraus, 2001). Another example of the influence of international organizations is UNESCO's approach of 'educational multilateralism' (Mundy, 1999). Furthermore, in domestic politics, the international level can be used instrumentally as an argument for reforms that are, in fact, more or less independent of the global agenda (Gonon, 2008).

The changing role of the nation state as *the* political actor of the nineteenth and twentieth centuries changes the conditions for policy analysis in education. We face an increasing Europeanization and internationalization of education policy, meaning that international organization gains more and more importance, and the agenda for education reform is increasingly a global one. But beneath the relationship between international and national levels, we also find related political processes on other specific levels, for instance, at the level of regions (see, for example, Drodge, 2004), institutions (see ibid. and Fend, 2006), and professions (see, for example, Henriksson et al., 2006). Like the nation state and international organizations, they are important political arenas, too.

Therefore, in *research*, it is not only important to pay more attention to the international level, and the relationship between the international and the national levels, but more generally to differentiate clearly between the distinct levels of political processes. The single levels are autonomous political arenas, each following its own rules but being at the same time highly interrelated with the others. However, a proper understanding of the nature of the relationship and mutual influences between the different arenas is still a desideratum for policy analyses. The decentralization and redistribution of power previously located at the level of the nation state in the nineteenth and twentieth centuries can no longer be understood using theoretical and empirical approaches that were developed for policy analysis when the nation state was the clear centre of power. To meet the new situation, new approaches must be developed, ones that analyse both the consequences of this redistribution of power for education policy and the political processes under the new conditions. In research, it is necessary to focus on both the distinct conditions at each level and the relationship and transfer between the different politico-spatial levels. Concerning the relation between different levels, we must also consider the influence of different contexts on the 'receiving' side, seeing the transfer – for instance, from the international to the national level (Kraus, 2008; Phillips/Ochs, 2003; Schriewer,

2003; Steiner-Khamsi, 2004) – as an interpretation rather than a simple import. The relationships and transfer processes between different levels must be understood in more detail and be made a focus of policy analysis. This focus calls for multilayered and context-sensitive approaches in policy analysis, paying attention to processes of mutual influence between different political arenas, transfer processes, and the influence of different contexts and distinct conditions on each level.

Capturing the process dimension of policy

Beyond linearity in the understanding of policy

Recently, we can observe the rise of a new paradigm of research in education that is mainly enhanced by international organization. For instance, the OECD regularly conducts studies such as PISA or IALS (International Adult Literacy Survey), comparing the performance of specific population groups in different countries in special fields of competence. Moreover, it publishes annual reports called 'Education at a Glance', evaluating and monitoring participation rates, financing and performance in national systems of education. Additionally, the EU makes member states deliver annual national reports according to outcome-based indicators which the EU has agreed, on the basis of the OMC, will be benchmarks for the measurement of the development of the EU and its member states (for example, Kraus, 2007a, b). This indicator-based approach to policy analysis, mainly conducted through quantitative surveys, might be satisfying as long as policy is understood narrowly as the outcome of institutions and systems; however, policy is not adequately addressed by such a linear model. The perspective is characterized by a more or less linear cause-and-effect chain, in which policies establish institutions producing a measurable outcome against which the quality of the institutions and policies behind the system can be measured. However, policy is a much more complex phenomenon than that, as other approaches show.

What is necessary as an alternative to the dominance of large-scale, accountability- and steering-oriented surveys conducted by international organizations is research that treats policy as the effect of interactions between actors in interplay with institutional structures, cultural traditions, and changing framework conditions. These actors have different interests and power; they interact in diverse constellations, and the bargaining between them takes place in complex contexts influenced by culture, history, social conditions, and economic developments.

In the contemporary work of several authors, policy is considered as a complex phenomenon that cannot be understood purely by indicator-led measurements. The multifaceted development of institutions is investigated with a focus on topics such as the question of convergence and divergence of education systems in the tension field between national traditions and globally converging conditions (Aarkrog and Jørgensen, 2008; Green et al., 1999); the development of a world culture and in its wake a new institutionalism in education (Meyer and Ramirez, 2007; Meyer and Rowan, 2006); the role of education in the process of an increasing European integration (Alexiadou, 2007; Kuhn and Sultana, 2006; Kraus, 2004b); and the approach of 'path dependence' in the development of education institutions (Powell and Solga, 2008; Thelen, 2004). These authors show the importance of and complex relations between developmental pathways, institutional persistency, feedback effects, power, and social and political contexts in conjunction with the conditioning influences of broader developments and global changes. The interplay of global and national policy levels is analysed as a complex relationship through a focus on transfer processes (Kaelble and Schriewer, 2003; Phillips and Ochs, 2003; Schriewer, 2003; Kraus, 2008) and the perspective of borrowing and lending in education policy (Phillips, 2005; Steiner-Khamsi, 2004). Moreover, authors such as Meuret and Duru-Bellat (2003) stress the influence of different modes of regulation on policy processes within education systems, as others stress the role that discourses play on and between different levels (Edwards et al., 2005; Field, 2000; Kraus, 2001; Schriewer, 2003). Authors also tackling the issue of education policy in a more multifaceted way include Clarke and Winch (2006, 2007), Heikkinen (2004), Schriewer and Harney (2000), and Kraus (2007c) emphasizing the role of concepts, values, cultural backgrounds, and traditions in understanding education, education systems, and policies.

These authors have different foci in their analysis of education policy but what they share is the desire to understand policy as a complex, multifaceted, and dynamic process that cannot be reduced to the level of national systems of education and their performance, even though national systems still play a crucial role in education. They investigate different topics and follow different theoretical approaches, but they all try to capture the process dimension of policy with a dynamic understanding of it, taking into account a range of factors and going explicitly beyond linear models of steering, performance, and accountability. In doing so, they highlight the necessity of contextualizing political processes. The contextualizing can be done in diachronic and synchronic ways. *Contextualizing in a diachronic sense* means taking seriously the impact of the historical developments and cultural traditions in which the topic under consideration is situated. *Contextualizing it in a synchronic sense* means exploring the influence of contemporary social, political, and economic conditions and developments on the research topic. Therefore, if policy is not to be reduced to linear steering procedures measured by outcome benchmarks, then contextualizing can be seen as a *sine qua non* in policy analysis.

The model of policy circle as a basis for policy analysis

Policy is not a static but a dynamic process, which requires an attentive attempt to capture its process dimension with adequate models, methods, and principles of research. Analytically, it presents the challenge to differentiate between different phases in the process without losing perspective of the whole process. To master this challenge, a model that encompasses the whole process but which allows distinction between different phases within it could be helpful. The policy circle, introduced in the following, should provide such a model, which tries both to consider policy inherently as a dynamic process and to differentiate between separate phases in that process. It should help to focus analysis on single phases in depth without losing the wider process dimension. The intention of the model is explicitly not to create a feature for research executed schematically phase by phase, but rather to keep us alert to the dynamics and complexity of policy, even if a single study concentrates on one phase. Figure 9.1 below shows this.

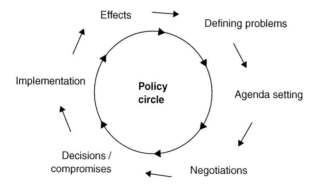

Figure 9.1   The policy circle with six different phases

Defining problems

Meyer (2003) and Tillmann (1991) emphasize that the definition of problems belongs already to the political process: any agreement that something should be changed is already a political decision since it immediately opens the space for change. The question is whether the need for action is accepted in the society and especially among the relevant political actors, which opens the political arena in readiness for the following steps. The inclusion of this phase into the policy circle highlights the importance of the role of the public in creating the legitimacy for change. Rhetoric is generally an important aspect of policy (Edwards et al., 2004), but for the stage of 'defining problems' the role of political rhetoric cannot be overestimated because the crucial question is how far actors are successful in persuading a wider audience of their definition of problems and the need for political action. Discourses and language are important aspects at this stage; accordingly, discourse analysis and the examination of rhetorical strategies are important research foci.

Agenda setting

Once a problem is defined, in other words a consensus about the necessity of political action is reached, the initiator(s) of this first phase, along with other actors can articulate their vision of how the problem might or should be solved in the future. What Phillips and Ochs (2003) describe for the phenomenon of cross-cultural policy borrowing in education is also true for the implementation of new policy more generally; before a decision for and implementation of the new policy is reached, there must be an attraction towards the new policy. It must be promising as the solution of the 'defined problem'. This process could be described as 'agenda setting', wherein different actors formulate what should be reached to solve the problem and try to make it attractive to a wider audience, seeking support for their aims and programmes. Different actors have different and often conflicting aims, and consequently follow different agendas. In this phase of the political process, all try to make their particular solution and agenda the common reform agenda. For critical policy analysis, it is important to differentiate between official agendas – what is expressed clearly and openly – and 'hidden agendas' which are (also) followed but not expressed as frankly. Therefore, the societal and historical contexts must be taken into account, because only by looking at these contexts can the hidden agendas be revealed. Besides analysing the content of the different programmes, it is essential to look at the position of actors in the society, and to contextualize the aims and contents of the agendas from diachronic and synchronic perspectives.

Negotiations

The differences between the actors and their interests on the one hand, and the principal non-deterministic nature of a society in the way it organizes itself on the other, are the foundation for politics as the bargaining between different positions, visions, and agendas. The relevant and powerful actors in the field negotiate over their agendas within institutional frameworks and social contexts, trying to bring as much as possible from their particular agenda into the general reform agenda. Only actors who 'know the ropes' are potentially influential in the political field. They try to influence the agenda setting and strengthen their own position in the field (Bourdieu, 2001). Furthermore, the position of the actor in the society and the political field itself is an important factor and related to that is the question of power. Beside position, power, and interest of each single actor, the constellation of actors and (possible) coalitions of interests as well as institutional frameworks are important factors in this stage. Accordingly, research can focus on power, positions, resources, and strategies through observation, interviews and again, analysis of rhetorical strategies. But the foundation of institutional frameworks, for instance through the law, is also important to understanding the framework for negotiations and the range of scope and influence of single actors.

Decisions/compromises

This stage is about making decisions about what will be implemented in the next phase (Phillips, 2005). The agreement is, by nature, a compromise, meaning that political decisions usually represent a compromise between different positions, visions, and agendas. This compromise must allow the involved actors to find their own position at least partly in the decision. Of course, the process of decision-making knows winners and losers. But even those who at first seem to have lost can in the long-run profit from decisions taken (Thelen, 2004), which again highlights the non-deterministic and non-linear nature of political processes. Besides analysing the content of the decisions taken, policy analysis can focus on the results as well as the nature of the decision-making process in the political field, for instance by observations, interviews, or document analysis.

Implementation

The 'politics of education policy' and the 'politics of pedagogical practice' are different (Kraus, 2002; Tillmann, 1991), but both must be considered part of the political process since, as a rule, education policy aims to set institutional frameworks for education and changing pedagogical practices. But there are limits to how far policy can dictate pedagogical practice and the implementation of a political programme does not automatically mean that pedagogical practice has changed in the intended direction. Therefore, the way from education policy to pedagogical practice has to be understood as a translation during which the political programme will be adapted to the conditions of practice, the interpretations (and again, interests) of the corresponding actors, and institutional traditions. The differences and contradictions between policy and practice in the realization of a specific programme are an important aspect of research which will best be covered by interviews with partners from both sides. Additionally, contrasting existing ideas in the political sphere about how a programme should be put into effect and how the practice deals with it is illuminating and could be targeted by document analysis and interviews, combined with observations of the process of implementation in pedagogical settings.

Effects

Policy reforms create effects on many different levels, such as the national state, international relations, states, regions, society, systems, organizations, institutions, pedagogical situations, and individuals. They can be divided between intended effects (having been part of the official or hidden agenda) and unintended consequences. Policy can fail, and its success and effects are not independent of the cultural and structural formation of a society and the general direction of social and economical change. Additionally, Ball (2006) differentiates between first order effects as 'changes in practices or structure' (p. 51) and second order effects as 'the impact of these changes' (ibid.) from the perspective of the society as a whole, especially with regard to social structure.

The aforementioned quantitative surveys can play a role in analysing effects of education policy, for instance, in evaluating measurements against objectives such as the percentage of early school leavers. To go beyond an evaluative perspective, a broader methodological approach is necessary. Only thus is it possible to contextualize the benchmarks, to discover why these particular benchmarks have been chosen, to interpret their unintended and unexpected effects, to understand the driving forces and barriers to change, and to work out the contradictions in the political process. Therefore, aside from changes to institutional structures – for instance, through the law or the constellations of influential actors – interviews with people being concerned, targeted, or affected by the reforms in different ways are essential. Furthermore, research questions and interpretations must be informed by social theory in order that their effects in their broader social context might be understood.

Even if we consider 'defining problems' as the first step in the political process, we cannot consider the effects as its end, since under no circumstances is everybody satisfied with the decision taken and its effects, and the last phase of the policy circle shifts seamlessly into the stage of 'defining problems' again. The policy circle presented here is an ideal-typical model of policy processes and does not necessarily turn out as well ordered chronology of clearly separated phases. Additionally, an overlap between different sequences is possible (Trampusch, 2006). Nevertheless, with the differentiation of the phases the complexity of the circle can be broken down into single elements on which analysis could concentrate without losing sight of the fact that the single phases are not isolated acts, but rather are part of the dynamic of the policy circle with its different phases and the endless dynamic of political process.

Multiplicity as a key principle of policy analysis

The intense relation between education policy and social change, and the non-linear nature of policy processes, discussed in the previous sections, call for an orientation in policy analysis that considers policy as a complex and dynamic process. There are two main pitfalls for research dealing with such complex and dynamic subjects: on the one hand, defining the subject of research too simply and narrowly, to capture it properly with ever-limited research methods, and on the other hand, creating too complex a design which, in the end, is impossible to handle in the research process. It is the balance between the complex and dynamic nature of education policy on the one hand, and the limits inherent to the research process on the other, that is the major challenge for policy analysis in education.

An orientation of multiplicity as a key principle of policy analysis is one way to meet this challenge. Multiplicity is to be understood as a general orientation guiding research and decision about designs and methods. This general orientation could be expressed in several principles of research in education policy, some of the most important of which are discussed in the following sections.

Multiperspectivity

Multiperspectivity as a principle of policy analysis is understood as concerning both the sources analysed and the researchers involved. *Sources* represent different actors, interests, and perspectives related to the topic under consideration, and therefore selection of sources is a critical moment for policy analysis: whose voice will be heard in the research through the selected sources? As *researchers*, people have different disciplinary, personal, social, theoretical, and methodological backgrounds that influence all stages of research from the formulation of the research question to the interpretation of the findings. The critical question in this case is 'who has the opportunity to define the research perspective?' Sources and researchers always bring and use 'situated knowledges' (Haraway, 1988) and therefore both their place in the research process and the position they are representing must be explicitly identified. Furthermore, it is crucial that research is not based either on only one research perspective, or on one kind of sources. A systematic use of multiperspectivity is made, for instance, in the triangulation of perspectives and methods, and if the combination of different perspectives is systematically international or cross-cultural it can even serve as the basis for comparisons.

The plurality of sources

In general, there are two kinds of sources for policy analysis: documents and persons. *Documents* for policy analysis can be laws, statutes, leaflets, declarations, recommendations, statistics, statements, and material presented by mass media, including even blogs and homepages (for the latter see, for instance, Kraus, 2006b) Additionally, there are area-specific documents, for example, curricula in analysis of education policy. These documents are not usually produced as material for research, originally serving other purposes. They must be selected as material, contextualized and analysed using different kinds of content analysis.

Persons involved in research as 'sources' inform the analysis with their specific knowledge and interpretations. Different 'informants' represent different perspective on a topic, for instance, belonging to different parties, professions, status, and age groups. They have different positions, aims, and influence in the political process and are situated at different levels and in different areas. Additionally, the consequences of policy for them, as well as their interpretations, might be different. To make the 'situated knowledge' and interpretations of the informant available for research, usually interviews are conducted, analysed, and interpreted. A careful, broad, and systematic selection of informants is crucial for a more complete picture of political processes.

The application of different methods

The representation and positioning of different perspectives via persons and documents is accompanied by a variety of potentially appropriate methods with a strong emphasis on a multimethod approach. Discussion about the phases of the policy circle and the research that could be applied in analysing them reveals that it is mainly a *qualitative approach* that is applied in policy analysis. One reason for this preference is that it is important to address the actors' strategies in rhetoric and acting, and to understand the rationales and boundaries of both. This can only be done using qualitative methods to reconstruct the intentions and implications of actions and strategies. Qualitative methods also allow us to engage with the temporality of actions and strategies as chains of situations, interpretations, and decisions embedded in several influential contexts, whereas quantitative methods focus necessarily on specific points in time. Likewise, tracing processes, meanings, and contexts requires a qualitative perspective. Nevertheless, *quantitative methods* also play a role in policy analysis; for example, they are sometimes applied in discourse analysis even if it is mainly a qualitative approach, and they are used in the evaluation of effects and in order to find out the impact of specific factors.

However, the decision about methods and their combination must be taken according to the questions and subjects under consideration and not as a pre-selection of methods. Different methods have different strengths and weaknesses, and to make best use of the first and compensate for the latter it is reasonable to combine different methods. A multimethod design does not necessarily mean a combination of qualitative and quantitative methods. In policy analysis, it is often a combination of different qualitative methods that is appropriate, such as the combination of interviews and document analysis (Kraus, 2007d).

Multilayered and intersectional approaches

Multilayered and intersectional approaches are necessary because of the interrelatedness of different political arenas. This interrelatedness can be differentiated in vertical and horizontal dimensions. In the *vertical dimension*, it is the linkage and transfer between different levels of policy, that is, *inter alia*, between national and international levels and between national policy and professional organizations. Which ideas, procedures, or models travel between the different levels, why and how do they do that, and how are they transformed in this process, according to the different conditions at each level? The *horizontal dimension* describes the interrelatedness of different sections on the same level, for instance, different areas of policy such as education and social policy, and the education system and the labour market. The complementarities, differences, and contradictions between the interrelated sections have a mutually influencing effect on the policy process in each section. The process of transfer can also be observed in a horizontal dimension, for example, the adoption of economic language and concepts in education (Ball, 2006). The interrelatedness in both dimensions call for multilayered and intersectional approaches.

Multiple contexts and the necessity of contextualizing

Policy itself is multifaceted and embedded in a whole range of influencing contexts that must be taken into account when analysing policy. That the policy circle can be identified on every level at which political processes take place allows researchers to contextualize policy in three ways: first, *within the model of the policy circle* itself because each phase can be set in the context of the comprehensive model. Second, the policy circle can be contextualized *against the background of previous, as well as parallel and consequent policy circles*. Finally, the policy circle can be situated *in a wider framework of influential conditions*, in a structure of higher and lower levels, legislative and institutional settings, the distribution of competences and cultural traditions, as well as in relation to changes in economy, politics, and society. All three ways of contextualizing ensure that policy is not seen as an isolated act. It is not necessary that all aspects be included in every analysis, but an awareness of this multiple embeddedness is necessary even when concentrating on one phase, level, or aspect in depth. Investigating contexts means to take seriously the historical dimension as well as the influence of global agendas, cultural and institutional settings, social structures, and economic developments on policy. The meaning and influence of contexts is not always obvious at first glance and requires theoretical as well as empirical efforts.

Conclusion

Multiplicity has been presented in this chapter as a consequence for the orientation of research of the complex and dynamic nature of education policy as a subject of analysis.

Policy analysis can have a *feedback effect on the political process*, if it is successful in making political processes more transparent by the reconstruction of 'defining problems', 'agenda setting', 'negotiations', 'decisions/compromises', 'implementation', and 'effects'. Transparency in how political processes take place might give other actors the opportunity to participate or to influence in policy-making.

For the research process, the orientation to multiplicity allows the teasing out of contradictions through the giving of voice to different actors, problematizing the functional approach that policy-makers often take to education, showing the options and limits for political actions and education, revealing hidden agendas and unintended effects, and analysing the effects of policy in a broader context. Following this principle in research means avoiding a linear and one-dimensional conceptualization of policy that narrows the analysis and thus hinders understanding of political processes. But to understand political processes in their dynamics, complexity and embeddedness is crucial for policy analysis.

Policy analysis can only understand, inform, and challenge education policy if it takes seriously the complex and dynamic nature of its subject. For the questions if and how far policy analysis can inform and challenge education policy, the resonance of research findings among the public and their adoption by influential political actors is decisive.

Bibliography

Aarkrog, V. and C. H. Jørgensen (eds) *Divergence and Convergence in Education and Work.* (Bern, New York: Peter Lang, 2008).

Alcoff, L. 'The Problem of Speaking for Others'. *Cultural Critique* (1991, Winter 1991–1992) 5–32.

Aldrich, R. *Education for the Nation.* (London: Cassell, 1996).

Aldrich, R. 'From Board of Education to Department for Education and Employment'. In R. Aldrich (ed.) *Lessons from History of Education.* (London and New York: Routledge, 2006), pp. 63–75.

Alexiadou, N. 'The Europeanisation of education policy: researching changing governance and "new" modes of coordination'. *Research in Comparative and International Education*, 2(2) (2007) 102–116.

Alldred, P. and V. Gillies. 'Eliciting Research Accounts: Re/Producing Modern Subjects?' In M. Mauthner, M. Birch, J. Jessop, and T. Miller (eds) *Ethics in Qualitative Research.* (London: Sage, 2002), pp. 146–165.

Alvesson, M. and K. Sköldberg. *Reflexive Methodology: New Vistas for Qualitative Research.* (London: Sage, 2000).

Andrews, G. Technocrats or Intellectuals? signsofthetimes, http://www.signsofthetimes.org.uk/pamphlet1/techno.html, 2001, Access Date: 20 April 2008.

Antaki, C., M. Billig, D. Edwards, and J. Potter. Discourse analysis means doing analysis: a critique of six analytic shortcomings, Discourse Analysis Online, http://extra.shu.ac.uk/daol/articles/open/2002/002/antaki2002002–01.html, 2002, Access Date: 29 July 2007.

Apple, M. W. 'Rhetorical reforms: markets, standards and inequality'. *Current Issues in Comparative Education*, 1(2) (1999) 6–18.

Applin, C. and M. Ward. *The Unlearned Lesson.* (London: Wynne Howard Books, 1998).

Arendt, H. *Über die Revolution.* (München: Piper, 1994).

Arendt, H. *Vita activa.* (München: Piper, 1996).

Arnstein, S. R. 'A ladder of citizen participation in the USA'. *Journal of the Royal Town Planning Institute*, 57(4) (1971) 176–182.

Atkinson, P. and W. Housley. *Interactionism: An Essay in Sociological Amnesia.* (London: Sage Publications, 2003).

Aubrey, R. and M. Hough. *Assessing Offenders' Needs: Assessment Scales for the Probation Service.* (London: Home Office, 1997).

Augoustinos, M., A. Lecouteur, and J. Soyland. 'Self-sufficient arguments in political rhetoric: constructing reconciliation and apologizing to the stolen generations'. *Discourse and Society*, 13(1) (2002) 105–142.

Augoustinos, M., K. Tuffin, and D. Every. 'New racism, meritocracy and individualism: constraining affirmative action in education'. *Discourse and Society*, 16(3) (2005) 315–340.

Baldwin, S. (ed.) *Needs Assessment and Community Care. Clinical Practice and Policy Making.* (Oxford: Butterworth-Heinemann, 1998).

Ball, S. *Education Policy and Social Class*. (London and New York: Routledge, 2006).

Banks, S. *Ethics, Accountability and the Social Professions*. (Basingstoke, Hampshire: Palgrave Macmillan, 2004).

Barr, A. *Practising Community Development*. (London: Community Development Foundation, 1991).

Barrett, P. H., P. J. Gautrey, S. Herbert, D. Kohn, and S. Smith (eds) *Charles Darwin's Notebooks, 1836–1844: Geology, Transmutation of Species, Metaphysical Enquiries*. (Ithaca, NY; London: Cornell University Press and British Museum (Natural History); Cambridge University Press and British Museum (Natural History), 1987).

Barwick, S. 'Still a Slum' (*The Spectator*, 11 May 1991), 26.

Bateson, G. *Steps to an Ecology of Mind*. (New York: Ballantine Books, 1972).

Bateson, G. *Mind and Nature a Necessary Unity*. (New York: Bantam Books, 1979).

Bateson, G. *Steps to an Ecology of Mind* 2nd ed. (Chicago, IL and London: The University of Chicago Press, 2000).

Bateson, G. and M. Bateson. *Where Angels Fear: Towards an Epistemology of the Sacred*. (New York: Macmillan, 1987).

Bauman, Z. 'Glokalisierung oder: Was fur die einen Globalisierung, ist fur die anderen Lokalisierung'. *Das Argument* 217.5–6 (1996) 653–664.

Bauman, Z. *Modernity and Ambivalence*. (Cambridge and Oxford: Polity Press, 1991).

Bauman, Z. *Ansichten der Postmoderne*. (Hamburg and Berlin: Argument Verlag, 1995).

Becker, H. 'Whose Side Are We on?' *Sociological Work, Method and Substance*. (London: Allen Lane, 1970), pp. 123–126.

Bekerman, Z. 'Hidden dangers in multicultural discourse'. *Race Equality and Teaching*, 21(3) (2003a) 36–42.

Bekerman, Z. 'Never free of suspicion'. *Cultural Studies and Critical Methodologies*, 3(2) (2003b) 136–147.

Bekerman, Z. 'Multicultural approaches and options in conflict ridden areas: Bilingual Palestinian-Jewish education in Israel'. *Teachers College Record*, 106(3) (2004) 574–610.

Bekerman, Z. 'Complex contexts and ideologies: Bilingual education in conflict-ridden areas'. *Journal of Language Identity and Education*, 4(1) (2005) 1–20.

Bell, V. *Interrogating Incest: Feminism, Foucault and the Law*. (London: Routledge, 1993).

Belloni, F. and J. Hodgson. *Criminal Injustice: An Evaluation of the Criminal Justice Process in Britain*. (London: Macmillan, 1999).

Benhabib, S., J. Butler, D. Cornell, and N. Fraser. *Der Streit um Differenz*. (Frankfurt am Main: Fischer Taschenbuch Verlag, 1993).

Benjamin, W. *Illuminationen*. (Frankfurt am Main: Suhrkamp, 1977).

Beresford, P. and C. Evans. 'Research note: Research and empowerment'. *British Journal of Social Work*, 29 (1999) 671–677.

Beresford, P., D. Green, R. Lister and K. Woodward. *Poverty First Hand! Poor People Speak for Themselves*. (London: CPAG, 1999).

Berger, P. L. *Facing Up To Modernity*. (New York: Basic Books, 1977).

Berliner, D. C. 'Our impoverished view of educational reform'. *Teachers college Record*, 108(6) (2006) 949–995.

Bernfeld, S. 'Sozialismus und Psychoanalyse'. In S. Bernfeld, W. Reich, W. Jurinetz, I. Sapir, and A. Stoljarov (eds) *Psychoanalyse und Marxismus*. (Frankfurt am Main: Suhrkamp, 1971), pp. 46–55.

Best, S. and D. Kellner. *Postmodern Theory: Critical Interrogations*. (Basingstoke, Hampshire: Palgrave Macmillan, 1991).

Bhabha, H. K. (ed.) *Nation and Narration*. (London and New York: Routledge, 1995).

Bhui, H. S. 'Race, racism and risk assessment: linking theory to practice with black mentally disordered offenders'. *Probation Journal*, 46 (1999) 171–181.

Bhui, H. S. 'Probation in England and Wales: from rehabilitation to risk'. *Journal of Forensic Psychiatry*, 13 (2002) 231–239.

Billig, M. *Banal Nationalism*. (London: Sage Publications, 1995).

Billig, M. *Arguing and Thinking: A Rhetorical Approach to Social Psychology* 2nd ed. (Cambridge: Cambridge University Press, 1996).

Blackburn, J. 'Understanding Paulo Freire: Reflections on the origins, concepts, and possible pitfalls of his educational approach'. *Community Development Journal*, 35(1) (2000) 3–15.

Blackman, T. 2001 'Complexity theory and the new public management.' *Social Issues, Vol. 1*(2) Special Issue on Complexity Science and Social Ploicy: http://www.whb.co.uk/socialissues

Bloor, M. 'Addressing social problems through qualitative research'. In D. Silverman (ed.) *Qualitative Research: Theory, Methods and Practice*. (London: Sage Publications, 2004), pp. 305–324.

BMRB. *A Study of the Quality of Life in Greenwich: Breadline Greenwich Report*. (London: BMRB International Ltd, 1994).

Boal, A. *Games for Actors and Non-Actors*. (London/ New York: Routledge, 1992).

Boal, A. *The Rainbow of Desire: The Boal Method of Theatre and Therapy*. (London/ New York: Routledge, 1995).

Boal, A. *Legislative Theatre: Using Performance to Make Politics*. (London/ New York: Routledge, 1998).

Bochner, A. P. 'Love Survives'. In N. K. Denzin and Y. S. Lincoln (eds) *9/11 in American Culture*. (Walnut Creek, CA: Altamira Press, 2003), pp. 180–187.

Bourdieu, P. *Sozialer Sinn. Kritik der theoretischen Urteilskraft*. (Frankfurt am Main: Suhrkamp, 1993).

Bourdieu, P. *Die feinen Unterschiede. Kritik der gesellschaftlichen Urteilskraft*. (Frankfurt am Main: Suhrkamp, 1999).

Bourdieu, P. 'The Biographical Illusion'. In P. DuGay, J. Evans, and P. Redman (eds) *Identity: A reader*. (London: Sage Publications, 2000), pp. 297–303.

Bourdieu, P. *Das politische Feld*. (Konstanz: UVK-Verlagsgesellschaft, 2001).

Bourdieu, P. *Wie die Kultur zum Bauern kommt. Über Bildung, Schule und Politik*. (Hamburg: VSA, 2001).

Bowcott, O. 'Council estates in downward spiral' (*The Guardian*, 13 February 1997), 6.

Brager, T. and H. Specht. 'Community Organising'. In Healthy Sheffield Support Team (ed.) *Community Development and Health: The way Forward in Sheffield* [Brager & Specht cited in 1993 report]. (Sheffield: Healthy Sheffield Support Team, 1973), p. 29.

Brah, A. 'Questions of Difference and International Feminism'. In S. Jackson, K. Atkinson, D. Beddoe, T. Brewer, S. Faulkner, A. Hucklesby, R. Pearson, H. Power, J. Prince, M. Ryan, and P. Young (eds) *Women's Studies: A Reader.* (Hemel Hempstead, Herts: Harvester Wheatsheaf, 1993), pp. 29–35.

Breckner, R. and S. Rupp. 'Discovering Biographies in Changing Social Worlds: the Biographical-Interpretative Method'. In P. Chamberlayne, M. Rustin, and T. Wengraf (eds) *Biography and Social Exclusion in Europe.* (Bristol, UK: Policy Press, 2002), pp. 289–308.

Brenner, C. *Grundzüge der Psychoanalyse.* (Frankfurt am Main: Fischer Taschenbuch Verlag, 1990).

British Sociological Association. *Statement of Ethical Practice.* (Durham: BSA Publications, 1996).

Britton, R. *Belief and Imagination.* (London: Routledge, 1977).

Bronfen, E., B. Marius, and T. Steffen (eds) *Hybride Kulturen.* (Tübingen: Stauffenburg Verlag, 1997).

Brookman, F., L. Noaks, and E. Wincup (eds) *Qualitative Research in Criminology.* (Aldershot: Ashgate, 1999).

Bruyn, S. T. *The Human Perspective in Sociology.* (Englewood Cliffs, NJ: Prentice Hall, 1966).

Bülow-Schramm, M. and D. Gipser (eds) *Der brüchige Habitus. Empirische Erforschung kooperativer Handlungsmöglichkeiten von StudentInnen und HochschullehrerInnen: vol. 41 of the series 'Theorie und Praxis', Fachbereich I.* (Hannover: Universität Hannover, 1991).

Bülow-Schramm, M. and D. Gipser (eds) *10 Jahre Lehr-/Lernprojekt Der brüchige Habitus: Hochschuldidaktische Arbeitspapiere no. 30.* (Hamburg: Universität Hamburg, 1997).

Burgess, R. G. *In the Field: An Introduction to Field Research.* (London: Allen and Unwin, 1984).

Burke, K. *A Rhetoric of Motives.* (Berkeley: University of California Press, 1969).

Burnett, R. 'One-to-One Ways of Promoting Desistance: In Search of an Evidence Base'. In R. Burnett and C. Roberts (eds) *What Works in Probation and Youth Justice: Developing Evidence Based Practice.* (Devon, UK: Willan Publishing, 2004), pp. 180–197.

Burnett, R. and F. McNeill. 'The place of the officer-offender relationship in assisting offenders to desist from crime'. *Probation Journal,* 52 (2005) 221–242.

Burton, C. 'Introduction to Complexity'. In K. Sweeney and F. Griffiths (eds) *Complexity and Healthcare – An Introduction.* (Oxford: Radcliffe Medical Press, 2002), pp. 1–18.

Butler, J. *Bodies that Matter.* (New York and London: Routledge, 1993).

Byrne, D. *Complexity Theory and the Social Sciences.* (London and New York: Routledge, 1998).

CAG Consultants. *Employment and Training Strategy for Kingsmead and Sherry Wharf.* (London: CAG Consultants, 1997).

Calhoun, C. 'Social Theory and the Public Sphere'. In B. S. Turner (ed.) *The Blackwell Companion to Social theory* 2nd ed. (Oxford: Blackwell Publishers, 2000), pp. 505–544.

Canton, R. 'Risk Assessment and Compliance in Probation and Mental Health Practice'. In B. Littlechild and D. Fearns (eds) *Mental Disorder and Criminal*

Justice: Policy, Provision and Practice. (Dorset, UK: Russell House Publishing, 2004), pp. 137–158.

Carabine, J. 'Unmarried Motherhood 1839–1900: A Genealogical Analysis'. In M. Wetherell, S. Taylor, and Y. S. J. (eds) *Discourse as Data: A Guide for Analysis*. (London: Sage Publications, 2001), pp. 267–310.

Carter, G. W. 'Measurement of Need'. In N. A. Polansky (ed.) *Social Work Research*. (Chicago, IL: University of Chicago, 1960), pp. 114–128.

Castel, R. 'From Dangerousness to Risk'. In Burchell.G (ed.) *The Foucault Effect. Studies in Governmentality.* (Brighton, UK: Harvester Wheatsheaf, 1991), pp. 281–298.

Castel, R. *From Manual Workers to Wage Labourers: Transformation of the Social Question.* (Edison, NJ : Transaction Publishers, 2002).

Castles, S. and M. J. Miller. *The Age of Migration: International Population Movements in the Modern World* 3rd ed. (Basingstoke, Hampshire: Palgrave Macmillan, 2003).

Chaiklin, S. and J. Lave. *Understanding Practice*. (Cambridge: Cambridge University press, 1996).

Chamberlyne, P. and A. Spano. 'Modernisation as Lived Experience: Contrasting Case Studies from the Sostris Project'. In P. Chamberlayne, J. Bornat, and T. Wengraf (eds) *The Turn to Biographical Methods in Social Science: Comparative Issues and Examples.* (London: Routledge, 2000), pp. 321–336.

Chamberlayne, P., J. Bornat, and T. Wengraf (eds) *The Turn Towards Biographical Methods in the Social Sciences: Comparative Issues and Examples.* (London: Routledge, 2000).

Chambers, R. *Rural Development: Putting the Last First.* (London: Longman, 1983).

Cheek, J. *Postmodern and Poststructural Approaches to Nursing Research.* (Thousand Oaks, CA: Sage Publications, 2000).

Churchman, C. W. *Challenge to Reason.* (New York: McGraw-Hill, 1968).

Churchman, C. W. *The Systems Approach* 2nd ed. (New York: Dell Publishing, 1979).

Cilliers, P. *Complexity and Postmodernism: Understanding Complex Systems.* (London: Routledge, 1998).

Clarke, C. Where Next for Penal Policy. Prison Reform Trust Annual Lecture, Prison reform Trust, http://www.prisonreformtrust.org.uk/uploads/documents/factfile1807lo.pdf, 2005, Access Date: 30 November 2007.

Clarke, L. and C. Winch. 'A European skills framework? But what are skills'. *Journal of Education and Work*, 19 (2006) 255–269.

Clarke, L. and C. Winch (eds) *Vocational Education.* (London and New York: Routledge, 2007).

Clarke, S. 'Learning from experience: psycho-social research methods in the social sciences'. *Qualitative Research*, 2(2) (2002) 173–194.

Clarke, S. 'Theory and practice: Psychoanalytic sociology as psycho-social studies'. *Sociology*, 40 (2006, 6 December) 1153–1169.

Cohen, D. 'What is the system in systemic reform?' *Educational Researcher*, 24(9) (1995) 11–31.

Cohen, J. and I. Stewart. *The Collapse of Chaos: Discovering Simplicity in a Complex World.* (Harmondsworth: Penguin, 1994).

Cohen, L., L. Manion, and K. Morrison. *Research Methods in Education.* (London: Routledge Falmer, 2000).

Conant, J. B. *Science and Common Sense*. (New Haven, CT: Yale University Press, 1951).

Coombs, P. *The World Educational Crisis*. (New York: Oxford University Press, 1968).

Cooper, A. and J. Lousada. *Borderline Welfare: Feeling and Fear of Feeling in Modern Welfare*. (London: Karnac, 2005).

Corbetta, P. *Social Research: Theory, Methods and Techniques*. (London: Sage Publications, 2003).

Cox, P. 'Young People, Migration and Metanarratives: Arguments for a Critical Theoretical Approach'. In T. Geisen and C. Riegel (eds) *Jugend, Partizipation und Migration: Orientierung im Kontext von Integration und Ausgrenzung*. (Wiesbaden: VS Verlag fur Sozialwissenschaft, 2007), pp. 51–66.

Cox, P., R. Hopkins, M. McKeown, L. Malihi-Shoji, and S. Downe. 'User and Carer Involvement: The Relevance of Social Movement Theory'. (In press)

Craissati, J., L. Webb, and S. Keen. *Personality Disordered Sex Offenders- Bracton Centre (Oxleas NHS Trust)*. (London: London Probation Service and Home Office, 2005).

Crang, M. and I. Cook. *Doing Ethnographies*. (London: Sage Publications, 2007).

Crime Concern. *Youth Crime in Hackney – Analysis and Options*. (London: Crime Concern, 1993).

Cromby, J. and D. J. Nightingale. 'What's Wrong with Social Constructionism'. In D. J. Nightingale and J. Cromby (eds) *Social Constructionist Psychology: A Critical Analysis of Theory and Practice*. (Buckingham: Open University Press, 1999), pp. 1–19.

Cronin, B., S. Roth, and M. Wrentschur (eds). *Training Manual for Theatre Work in Social Fields*. (Frankfurt am Main: Brandes & Apsel, 2005).

Cutler, T. and B. Waine. *Managing the Welfare State*. (Oxford: Berg, 1997).

Damasio, A. *Descartes' Error: Emotion, Reason and the Human Brain* 2nd ed. (London: Vintage Books, 2006).

Delanty, G. *Modernity and Postmodernity: Knowledge, Power and the Self.* (London: Sage, 2000).

Denzin, N. K. *Sociological Methods: A Sourcebook*. (New York: McGraw-Hill, 1978).

Denzin, N. K. *Interpretive Biography*. (London: Sage, 1989).

Denzin, N. K. *Interpretive Ethnography: Ethnographic Practices for the 21st Century*. (Thousand Oaks, CA: Sage, 1997).

Denzin, N. K. and Y. S. Lincoln (eds). *Handbook of Qualitative Research* 2nd ed. (London: Sage, 2000).

Denzin, N. K. and Y. S. Lincoln (eds). *9/11 in American Culture*. (Walnut Creek, CA: Altamira Press, 2003a).

Denzin, N. K. and Y. S. Lincoln (eds). *Collecting and Interpreting Qualitative Materials* Vol. 3. (Thousand Oaks, CA: Sage, 2003b) 3 vols.

Department of Communities and Local Government, New Deal for Communities, Neighbourhood Renewal Unit, Department of Communities and Local Government, London, http://www.neighbourhood.gov.uk/page.asp?id=617, 2008, Access Date: 20 March 2008.

Department of the Environment Transport and the Regions. *Indices of Deprivation 2000*. (London: Department of the Environment Transport and the Regions, 2000).

Derrida, J. *The Truth in Painting* [Trans.: G. B. a. I. McLeod]. (Chicago, IL: Chicago University Press, 1987).

Dockery, G. 'Participatory Research: Whose Roles, Whose Responsibilities?' In C. Truman, D. M. Mertens, and B. Humphries (eds). *Research and Inequality.* (London: UCL Press, 2000), pp. 95–110.

Dogbe, T. ' "The One Who Rides the Donkey Does Not Know the Ground Is Hot": Centre for the Development of People's Involvement in the Ghana Participatory Poverty Assessment'. In J. Holland and J. Blackburn (eds) *Whose Voice? Participatory Research and Policy Change.* (London: Intermediate Technology Publications, 1998), pp. 91–102.

Drodge, S. 'Institutional, Local, Regional and National Dynamics in the New English Skill System'. In R. Husemann and A. Heikkinen (eds) *Governance and Marketisation in Vocational and Continuing Education.* (Bern, NY: Peter Lang, 2004), pp. 103–121.

Duce, R. 'Council uses civil court to end family's terror reign' (*The Times,* 1993), 11.

Dudley, E. *The Critical Villager. Beyond Community Participation.* (London: Routledge, 1993).

Duro, P. *The Rhetoric of the Frame.* (Cambridge, MA: Cambridge University Press, 1996).

Durston, S. *The Kingsmead Kabin: An Independent Evaluation.* (London: Kingsmead Kabin, 1997).

Eagleton, T. *After Theory.* (London: Allen Lane, 2003).

Edwards, D. *Discourse and Cognition.* (London: Sage, 1997).

Edwards, D., M. Ashmore, and J. Potter. 'Death and furniture: The rhetoric, politics and theology of bottom line arguments against relativism'. *History of Human Sciences,* 8(2) (1995) 25–49.

Edwards, R., K. Nicoll, N. Solomon and R. Usher. *Rhetoric and Educational Discourse: Persuasive Texts?* (London and New York: Routledge, 2004).

Elias, N. *Über den Prozess der Zivilisation.* (Frankfurt am Main: Suhrkamp, 1976, 2 vols).

Elias, N. *The Society of Individuals* [Trans.: E. Jephcott]. (Oxford: Blackwell, 1991).

Elias, N. 'Civilization, Culture, Identity: "Civilization" and "Culture": Nationalism and Nation State Formation: An Extract from the Germans'. In J. Rundell and S. Mennell (eds) *Classical Readings in Culture and Civilization.* (New York: Routledge, 1998), pp. 225–240.

Ellis, C. ' "There are survivors": telling a story of sudden death'. *Sociological Quarterly,* 34 (1993) 711–730.

Ellis, C. 'Exploring Loss through Autoethnographic Inquiry: Autoethnographic Stories, Co-constructed Narratives and Interactive Interviews'. In J. H. Harvey (ed.) *Perspectives on Loss: A Sourcebook.* (Newbury Park, CA: Sage, 1998), pp. 49–62.

Ellis, C. 'Take No Chances'. In N. K. Denzin and Y. S. Lincoln (eds) *9/11 in American Culture.* (Walnut Creek, CA: Altamira Press, 2003), pp. 188–193.

Ellis, C. and A. P. Bochner. *Composing Ethnography: Alternative Forms of Qualitative Writing.* (Walnut Creek, CA: Altamira Press, 1996).

Ellis, C. and A. P. Bochner. 'Autoethnography, Personal Narrative, Reflexivity: Researcher as Subject'. In N. K. Denzin and Y. S. Lincoln (eds) *Collecting and Interpreting Qualitative Materials* 2nd ed. Vol. 3. (Thousand Oaks, CA: Sage, 2003), pp. 199–258 3 vols.

Ellis, K. and H. Dean (eds). *Social Policy and the Body: Transitions in Corporeal Discourse*. (Basingstoke, Hampshire: Macmillan, 2000).

Erdheim, M. *Die gesellscaftliche Produktion von Unbewussheit*. (Frankfurt am Main: Suhrkamp, 1992).

'Estate's clean up sets fine example'. (*Hackney Gazette*, 22 December 1994), 10.

Faraday, A. and K. Plummer. 'Doing life histories'. *Sociological Review*, 27(4) (1979) 773–798.

Fend, H. *Neue Theorie der Schule*. (Wiesbaden: VS-Verlag, 2006).

Field, J. *Lifelong Learning and the New Educational Order*. (Stoke on Trent: Trentham Books, 2000).

Fielding, N. 'Varieties of research interviews'. *Nurse Researcher*, 1(3) (1994) 188–197.

Filkin, N. and M. Naish. 'Whose Side Are We on? The Damage Done by Neutralism'. In G. Craig, N. Derricourt, and M. Loney (eds) *Community Work and the State: Towards a Radical Practice*. (London: Routledge and Kegan Paul, 1982), pp. 56–58.

Finch, J. ' "It's Great to Have Someone to Talk to": The Ethics and Politics of Interviewing Women'. In C. Bell and H. Roberts (eds) *Social Researching*. (London: Routledge and Kegan Paul, 1984), pp. 38–53.

Fitzgibbon, D. W. *Pre- emptive Criminalisation; Risk Control and Alternative Futures-Monograph*. (London: NAPO ICCJ, 2004).

Fitzgibbon, D. W. 'Institutional Racism, Pre-emptive Criminalisation and Risk Analysis'. *Howard Journal of Criminal Justice*, 46 (2007a) 128–144.

Fitzgibbon, D. W. 'Risk analysis and the new practitioner: Myth or reality?' *Punishment and Society*, 9 (2007b) 87–97.

Fitzgibbon, D. W. and A. Cameron. *E-OASys: A Helpful Assessment Tool for the Mentally Vulnerable Offender?* (London: London Probation Area, 2005).

Flick, U. *An Introduction to Qualitative Research: Theory, Method and Applications* 2nd ed. (London: Sage, 2002).

Forgacs, D. (ed.) *A Gramsci Reader*. (London: Lawrence and Wishart, 1988).

Foucault, M. *The Archeology of Knowledge*. (London: Tavistock, 1969).

Foucault, M. *The Order of Things: An Archaeology of the Human Sciences*. (New York: Vintage Books, 1973).

Foucault, M. *Überwachen und Strafen. Die Geburt des Gefängnisses*. (Frankfurt am Main: Suhrkamp, 1977).

Foucault, M. *Dispositive der Macht. Über Sexualität, Wissen und Wahrheit*. (Berlin: Merve, 1978).

Foucault, M. *Herculine Barbin: Being the Recently Discovered Memoirs of a Nineteenth-Century French Hermaphrodite* [First Pub. 1978]. (New York: Pantheon Books, 1980a).

Foucault, M. 'Two Lectures'. In C. Gordon (ed.) *Power/Knowledge: Selected Interviews and Other Writings, 1972–1977*. (Brighton, UK: Harvester Press, 1980a), pp. 78–108.

Foucault, M. 'The Order of Discourse'. In R. Young (ed.) *Untying the Text: A Poststructuralist Reader* [First Pub. 1971]. (Boston, MA: Routledge & Kegan Paul, 1981), pp. 48–78.

Foucault, M. *The History of Sexuality, Volume 2: The Use of Pleasure* [First Pub. 1984]. (London: Penguin, 1987).

Foucault, M. *The History of Sexuality, Volume 1: An Introduction* [First Pub. 1978]. (London: Penguin, 1990a).

Foucault, M. *The History of Sexuality, Volume 3: The Care of the Self* [First Pub. 1984]. (London: Penguin, 1990b).

Foucault, M. *Discipline and Punish: The Birth of the Prison* [First Pub. 1975]. (Harmondsworth: Penguin, 1991).

Foucault, M. 'Nietzsche, Genealogy, History'. In J. D. Faubion (ed.) *Essential Works of Foucault 1954–1984, Volume 2: Aesthetics, Method, and Epistemology* [First Pub. 1971]. (London: Penguin, 2000a), pp. 369–391.

Foucault, M. 'On the Genealogy of Ethics: an Overview of Work in Progress'. In P. Rabinow (ed.) *Essential Works of Foucault 1954–1984, Volume 1: Ethics, Subjectivity, and Truth* [First Pub. 1982]. (London: Penguin, 2000b), pp. 253–280.

Foucault, M. 'The Social Triumph of the Sexual Will'. In P. Rabinow (ed.) *Essential Works of Foucault 1954–1984, Volume 1: Ethics, Subjectivity, and Truth*. (London: Penguin, 2000c), pp. 157–162.

Foucault, M. *The Archaeology of Knowledge* [First Pub. 1969]. (London: Routledge, 2002).

Francis, D. and S. Hester. *An Invitation to Ethnomethodology: Language, Society and Interaction*. (London: Sage, 2004).

Frank, A. *The Wounded Storyteller: Body, Illness, and Ethics*. (Chicago, IL: University of Chicago Press, 1995).

Frank, A. 'Illness and autobiographical work: Dialogue as narrative destabilization'. *Qualitative Sociology*, 23(1) (2000) 135–156.

Frank, A. 'Asking the right question about pain: Narrative and phronesis'. *Literature and Medicine*, 23(2) (2004) 209–225.

Franko Aas, K. 'From Narrative to Database: technological change and penal culture'. *Punishment and Society* 6 (2004) 379–393.

Freire, A. and D. Macedo (eds). *The Paulo Freire Reader*. (New York: Continuum, 1998).

Freire, P. 'Cultural action and conscientization'. *Harvard Educational Review*, 40(3) (1970a) 452–477.

Freire, P. *Cultural Action for Freedom*. (Cambridge, MA: Harvard Educational Review Press, 1970b).

Freire, P. *Pedagogy of the Oppressed*. (London: Penguin, 1972).

Freire, P. *Education for Critical Consciousness*. (New York: Seabury, 1973).

Freire, P. *Pädagogik der Unterdrückten. Erziehung als Praxis der Freiheit*. (Reinbek bei Hamburg: Rowohlt, 1982).

French, R. and P. Simpson. 'Learning at the edges between knowing and not-knowing: "Translating" Bion'. *Organisational and Social Dynamics*, 1(1) (2001) 54 77.

Freud, S. *Complete Edition* [Volume 9 (Fragen der Gesellschaft. Ursprünge der Religion)]. (Frankfurt am Main: Fischer Taschenbuch Verlag, 2000).

Freud, S. 'Die Zukunft einer Illusion'. *Complete Edition* [Volume 9 (Fragen der Gesellschaft. Ursprünge der Religion)]. (Frankfurt am Main: Fischer Taschenbuch Verlag, 1999), pp. 135–190.

Freud, S. 'Totem und Tabu'. *Complete Edition* [Volume 9 (Fragen der Gesellschaft. Ursprünge der Religion)]. (Frankfurt am Main: Fischer Taschenbuch Verlag, 1999), pp. 287–444.

Fritz, C. *Because I Speak Cockney They Think I'm Stupid: An Application of Paulo Freire's Concepts to Community Work with Women*. (London: Association of Community Workers, 1982).

Froggett, L. *Love, Hate and Welfare: Psychosocial Approaches to Policy and Practice*. (Bristol, UK: Policy Press, 2002).

Frosh, S. 'Psychosocial studies and psychology: Is a critical approach emerging?' *Human Relations*, 56(12) (2003) 1545–1567.

Frosh, S. and P. Emerson. 'Interpretation and over-interpretation: Disputing the meaning of texts'. *Qualitative Research*, 5(3) (2005) 307–324.

Fuchs-Heinritz, W. *Biographische Forschung*. (Wiesbaden: VS Verlag für Sozialwissenschaften, 2005).

Gadd, D. 'Making sense of the interviewee-interviewer dynamic in narratives about violence in intimate relationships'. *International Journal of Social Research Methodology, Theory and Practice*, 7 (2004, 5, December) 383–402.

Gamson, J. 'Sexualities, Queer Theory, and Qualitative Research'. In N. K. Denzin and Y. S. Lincoln (eds) *Handbook of Qualitative Research* 2nd ed. (Thousand Oaks, CA: Sage, 2000), pp. 347–365.

Gardiner, M. 'Ecology and carnival: Traces of a "green'" social theory in the writings of M. Bakhtin'. *Theory and Society*, 22 (1993) 765–812.

Garfinkel, H. *Studies in Ethnomethodology*. (Oxford: Polity Press, 1985).

Garland, D. *The Culture of Control: Crime and Social Order in Contemporary Society*. (Oxford: Oxford University Press, 2001).

Geertz, C. *The Interpretation of Culture*. (New York: Basic Books Inc., 1973).

Geisen, T. 'Grenze und Ambivalenz'. In T. Geisen and A. Karcher (eds) *Grenze: Sozial – Politisch – Kulturell*. (Frankfurt am Main: IKO Verlag, 2003), pp. 99–126.

Geisen, T. 'People on the Move: The Inclusion of Migrants in Labour Transfer Systems.' T. Geisen, A. A. Hickey, and A. Karcher (eds) *Migration, Mobility and Borders: Issues of Theory and Policy*. (Frankfurt am Main: IKO Verlag, 2004a), pp. 35–80.

Geisen, T., A. A. Hickey, and A. Karcher (eds). *Migration, Mobility and Borders: Issues of Theory and Policy*. (Frankfurt am Main: IKO Verlag, 2004b).

Gellner, E. *Nations and Nationality*. (Oxford: Basic Blackwell, 1983).

Geyer, R. 'European integration, the problem of complexity and the revision of theory'. *Journal of Common Market Studies*, 41 (2003) 15–35.

Geyer, R. and S. Rihani. 'Complexity: An appropriate framework for development?' *Progress in Development Studies*, 1 (2001) 237–245.

Giddens, A. *Modernity and Self-Identity*. (Cambridge: Polity, 1991).

Giddens, A. *Die Konstitution der Gesellschaft*. (Frankfurt am Main and New York: Campus Verlag, 1997).

Gilbert, G. N. and M. Mulkay. *Opening Pandora's Box: A Sociological Analysis of Scientists' Discourse*. (Cambridge, UK: Cambridge University Press, 1984).

Gill, R. 'Justifying Injustice: Broadcasters' Accounts of Inequality in Radio'. In E. Burman and I. Parker (eds). *Discourse Analytic Research: Repertoires and Readings of Texts in Action*. (London: Routledge, 1993), pp. 75–93.

Gill, R. 'Relativism, Reflexivity and Politics: Interrogating Discourse Analysis from a Feminist Perspective'. In S. Wilkinson and C. Kitzinger (eds). *Feminism and Discourse: Psychological Perspectives*. (London: Sage, 1995), pp. 165–186.

Gill, R. 'Discourse Analysis: Practical Implementation'. In J. T. E. Richardson (ed.) *Handbook of Qualitative Research Methods for Psychology and the Social Sciences*. (Leicester: BPS Books, 1996), pp. 141–158.

Gipser, D. 'Grenzüberschreitungen. Theater der Unterdrückten an Hochschulen in Nah-Ost und West – Emanzipatorische Forschungsprozesse'. *Zeitschrift für befreiende Pädagogik*, X (1996, June) 26–31.

Glaser, B. G. and A. L. Strauss. *Grounded Theory.* (Bern: Verlag Hans Huber, 2005).
Glinka, H. -J. *Das Narrative Interview.* (Weinheim und Munchen: Juventa Verlag, 1988).
Goldschmidt, H. L. *Freiheit für den Widerspruch.* (Wien: Passagen Verlag, 1993).
Gonon, P. 'The Internationalization of Vocational Education Reform-concepts: a Rhetorical Perspective'. In A. Heikkinen and K. Kraus (eds) *Re-working Vocational Education* [in press]. (Bern, New York: Peter Lang, 2008).
Goodman, A. 'Probation into the Millennium: The Punishing Service'. In R. Matthews and J. Young (eds) *The New Politics of Crime and Punishment.* (Cullompton, UK: Willan Publishing, 2003), pp. 199–222.
Gordon, E. W. and M. A. Rebell. 'Toward a comprehensive system of education for all children'. *Teachers College Record*, 109(7) (2007) 1836–1843.
Gough, B. 'Men and the discursive reproduction of sexism: Repertoires of difference and equality'. *Feminism and Psychology*, 8(1) (1998) 25–49.
Gouldner, A. *The Coming Crisis of Western Sociology.* (New York: Basic Books, 1970).
Gouldner, A. *For Sociology: Renewal and Critique in Sociology Today.* (Harmondsworth: Penguin, 1973).
Gramsci, A. *Selections from the Prison Notebooks* [edited by Q. Hoare & G. N. Smith]. (London: Lawrence and Wishart, 1971).
Gray, N., J. Laing and L. Noaks (eds) *Criminal Justice, Mental Health and the Politics of Risk.* (London: Cavendish, 2002).
Grbich, C. *Qualitative Research in Health: An Introduction.* (London: Sage, 1999).
Green, A. *Education and State Formation.* (London: Macmillan, 1990).
Green, A., A. Wolf, and T. Leney. *Convergence and Divergence in European Education and Training Systems.* (London: Institute of Education, University of London, 1999).
Greene, B. *The Elegant Universe: Superstrings, Hidden Dimensions and the Quest for the Ultimate Theory* 2nd ed. (London: Vintage, 2005).
Green, R. *Community Action against Poverty: A Poverty Profile of the Kingsmead Estate.* (London: Kingsmead Kabin, 1997).
Green, R. 'Why New Labour's Social Exclusion Unit is in danger of getting it wrong'. *Benefits Journal*, 22 (1998) 38–40.
Green, R. 'Applying a community needs profiling approach to tackling service user poverty'. *British Journal of Social Work*, 30(3) (2000) 287–303.
Green, R. 'Rebuilding a sense of community: Community research as part of a community development process'. *Community Development Society in Association with the International Association for Community Development.* (Ithaca, NY: Cornell University, 2003).
Green, R. *Voices from the Mead: People's Stories of the Kingsmead Estate.* (Bury St Edmunds: Arima Publishing, 2005).
Green, R. 'Researching Social Exclusion'. (Unpublished paper delivered to a seminar at Macquarie University, Sydney, Australia, 2006a).
Green, R. 'Voices from the Mead: building a community archive', in *Knowledge and Inspiration: A Strategy for Archive, Library and Museum Collections in London* (London: ALM, 2006b).
Green, R. and A. Turner. 'Challenging the Power of Professionals: Involving the Community in Tackling Poverty'. In H. Payne and B. Littlechild (eds) *Ethical*

Practice and the Abuse of Power in Social Responsibility. (London: Jessica Kingsley, 1999), pp. 16–36.

Green, R. and A. Watson. 'Kingsmead Community History Project'. *Islington Local History Project.* (2006).

Green, R. and B. Hammond. 'The Kabin: Community Development Work in Practice'. *Talking Point, Association of Community Workers,* 215 (2005) 1–4.

Green, R. and H. Sender. 'Supporting young people: A community response to dispersal orders for young people'. *Talking Point, Association of Community Workers,* 214 (2005) 1–4.

Green, R., M. Broome, and K. Diosi. Local Solutions to Local Needs: A Community Needs Survey of the Kingsmead Estate, Hackney Marsh Partnership/Kingsmead Homes Housing Association, London, http://www.hmp.org.uk, 2007, Access Date: 20 March 2008.

Green, R. and S. Dicks. 'Counselling in the inner city: A community research project'. *Journal of Social Work* (in press).

Greinert, W. D. *Das "deutsche System"der Berufsausbildung.* (Baden-Baden: Nomos, 1998).

Gribbin, J. *Deep Simplicity: Chaos, Complexity and the Emergence of Life.* (London: Allen Lane, 2004).

Griffiths, F. 'Complexity and Primary Healthcare Research'. In K. Sweeney and F. Griffiths (eds) *Complexity and Healthcare: An Introduction.* (Oxford: Radcliffe Medical Press, 2002), pp. 149–166.

Griffiths, S. *The Challenge: A Profile of Poverty in Hackney.* (London: London Borough of Hackney, 1996).

Griffiths, S. *Waltham Forest, the Way It Is: A Profile of Poverty in Waltham Forest.* (London: London Borough of Waltham Forest, 1997).

Grounds, A. 'Risk Assessment and Management in Clinical Context'. In J. Crichton (ed.) *Psychiatric Patient Violence: Risk and Relapse.* (London: Duckworth, 1995), pp. 58–72.

Grover, S. 'Why won't they listen to us?' *Childhood,* 11(1) (2004) 81–116.

Gubrium, J. F. and J. A. Holstein. *The New Language of Qualitative Method.* (Oxford: Oxford University Press, 1997).

Gubrium, J. F. and J. A. Holstein. 'From the Individual Interview to the Interview Society'. In J. F. Gubrium and J. A. Holstein (eds) *Postmodern Interviewing.* (Thousand Oaks, CA: Sage Publications, 2003), pp. 21–49.

Gubrium, J. F. and J. A. Holstein (eds) *Postmodern Interviewing.* (Thousand Oaks, CA: Sage Publications, 2003).

Gutting, G. *Foucault: A Very Short Introduction.* (Oxford: Oxford University Press, 2005).

H.M Inspectorate of Probation. *An Independent Review of a Serious Further Offence Case: Damien Hanson & Elliot White.* (London: Stationery Office, 2006).

Habermas, J. *Theory and Practice.* (Boston, MA: Beacon Press, 1973).

Habermas, J. *The Theory of Communicative Action, Volume 1: Reason and the Rationalization of Society.* (London: Heinemann, 1984).

Habermas, J. *The Theory of Communicative Action, Volume 2: Lifeworld and System: A Critique of Functionalist Reason.* (Cambridge: Polity Press, 1987).

Hacking, I. 'Making up People'. In T. C. Heller, M. Sosna, and D. E. Wellbery (eds) *Reconstructing Individualism: Autonomy, Individuality, and the Self in Western Thought.* (Stanford: Stanford University Press, 1986), pp. 222–236.

Hackney Marsh Partnership. *A Year Filled with Life*. (London: Hackney Marsh Partnership, 2005).

Hale, J. N. 'On the Origins of Participatory Action Research'. *Action Research Journal*, June 2007, http://www.montana.edu/arexpeditions/articlereviewer.php?AID=101

Halfpenny, P. 'Positivism in the Twentieth Century'. In G. Ritzer and B. Smart (eds) *Handbook of Social Theory*. (London: Sage Publications, 2001), pp. 371–385.

Hall, S. *Rassismus und Kulturelle Identitat*. (Hamburg: Argument Verlag, 1994a).

Hall, S. 'Der Westen und der Rest: Diskurse der Macht'. *Rassismus und Kulturelle Identitat*. (Hamburg: Argument Verlag, 1994b), pp. 137–179.

Halperin, D. M. *Saint Foucault: Towards a Gay Hagiography*. (New York: Oxford University Press, 1995).

Hannah-Moffat, K. 'Criminogenic needs and the transformative risk subject: Hybridisations of risk/need in penalty'. *Punishment and Society*, 7 (2005) 29–61.

Haraway, D. 'Situated knowledges: The science question in feminism and the privilege of partial perspective'. *Feminist Studies*, 13(3) (1988) 575–599.

Hardcastle, D. A., S. Wencour, and P. R. Powers. *Community Practice: Theories and Skills for Social Workers*. (New York: Oxford University Press, 1997).

Hardiman, M. 'People's Involvement in Health and Medical Care'. In J. Midgley (ed.) *Community Participation, Social Development and the State*. (London: Methuen, 1986), pp. 69–82.

Harding, S. *The Science Question in Feminism*. (Ithaca, NY: Cornell University Press, 1986).

Harding, S. *Whose Science? Whose Knowledge? Thinking from Women's Lives*. (Ithaca, NY: Cornell University Press, 1991).

Haug, F. 'Functions of the Private Sphere in Social Movements'. In C. W. Tolman and W. Maiers (eds) *Critical Psychology: Contributions to an Historical Science of the Subject*. (Cambridge, UK: Cambridge University Press, 1991), pp. 234–250.

Hawtin, M., G. Hughes, and J. Percy-Smith. *Community Profiling: Auditing Social Needs*. (Buckingham: Open University Press, 1994).

Hazelrigg, L. *Cultures of Nature*. (Tallahassee, FL: Florida State University Press, 1995).

Hegel, G. W. F. *Phänomenologie des Geistes*. (Hamburg: Felix Meiner Verlag, 1988).

Heikkinen, A. 'Models, Paradigms or Cultures of Vocational Education'. *European Journal of Vocational Education*, 32 (2004) 32–44.

Heinze, T. *Qualitative Sozialforschung*. (Opladen: Westdeutscher Verlag, 1987).

Henriksson, L., S. Wrede, and V. Burau. 'Understanding professional projects in welfare service work: revival of old professionalism?' *Gender, Work and Organization*, 13 (2006) 174–192.

Henriques, J., W. Hollway, C. Urwin, C. Venn, and V. Walkerdine. *Changing the Subject*. (London: Methuen and Co. Ltd, 1984).

Hepburn, A. 'Teachers and secondary school bullying: a postmodern discourse analysis'. *Discourse & Society*, 8(1) (1997) 27–48.

Heritage, J. 'Explanations As Accounts: a Conversation Analytic Perspective'. In C. Antaki (ed.) *Analysing Everyday Explanation: A Casebook of Methods*. (London: Sage Publications, 1988), pp. 127–144.

Heron, J. 'Philosophical Basis for the New Paradigm'. In P. Reason and J. Rowan (eds) *Human Enquiry: A Sourcebook of New Paradigm Research*. (New York: John Wiley, 1981), pp. 92–110.

Herrnstein Smith, B. 'The Unquiet Judge: Activism without Objectivism'. In A. Megill (ed.) *Rethinking Objectivity*. (Durham, NC: Duke University Press, 1994), pp. 289–311.

Hicks, S. 'Sexuality: Social Work Theories and Practice'. In R. Adams, L. Dominelli, and M. Payne (eds) *Social Work Futures: Crossing Boundaries, Transforming Practice*. (Basingstoke, Hampshire: Palgrave Macmillan, 2005), pp. 141–153.

Hicks, S. 'Thinking through sexuality'. *Journal of Social Work*, 8(1) (2008) 65–82.

Hill Collins, P. *Black Feminist Thought: Knowledge, Consciousness and the Politics of Empowerment*. (London: Routledge, 1991).

Hills, G. 'Diverting tactics'. *Nursing Times*, 89 (1993) 24–27.

Hirschland, M. J. and S. Steinmo. 'Correcting the record: Understanding the history of federal intervention and failure in securing U.S. educational reform'. *Educational Policy*, 17 (2003) 343–364.

Hoggett, P. *Emotional Life and the Politics of Welfare*. (Basingstoke, Hampshire: Palgrave Macmillan, 2000).

Hoggett, P., P. Beedell, L. Jimenez, M. Mayo, and C. Miller. 'Identity, life history and commitment to welfare'. *Journal of Social Policy*, 35(4) (2006) 689–704.

Holland, J. H. *Adaptation in Natural and Artificial Systems*. (Ann Arbor, MI: University of Michigan Press, 1975).

Holland, J. H., K. J. Holyoak, R. E. Nisbet, and P. R. Thagard. *Induction: Processes of Inference, Learning and Discovery*. (Cambridge, MA: MIT Press, 1986).

Hollway, W. 'The psycho-social subject in evidence-based practice'. *Journal of Social Work Practice*, 15(1) (2001) 9–22.

Hollway, W. and T. Jefferson. *Doing Qualitative Research Differently: Free association, Narrative and the Interview Method*. (London: Sage Publications, 2000).

Holman, B. *Kids at the Door*. (Oxford: Basil Blackwell, 1981).

Holman, B. *Kids at the Door Revisited*. (Lyme Regis, Russell House Publishing 2000).

Holman, B. *A New Deal for Social Welfare*. (London: Lion, 1993).

Holman, B. *FARE Dealing: Neighbourhood Involvement in a Housing Scheme*. (London: Community Development Foundation, 1997).

Home Office. *Provision for mentally disordered offenders: Home Office Circular No 66/90*. (London: Home Office, 1990).

Home Office. *Mentally Disordered Offenders: Inter-Agency Working: Home Office Circular No 12/95*. (London: Home Office, 1995).

Home Office. *OASys User Manual*. (London: National Probation Directorate, 2002 2 vols).

Home Office. *Reducing Re-offending National Action Plan*. (London: Home Office Communications Directorate, 2004).

Home Office. *A Five Year Strategy for Protecting the Public and Reducing Re-offending*. (London: Stationery Office, 2006).

Honig, B. 'Difference, Dilemmas and the Politics of Home'. In S. Benhabib (ed.) *Democracy and Difference: Contesting the Boundaries of the Political*. (Princeton, NJ: Princeton University Press, 1996), pp. 257–277.

Hopf, C. and E. Weingarten (eds). *Qualitative Sozialforschung*. (Stuttgart: Klett-Cotta, 1979).

Horkheimer, M. and T. Adorno. *Dialektik der Aufklärung*. (Frankfurt am Main: Fischer Taschenbuchverlag, 1988).

Hough, M., R. Allen, and U. Patel (eds). *Reshaping Probation and Prisons: The New Offender Management Framework.* (Bristol, UK: Policy Press, 2006).

Hudson, B. 'Punishment, Rights and Difference: Defending Justice in the Risk Society'. In K. Stenson and R. Sullivan (eds) *Crime, Risk and Justice.* (Devon, UK: Willan Publishing, 2001), pp. 144–172.

Hudson, B. *Justice in the Risk Society.* (London: Sage Publications, 2003).

Hudson, B. and G. Bramhall. 'Assessing the "other": Constructions of "Asianness" in risk assessments by probation officers'. *British Journal of Criminology*, 45 (2005) 721–740.

Humphries, B. 'From Critical Thought to Emancipatory Action: Contradictory Research Goals'. In C. Truman, D. M. Mertens, and B. Humphries (eds) *Research and Inequality.* (London: UCL Press, 2000), pp. 179–190.

Hunt, J. *Psychoanalytic Aspects of Fieldwork, Qualitative Research Methods Series 18.* (Thousand Oaks, CA: Sage Publications, 1989).

Institut für Sozialforschung Frankfurt. *Geschlechterverhältnisse und Politik.* (Frankfurt am Main: Suhrkamp, 1994).

Jakobi, A. P. 'Die Bildungspolitik der OECD: Vom Erfolg eines scheinbar machtlosen Akteurs'. *Zeitschrift für Pädagogik*, 53 (2007) 166–181.

James, A. and J. Raine (eds). *The New Politics of Criminal Justice.* (London: Longman, 1998).

Janesick, V. J. 'The Dance of Qualitative Research Design: Metaphor, Methodolatory and Meaning'. In N. K. Denzin and Y. S. Lincoln (eds) *The Handbook of Qualitative Research.* (Thousand Oaks, CA: Sage Publications, 1996), pp. 209–219.

Jensen, R. 'Using Pornography'. In G. Dines, R. Jensen, and A. Russo (eds) *Pornography: The Production and Consumption of Inequality.* (New York: Routledge, 1998), pp. 101–146.

Johnstone, K. *Improvisation und Theater.* (Berlin: Alexander Verlag, 1993).

Jouhy, E. *Bleiche Herrschaft – Dunkle Kulturen.* (Frankfurt am Main: IKO Verlag, 1996).

Kaelble, H. and J. Schriewer (eds). *Vergleich und Transfer.* (Frankfurt am Main and New York: Campus, 2003).

Kamper, D. and C. Wulf (eds). *Die Wiederkehr des Körpers.* (Frankfurt am Main: Suhrkamp, 1982).

Kant, I. *Kritik der reinen Vernunft.* (Köln: Könemann, 1995).

Kaufman, C. *Ideas for Action: Relevant Theory for Radical Change.* (Cambridge, MA: South End Press, 2003).

Kelle, U. and S. Kluge. *Vom Einzelfall zum Typus.* (Wiesbaden: VS Verlag für Sozialwissenschaften, 2007).

Kemshall, H. *Understanding Risk in Criminal Justice.* (Berkshire: Open University, 2003).

Kendall, G. and G. Wickham. *Using Foucault's Methods.* (London: Sage Publications, 1999).

Kendall, G. and G. Wickham. 'The Foucaultian Framework'. In C. Seale, G. Gobo, J. F. Gubrium, and D. Silverman (eds) *Qualitative Research Practice.* (London: Sage Publications, 2007), pp. 141–150.

Kennedy, H. *Just Law.* (London: Chatto & Windus, 2004).

Kiel, L. D. and E. Elliott (eds). *Chaos Theory in the Social Sciences: Foundations and Applications.* (Ann Arbor, MI: The University of Michigan Press, 1997).

Kingsmead Community Trust. *Annual Report 1994–1995*. (London: Kingsmead Community Trust, 1995).

Kingsmead Homes. *Annual Report*. (London: Kingsmead Homes, 2005).

Klein, M. *Love, Guilt and Reparation and Other Works, 1921–1945*. (London: Virago, 1988).

Koch, G. *Lernen mit Bert Brecht. Bertolt Brechts politisch-kulturelle Pädagogik*. (Frankfurt am Main: Brandes & Apsel, 1988).

Koch, G. 'Theater-Spiel als szenische Sozialforschung'. In J. Belgrad (ed.) *Theaterspiel Ästhetik Des Schul- Und Amateurtheaters*. (Hohengehren: Schneider, 1997), pp. 81–96.

Kraus, K. *Lebenslanges Lernen – Karriere einer Leitidee*. (Bielefeld: Bertelsmann, 2001).

Kraus, K. 'Lifelong Learning between Educational Policy and Pedagogy'. In K. Harney, A. Heikkinen, S. Rahn, and M. Schemmann (eds) *Lifelong Learning: One Focus, Different Systems*. (Bern, NY: Peter Lang, 2002), pp. 33–43.

Kraus, K. 'Education, Social Policy and Governance – An Analysis of the Third Way'. In R. Husemann and A. Heikkinen (eds) *Governance and Marketisation in Vocational and Continuing Education*. (Bern, NY: Peter Lang, 2004a), pp. 31–48.

Kraus, K. 'Constructing "Europe" and "European Identity": The Role of Education in the Process of European Unification'. In T. Geisen, A. A. Hickey, and A. Karcher (eds) *Migration, Mobility and Borders: Issues of Theory and Policy*. (Frankfurt am Main and London: IKO, 2004b), pp. 137–158.

Kraus, K. 'Better educated, but not equal – women between general education, VET, the labour market and the family in Germany'. *Journal of Vocational Education and Training*, 58 (2006a) 409–422.

Kraus, K. 'Work-Life Balance Campaigns and their Contribution to Re-define the Notion of Vocational Qualification'. In L. Mjelde and R. Daly (eds) *Working Knowledge in a Globalizing World*. (Bern, NY: Peter Lang, 2006b), pp. 237–353.

Kraus, K. '"Ältere Beschäftigte" als Zielgruppe von Beschäftigungspolitik und Berufsbildung'. In K. K and C. (eds) *Ältere Beschäftigte – Alternde Belegschaften: Wie regiert die Berufspädagogik auf diese Herausforderung?* (Bielefeld: Bertelsmann, 2007a), pp. 13–23.

Kraus, K. '"Funktionslogik" – Überlegungen zu einem Modell für die Weiterbildungsforschung'. In G. Wiesner, C. Zeuner, H. Forneck, and Hermann (eds) *Empirische Forschung und Theoriebildung in der Erwachsenenbildung*. (Baltmannsweiler: Schneider Hohengehren, 2007d), pp. 183–194.

Kraus, K. 'Die "berufliche Ordnung" im Spannungsfeld von nationaler Tradition und europäischer Integration'. *Zeitschrift für Pädagogik*, 53 (2007c) 381–397.

Kraus, K. The Establishment of "Elder Employees" as a new Target Group for Education, Paper presented to the Small Group Meeting on Aging and Work, University of Tilburg, http://www.tilburguniversity.nl/faculties/fsw/departments/HRS/SGM/papers, 2007b, Access Date: 20 April 2008.

Kraus, K. 'Understanding the Transfer of Concepts between the International and the National Levels: Import or Interpretation?' In V. Aarkrog and C. H. Jørgensen (eds) *Divergence and Convergence in Education and Work*. (Bern, NY: Peter Lang, 2008), pp. 77–99.

Kuhn, M. and R. G. Sultana (eds) *Homo Sapiens Europaeus?* (Bern, NY: Peter Lang, 2006).

Kuhn, T. *The Structure of the Scientific Revolution* 2nd ed. (Chicago, IL: University of Chicago Press, 1970).

Küsters, I. *Narrative Interviews*. (Wiesbaden: VS Verlag für Sozialwissenschaften, 2006).

Kvale, S. *InterViews: An Introduction to Qualitative Research Interviewing*. (Thousand Oaks, CA: Sage Publications, 1996).

Kvale, S. 'The psycho-analytic interview as qualitative research'. *Qualitative Inquiry*, 5(1) (1999) 87–113.

Lakatos, I. 'Falsification and the Methodology of Scientific Research Programmes'. In I. Lakatos and A. Musgraver (eds) *Criticism and the Growth of Knowledge*. (Cambridge: Cambridge University Press, 1970), pp. 91–196.

Lather, P. 'Postbook: Working the ruins of feminist ethnography'. *Signs*, 27(1) (2001) 199–228.

Lather, P. and C. Smithies. *Troubling the Angels: Women Living with HIV/AIDS*. (Boulder, CO: Westview, 1997).

Latour, B. *We Have Never Been Modern*. (Hemel Hempstead, Hertfordshire: Harvester Wheatsheaf, 1993).

Latour, B. 'When things strike back – a possible contribution of 'science studies' to the social sciences'. *British Journal of Sociology*, 51(1) (2000) 107–122.

Lea, J. *Crime and Modernity*. (London: Sage Publications, 2002).

Ledwith, M. *Participation in Transformation: Towards a Working Model of Community Development*. (Birmingham: Venture Press, 1997).

Ledwith, M. *Community Development: A Critical Approach* 2nd ed. (Birmingham: BASW/Policy Press, 2005).

Lee, R. 'Structures of Knowledge'. In T. K. Hopkins and I. Wallerstein (eds) *The Age of Transition*. (London and New Jersey: Zed Books, 1996), pp. 178–206.

Leschinsky, A. 'Vom Bildungsrat (nach) zu PISA'. *Zeitschrift für Pädagogik*, 51 (2005) 818–839.

Lincoln, Y. S. 'Emerging criteria for quality in qualitative and interpretive inquiry'. *Qualitative Inquiry*, 1 (1995) 275–289.

Lincoln, Y. S. and E. G. Guba. *Naturalistic Inquiry*. (Beverly Hills, CA: Sage, 1985).

Lincoln, Y. S. and E. G. Guba. 'Paradigmatic Controversies, Contradictions, and Emerging Confluences'. In N. K. Denzin and Y. S. Lincoln (eds) *Handbook of Qualitative Research* 2nd ed. (London: Sage, 2000), pp. 163–188.

Lindley, D. 'The philosophy of statistics'. *Journal of the Royal Statistical Society: Series D (The Statistician)*, 49(3) (1999) 293–337.

Locke, A. and D. Edwards. 'Bill and Monica: Memory, emotion and normativity in Clinton's Grand Jury testimony'. *British Journal of Social Psychology*, 42 (2003) 239–256.

Loftland, J. and L. H. Loftland. *Analysing Social Settings* 2nd ed. (Belmont, CA: Wadsworth, 1984).

London Borough of Hackney. *Putting the Heart Back into Kingsmead Estate*. (London: London Borough of Hackney, 1994).

London Borough of Hackney, Research and Statistics Team. *Hackney Key Facts*. (London: London Borough of Hackney, 2004).

London Research Centre. *The Capital Divided: Mapping Poverty and Social Exclusion in London*. (London: London Research Centre, 1996).

Lovett, T., C. Clarke, and A. Kilmurray. *Adult Education and Community Action*. (Kent: CroomHolm, 1983).

Lucey, H., J. Melody, and V. Walkerdine. 'Project 4:21 Transitions to womanhood: Developing a psychosocial perspective in one longitudinal study'. *International Journal of Social Research Methodology*, 6(3) (2003) 279–284.

Lyotard, J. F. *The Postmodern Condition: A Report on Knowledge.* (Manchester: Manchester University Press, 1984).

MacMartin, C. and C. D. Lebaron. 'Arguing and Thinking Errors: Cognitive Distortion as a Member's Category in Sex Offender Group Therapy Talk'. In A. Hepburn and S. Wiggins (eds) *Discursive Research: New Approaches to Psychology and Interaction.* (Cambridge: Cambridge University Press, 2007), pp. 147–165.

Mainzer, K. *Thinking in Complexity* 2nd ed. (New York: Springer-Verlag, 1996).

Marcus, G. E. 'A report on two initiatives in experiments with ethnography – ... a decade after the "writing culture" critique'. *Anthropological Journal of Field Work. Reflecting Cultural Practice. The Challenge of Field Work (1)*, VI(2) (1997) 9–23.

Marx, K. 'Der achtzehnte Brumaire des Louis Bonaparte'. *Marx-Engels-Werke* Vol. 8. (Berlin: Dietz Verlag, 1960), pp. 111–207 42 vols.

Mauthner, M., M. Birch, J. Jessop and T. Miller (eds) *Ethics in Qualitative Research.* (London: Sage, 2002).

May, T. *Social Research. Issues, Methods and Process* 3rd ed. (Buckingham: Open University Press, 2001).

Maykut, P. and R. Morehouse. *Beginning Qualitative Research: A Philosophic and Practical Guide.* (London: The Falmer Press, 1994).

Maynard-Moody, S., M. Musheno, and D. Palumbo. 'Street-wise social policy; resolving the dilemma of street-level influence and successful implementation'. *Western Political Quarterly*, 43 (1990) 831–846.

Mayr, E. *Toward a New Philosophy of Biology.* (Cambridge, MA: Belknap Harvard, 1988).

Mazzini, R. and M. Wrentschur. 'Theatre of the Oppressed in Social Fields/ Theater der Unterdrückten in sozialen Feldern'. In G. Koch, S. Roth, F. Vaßen, and M. Wrentschur (eds) *Theaterarbeitsozialen Feldern/theatre Worksocial Fields.* (Frankfurt am Main: Brandes & Apsel, 2004), pp. 174–186.

McDaniel, R. R. J. 'Strategic leadership: A view from quantum and chaos theories'. *Health Care Management Review* 22.1 (1997) 21–37.

Mcdermott, R. and J. D. Raley. 'From John Dewey to an anthropology of education'. *Teachers College Record*, 109(7) (2007) 1820–1835.

McGinn, M. *Wittgenstein and the Philosophical Investigations.* (London: Routledge, 1997).

McIntyre, A. *Participatory Action Research.* (Thousand Oaks, CA: Sage, 2008).

Mcsweeney, T., V. Herrington, M. Hough, P. J. Turnball, and J. Parsons. *From Dependency to Work – Addressing the Multiple Needs of Offenders with Drug Problems.* (London: Institute for Criminal Policy Research, 2004).

McTaggart, R. 'Issues for Participatory Action Researchers'. In O. Zuber-Skerritt (ed.) *New Directions in Action Research.* (London: Falmer Press, 1996), pp. 243–255.

Medd, W. 'Complexity and the Social World'. *International Journal of Social Research Methodology* 5.1 (2002) 71–81.

Megill, A. (ed.) *Rethinking Objectivity.* (Durham, NC: Duke University Press, 1994).

Meltzer, D. *The Kleinian Development: Part III, the Clinical Significance of the Work of Bion.* (Perthshire: Clunie Press, 1978).

Mendez, C. L., F. Coddou, and H. Maturana. 'The bringing forth of pathology'. *The Irish Journal of Psychology*, 9(1) (1988) 144–172.

Mergner, G. *Lernfähigkeit der Subjekte und gesellschaftliche Anpassungsgewalt.* (Berlin and Hamburg: Argument Verlag, 1999).

Mergner, G. *Social Limits to Learning.* (New York and Oxford: Berghahn Books, 2005).

Merry, U. *Coping with Uncertainty: Insights from the New Science of Chaos, Self-Organization and Complexity.* (Westport, CT: Praeger Publishers, 1995).

Meuret, D. and M. Duru-Bellat. 'English and French modes of regulation of the education system'. *Comparartive Education*, 39 (2003) 463–477.

Meyer, H. D. and B. Rowan (eds). *The New Institutionalism in Education.* (Albany, NY: Sate University of New York, 2006).

Meyer, J. W. and F. O. Ramirez. 'The World Institutionaliszation of Education'. In J. Schriewer (ed.) *Weltkultur und kulturelle Bedeutungswelten.* (Frankfurt am Main and New York: Campus, 2007), pp. 279–297.

Meyer, T. *Was ist Politik?* 2nd ed. (Opladen: Leske + Budrich, 2003).

Midgley, J. (ed.) *Community Participation: Social Development and the State.* (London: Methuen, 1986).

Mies, M. 'Towards a Methodology for Feminist Research'. In G. Bowles and R. D. Klein (eds) *Theories for Women's Studies.* (London: Routledge and Kegan Paul, 1983), pp. 117–139.

Milgram, S. *Obedience to Authority. An Experimental View.* (Harper: New York, 1974).

Mills, S. *Discourse.* (London: Routledge, 1997).

Mills, S. *Michel Foucault.* (London: Routledge, 2003).

Moore, B. *Risk Assessment: A Practitioner's Guide to Predicting Harmful Behaviour.* (London: Whiting and Birch, 1996).

Moore, H. '"Divided we stand": Sex, gender and difference'. *Feminist Review*, 47 (1994) 78–95.

Morgan, S. *Clinical Risk Management: A Clinical Tool and Practitioner Manual.* (London: Sainsbury Centre for Mental Health, 2000).

Morwitz, H. J. *The Emergence of Everything: How the World Became Complex.* (Oxford: Oxford University Press, 2002).

Mullender, A. and D. Ward. *Self-Directed Groupwork.* (London: Whiting and Birch, 1991).

Mundy, K. 'Educational Multilateralism in a Changing World Order: UNESO and the Limits of the Possible'. *International Journal of Educational Development*, 19 (1999) 27–52.

Murphy, K. and M. Fearon. *Devil's Island.* (London: Marshalls, 1985).

Murray, C. *The Emerging British Underclass.* (London: Institute of Economic Affairs, 1990).

Murray, C. *Underclass: The Crisis Deepens.* (London: Institute of Economic Affairs, 1994).

NACRO. *Crime, Community and Change. Taking Action on the Kingsmead Estate in Hackney.* (London: NACRO, 1996).

Nagel, T. *The View from Nowhere.* (New York: Oxford University Press, 1986).

Nellis, M. 'The Electronic Monitoring of Offenders in Britain: A Critical Overview'. In J. Buchanan (ed.) *Electronic Monitoring of Offenders: Key Developments* [Monograph]. (London: NAPO ICCJ, 2004), pp. 53–82.

Nguyen, T. *We Are All Suspects Now: Untold Stories from Immigrant Communities after 9/11.* (Boston, MA: Beacon Press, 2005).

Nightingale, D. J. and J. Cromby (eds). *Social Constructionist Psychology: A Critical Analysis of Theory and Practice.* (Buckingham: Open University Press, 1999).

Nitsch, W. and I. Scheller. 'Forschendes Lernen mit Mitteln des szenischen Spiels als aktivierende Sozial- und Bildungsforschung'. In B. Friebertshäuser and A. Prengel (eds) *Handbuch Qualitative Forschungsmethodender Erziehungswissenschaft.* (Weinheim-München: Juventa, 1997), pp. 704–710.

Nitsch, W. and I. Scheller. *Lehrkörper. Haltungen von Männern in der Lehre – erkundet mit Mitteln des szenischen Spiels.* (Oldenburg: Carl von Ossietzky Universität Oldenburg. Zentrum für pädagogische Berufspraxis, 1998).

Noaks, L. and E. Wincup. *Criminological Research: Understanding Qualitative Methods.* (London: Sage, 2004).

O'Brien, C.-A. 'Contested Territory: Sexualities and Social Work'. In A. S. Chambon, A. Irving and L. Epstein (eds) *Reading Foucault for Social Work.* (New York: Columbia University Press, 1999), pp. 131–155.

O'Farrell, C. *Michel Foucault.* (London: Sage, 2005).

Oakley, A. 'Interviewing Women: A contradiction in terms'. In H. Roberts (ed.) *Doing Feminist Research.* (London: Routledge and Kegan Paul, 1981), pp. 36–48.

OECD. *Economic Survey of Germany 2008.* (Paris: OECD, 2008).

Oelkers, J. *Einführung in die Theorie der Erziehung.* (Weinheim and Basel: Beltz, 2001).

Ohmacht, S. *Wohnungslos in Graz. Sozialwissenschaftliche Dokumentation der Sozialarbeit für wohnungslose Menschen in Graz, Analyse der Betreuungsangebote sowie Strategiekonzept Wohnungslosenhilfe Graz. Studie im Auftrag des Landes Steiermark und der Stadt Graz. Kurzfassung.* (Stadt Graz: Sozialamt, 2004).

Oldfield, M. *From Risk to Welfare: Discourse, Power and Politics in The Probation Service. Monograph.* (London: NAPO ICCJ, 2002).

Oliver, M. 'Changing the social relations of research production'. *Disability Handicap and Society,* 7(2) (1992) 101–114.

Opie, A. 'Qualitative research: Appropriation of the "other" and empowerment'. *Feminist Review,* 40 (1992) 52–69.

Osborn, S. and H. Shaftoe. *Safe Neighbourhoods? Successes and Failures in Crime Prevention.* (London: Safe Neighbourhood Unit, 1995).

Packham, C. 'Community auditing as community development'. *Community Development Journal,* 33(3) (1998) 249–259.

Parry-Davies, B. 'An end to estates of siege' (*The Times,* 29 June 1993), 4.

Payne, J. *Researching Health Needs.* (London: Sage, 1999).

Pearce, E. 'Commentary: Hackney's terror estate finding a civil cure' (*The Guardian,* 12 June 1993), 15.

Peay, J. 'Mentally Disordered Offenders'. In M. Maguire, R. Morgan, and R. Reiner (eds) *The Oxford Handbook of Criminology* 4th ed. (Oxford: Oxford University Press, 2002), pp. 496–527.

Percy-Smith, J. (ed.) *Needs Assessments in Public Policy.* (Buckingham: Open University Press, 1996).

Peshkin, A. (2003) 'The Goodness of Qualitative Research', *Educational Researcher* (22)2, 23–29.

Phillips, D. 'Policy Borrowing in Education'. In J. Zajda (ed.) *International Handbook of Globalisation, Education and Policy Research.* (Dordrecht: Springer, 2005), pp. 23–34.

Phillips, D. and K. Ochs. 'Processes of Policy Borrowing in Education'. *Comparative Education*, 39 (2003) 451–461.

Picht, D. *Die deutsche Bildungskatastrophe*. (Olten and Freiburg im Breisgau: Walter, 1964).

Pierce, C. S. 'Aus den Pragmatismus-Vorlesungen'. In J. Strübing and B. Schnettler (eds) *Methodologie interpretativer Sozialforschung*. (Konstanz: UVK Verlagsgesellschaft, 2004), pp. 201–222.

Plummer, K. *Documents of Life: An Introduction to the Problems and Literature of a Humanistic Method*. (London: George Allen and Unwin, 1983).

Plummer, K. *Documents of Life 2: An Invitation to a Critical Humanism*. (London: Sage Publications, 2001).

Poincaré, H. *Science and Method*. (London: T. Nelson and Sons, 1914).

Polanyi, M. *The Tacit Dimension*. (London: Routledge and Kegan Paul, 1967).

Pole, C., P. Mizen, and A. Bolton. 'Realising children's agency in research: Partners and participants?' *International Journal of Social Research Methodology*, 2(1) (1999) 39–54.

Porter, R. *The Hutchinson Dictionary of Scientific Biography* 2nd ed. (Oxford: Helicon Publishing Ltd, 1994).

Potter, J. *Representing Reality: Discourse, Rhetoric and Social Construction*. (London: Sage Publications, 1996).

Potter, J. 'Wittgenstein and Austin'. In M. Wetherell, S. Taylor, and S. J, Yates (eds) *Discourse and Theory: A Reader*. (London: Sage Publications, 2001), pp. 39–46.

Potter, J. 'Discourse Analysis As a Way of Analysing Naturally Occurring Talk'. In D. Silverman (ed.) *Qualitative Research: Theory, Method and Practice* 2nd ed. (London: Sage Publications, 2004), pp. 200–221.

Poulos, C. N. 'The Death of Ordinariness: Living, Learning and Relating in the Age of Anxiety'. In N. K. Denzin and Y. S. Lincoln (eds) *9/11 in American Culture*. (Walnut Creek, CA: Altamira Press, 2003), pp. 232–243.

Powell, J. J. W. and H. Solga, Internationalization of Vocational and Higher Education Systems, Discussion Paper SP I 2008–501, Social Science Research Center, Berlin, http://www.wzb.eu/bal/aam/discussion_papers.de.htm, 2008, Access Date: 20 April 2008.

Prigogine, I. *From Being to Becoming: Time and Complexity in the Physical Sciences*. (New York: W.H. Freeman and Co. Ltd., 1980).

Prigogine, I. *The End of Certainty*. (New York: The Free Press, 1997).

Prigogine, I. and I. Stengers. *Order Out of Chaos: Man's New Dialogue with Nature*. (London: Fontana, 1984).

Prins, H. *Will They Do It Again? Risk Assessment and Management in Criminal Justice and Psychiatry*. (London: Routledge, 1999).

Prins, H. 'Mental disorder and violent crime: A problematic relationship'. *Probation Journal*, 52 (2005) 333–357.

Prout, A. (ed.) *The Body, Childhood and Society*. (Basingstoke, Hampshire: Palgrave Macmillan, 2000).

Putnam, H. *Reason, Truth and History*. (Cambridge: Cambridge University Press, 1981).

Rabinow, P. (ed.) *Essential Works of Foucault 1954–1984, Volume 1: Ethics, Subjectivity & Truth*. (London: Penguin, 2000).

Ramazanoglu, C. and J. Holland. *Feminist Methodology: Challenges and Choices*. (London: Sage Publications, 2002).

Reason, P. (ed.) *Human Enquiry in Action: Developments in New Paradigm Research*. (London: Sage Publications, 1988).

Reason, P. and H. Bradbury (eds) *Handbook of Action Research: Participative Inquiry and Practice*. (London: Sage Publications, 2001).

Reason, P. and J. Rowan. *Human Enquiry: A Sourcebook of New Paradigm Research*. (New York: John Wiley, 1981).

Rees, M. '21st Century Science: Prospects, Threats and Ethical Challenges – Joseph Rotblat Memorial Lecture.' Unpublished Paper. *The Guardian Hay Festival 2006*. The Guardian Hay Festival, Hay on Wye, Herefordshire. (2006).

Renk, H. E. 'Authentizität als Kunst. Zur Ästhetik des Amateurtheaters oder: wenn sie gut sind, sind sie aufregend bei sich selber'. In J. Belgrad (ed.) *TheaterSpiel: Ästhetik des Schul- und Amateurtheaters*. (Hohengehren: Schneider, 1997), pp. 38–56.

Reviere, R., S. Berkowitz, C. C. Carter, and C. C. Ferguson. *Needs Assessments. A Creative and Practical Guide for Social Scientists*. (Washington, USA: Taylor and Francis, 1996).

Revolving Doors Agency. *Future Imperfect: Young People, Mental Health and the Criminal Justice System*. (London: Revolving Doors Agency, 2002).

Richardson, L. *Fields of Play: Constructing an Academic Life*. (New Brunswick, NJ: Rutgers University Press, 1997).

Richardson, L. 'Writing: A Method of Inquiry'. In N. K. Denzin and Y. S. Lincoln (eds) *Collecting and Interpreting Qualitative Materials* 2nd ed. Vol. 3. (Thousand Oaks, CA: Sage Publications, 2003), pp. 499–541 3 vols.

Rickford, D. and K. Edgar. *Troubled Inside: Responding to the Mental Health Needs of Men in Prison*. (London: Prison Reform Trust, 2005).

Riley, S. C. 'Constructions of equality and discrimination in professional men's talk'. *British Journal of Social Psychology*, 41(3) (2002) 443–461.

Robinson, G. 'Exploring risk management in probation practice: Contemporary developments in England and Wales'. *Punishment and Society*, 4 (2001) 5–25.

Robinson, G. 'Implementing OASys: Lessons from research into LSI-R and ACE'. *Probation Journal*, 50 (2003a) 30–40.

Robinson, G. 'Risk and Risk Assessment'. In W. H. Chui and M. Nellis (eds) *Moving Probation Forward*. (London: Pearson, 2003b), pp. 108–129.

Robinson, G. 'What works in offender management?' *The Howard Journal*, 44 (2005) 307–318.

Robson, C. *Real World Research*. (Oxford: Blackwell, 1993).

Roeder, P. M. 'TIMSS und PISA – Chancen eines neuen Anfangs in Bildungspolitik, -planung, -verwaltung und Unterricht. Endlich ein Schock mit Folgen?' *Zeitschrift für Pädagogik*, 49 (2003) 180–197.

Rorty, R. *The Linguistic Turn: Recent Essays in Philosophical Method*. (Chicago, IL: University of Chicago Press, 1967).

Rosenthal, G. 'Reconstruction of life stories: Principles of selection in generating stories for narrative biographical interviews'. *The Narrative study of Lives*, 1(1) (1993) 59–91.

Rosenthal, G. *Interpretative Sozialforschung*. (Weinheim and München: Juventa Verlag, 2005).

Rosenthal, G. and D. Bar-On. 'A biographical case study of a victimizer's daughter's strategy: pseudo-identification with the victims of the Holocaust'. *Journal of Narrative and Life History*, 2 (1992) 105–127.

Ruckerbauer, A. and M. Wrentschur. 'Theaterarbeit mit wohnungslosen Menschen am Beispiel von "wohnungs/LOS/theatern"/Theatre Work with Homeless People, e.g. "wohnungs/LOS/theatern" '. In G. Koch, S. Roth, F. Vaßen and M. Wrentschur (eds) *Theaterarbeit in sozialen Feldern/Theatre Work in Social Fields*. (Frankfurt am Main: Brandes & Apsel, 2004), pp. 199–205.

Rumgay, J. 'Partnerships in the Probation Service'. In W. H. Chui and M. Nellis (eds) *Moving Probation Forward: Evidence, Arguments and Practice*. (Harlow: Pearson Education Ltd, 2003), pp. 195–213.

Ryan, T. 'Perceived Risks Associated with Mental Illness: Beyond Homicide and Suicide'. *Social Science and Medicine*, 46(2) 1998 287–297.

Said, E. *Die Welt der Text und der Kritiker*. (Frankfurt am Main: S. Fischer Verlag, 1983).

Said, E. 'Representing the Colonized: Anthropology's Interlocutors'. *Critical Inquiry* (1989, Winter) 205–225.

Sartre, J. -P. *Marxismus und Existentialismus*. (Reinbeck bei Hamburg: Rowohlt Taschenbuch Verlag, 1964).

Scambler, G. 'Medical Sociology and Modernity: Reflections on the Public Sphere and the Roles of Intellectuals and Social Critics'. In G. Scambler and P. Higgs (eds) *Modernity, Medicine and Health: Towards Medical Sociology Towards 2000*. (London: Routledge, 1998), pp. 46–65.

Schriewer, J. 'Comparative Education Methodology in Transition'. In J. Schriewer (ed.) *Discourse Formation in Comparative Education*. (Bern, NY: Peter Lang, 2003), pp. 3–52.

Schriewer, J. and K. Harney. 'Beruflichkeit versus culture technique'. In P. Wagner, C. Didry, and B. Zimmermann (eds) *Arbeit und Nationalstaat*. (Frankfurt am Main and New York: Campus, 2000), pp. 128–168.

Schutz, A. *Der sinnhafte Aufbau der sozialen welt*. (Frankfurt am Main: Suhrkamp, 1993).

Schwandt, T. A. *Dictionary of Qualitative Inquiry* 2nd ed. (Thousand Oaks, CA: Sage Publications, 2001).

Scott, J. *A Matter of Record: Documentary Sources in Social Research*. (Cambridge, UK: Polity Press, 1990).

Scott, J. W. 'Evidence from Experience'. *Critical Inquiry* (1991, Summer) 775–797.

Seymour-Rolls, K. and I. Hughes. Participatory Action Research: Getting the Job Done, Action Research E-Reports, http://www.gpcontract.co.uk/, 2000, Access Date: 20 March 2008.

Shacklock, G. and J. Smyth (eds). *Being Reflexive in Critical Educational and Social Research*. (London: Falmer, 1993).

Shortall, S. 'Participatory Action Research'. In R. L. Miller and J. D. Brewer (eds) *The A-Z of Social Research*. (London: Sage Publications, 2003), pp. 225–227.

Silverman, D. *Interpreting Qualitative Data: Methods for Analysing Talk, Text and Interaction*. (London: Sage Publications, 1993).

Silverman, D. 'Qualitative/Quantitative'. In C. Jenks (ed.) *Core Sociological Dichotomies*. (London: Sage Publications, 1998), pp. 78–95.

Silverman, D. (2nd edition). *Interpreting Qualitative Data: Methods for Analyzing Talk, Text and Interaction*. (London: Sage Publications, 2001).

Sinding, C. and J. Aronson. 'Exposing failures, unsettling accommodations: Tensions in interview practice'. *Qualitative Research*, 3(1) (2003) 95–117.

Smart, B. *Michel Foucault* Rev. ed. [First Pub. 1985]. (London: Routledge, 2002).

Smith, B. *Nationalism and Modernism*. (London: Routledge, 1998).

Smith, A. M. *New Right Discourse on Race & Sexuality, Britain 1968–1990*. (Cambridge: Cambridge University Press, 1994).

Smith, D. E. *Texts, Facts, and Femininity: Exploring the Relations of Ruling*. (London: Routledge, 1990).

Smith, D. E. *Writing the Social: Critique, Theory and Investigations*. (Toronto, Canada: University of Toronto Press, 1999).

Smith, D. 'Probation and social work'. *The British Journal of Social Work*, 35 (2005) 621–637.

Smith, D. and M. Vanstone. 'Probation and Social Justice'. *British Journal of Social Work*, 32(6) (1 September 2002) 815–830.

Soriano, F. I. *Conducting Needs Assessments. A Multidisciplinary Approach*. (Thousand Oaks, CA: Sage Publications, 1995).

Sparkes, A. 'Reciprocity in Critical Research? Some Unsettling Thoughts'. In G. Shacklock and J. Smyth (eds) *Being Reflexive in Critical Educational and Social Research*. (London: Falmer, 1993), pp. 67–82.

Sparkes, A. 'The fatal flaw: A narrative of the fragile body-self'. *Qualitative Inquiry*, 2 (1996) 463–494.

Speer, S. A. *Gender Talk: Feminism, Discourse & Conversation Analysis*. (London: Routledge, 2005).

Speer, S. A. and J. Potter. 'The management of heterosexist talk: Conversational resources and prejudiced claims'. *Discourse & Society*, 11(4) (2000) 543–572.

Spivak, G. C. 'Can the Subaltern Speak?' In C. Nelson and L. Grossberg (eds) *Marxism and the Interpretation of Culture*. (Chicago, IL: University of Illinois Press, 1988), pp. 271–313.

Squire, C. 'Situated Selves, the Coming-Out Genre and Equivalent Citizenship in Narratives of Hiv'. In P. Chamberlayne, J. Bornat, and T. Wengraf (eds) *The Turn to Biographical Methods in Social Science: Comparative Issues and Examples*. (London: Routledge, 2000), pp. 196–213.

Stanley, L. 'For Sociology: Gouldner's and Ours'. In J. Eldridge, J. MacInnes, S. Scott, C. Warhurst, and A. Witz (eds) *For Sociology: Legacies and Prospects*. (Durham: Sociology Press, 2000), pp. 56–82.

Steele, J. Four days in California: US Sociologists are finally challenging the intellectual stranglehold of economists, *The Guardian*, http://www.guardian.co.uk/world/2004/aug/24/usa.highereducation/print, Access Date: 24 August 2004, Access Date: 20 April 2008.

Steiner-Khamsi, G. (ed.) *The Global Politics of Educational Borrowing and Lending*. (New York and London: Teachers College Press, 2004).

Steinweg, R. *Gewalt in der Stadt. Wahrnehmungen und Eingriffe. Das Grazer Modell*. (Münster: Agenda, 1994).

Steinweg, R. *Lehrstück und episches Theater. Brechts Theorie und die theaterpädagogische Praxis.* (Frankfurt am Main: Brandes & Apsel, 1995).

Steinweg, R. H. W. and P. Petsch. *Weil wir ohne Waffen sind. Ein theaterpädagogisches Forschungsprojekt zur Politischen Bildung. Nach einem Vorschlag von Bertolt Brecht.* (Frankfurt am Main: Brandes & Apsel, 1986).

Stevens, I. and P. Cox, Complexity Theory: Developing New Understandings of Child Protection in Field Settings and in Residential Care, British Journal of Social Work, http://bjsw.oxfordjournals.org/cgi/reprint/bcm052, Access Date: 25 July 2007, Access Date: 25 July 2007.

Stopford, A. 'Researching postcolonial subjectivities: The application of relational psychoanalysis to research methodology'. *Critical Psychology*, 10 (2004) 13–35.

Strauss, A. L. and J. Corbin. *Grounded Theory: Grundlagen qualitativer Sozialforschung.* (Weinheim: Beltz, 1996).

Summit, R. C. 'Hidden Victims, Hidden Pain: Societal Avoidance of Child Sexual Abuse'. In G. E. Wyatt and G. J. Powell (eds) *Lasting Effects of Child Sexual Abuse.* (Newbury Park, CA: Sage Publications, 1988), pp. 39–60.

Sweeney, K. 'History of Complexity'. In K. Sweeney and F. Griffiths (eds) *Complexity and Healthcare: An Introduction.* (Oxford: Radcliffe Medical Press, 2002), pp. 19–34.

Taylor, C. 'Foucault on Freedom and Truth'. In D. Hoy (ed.) *Foucault: A Critical Reader.* (Oxford: Blackwell, 1986), pp. 63–103.

Taylor, C. *Sources of the Self.* (Cambridge MA: Harvard University Press, 1989).

Taylor, C. and S. White. *Practising Reflexivity in Health and Welfare: Making Knowledge.* (Buckingham: Open University Press, 2000).

Taylor, P. V. *The Texts of Paulo Freire.* (Buckingham: Open University Press, 1993).

te Molder, H. and J. Potter (eds). *Cognition and Conversation.* (Cambridge: Cambridge University Press, 2005).

Tendler, S. 'Hackney initiative cuts crime on estate' (*The Times*, 12 June 1993), 7.

Tennant, R., M. Shirkie, and K. Mcgarygle. *A Poverty Profile of Royston and Germiston.* (Glasgow: Glasgow Caledonian University and Save the Children, 1996).

'The people of Kingsmead are drawn mainly from lists of nominees from boroughs all over London' (*The Guardian*, 1973), 4.

Thelen, K. *How Institutions Evolve.* (Cambridge: Cambridge University Press, 2004).

Tillmann, K. J. 'Erziehungswissenschaft und Bildungspolitik'. *Zeitschrift für Pädagogik*, 37 (1991) 955–974.

Tillmann, K. J. 'Erziehungswissenschaft und Bildungspolitik – von den 1970er Jahren zur PISA-Zeit'. *Die Deutsche Schule*, 100(1) (2008) 31–43.

Tomlinson, S. *Education in a Post-Welfare Society.* (Buckingham: Open University Press, 2001).

Touraine, A. *Post-Industrial Society.* (New York: Random House, 1971).

Trampusch, C. 'Sequenzorientierte Policy-Analyse'. *Berliner Journal für Soziologie*, 16 (2006) 55–76.

Trinh, T. M. *Woman, Native, Other: Writing Postcoloniality and Feminism.* (Bloomington, IN: Indiana University Press, 1989).

Turner, B. S. 'An Outline of a General Sociology of the Body'. In B. S. Turner (ed.) *The Blackwell Companion to Social Theory* 2nd ed. (Oxford: Blackwell Publishers, 2000), pp. 481–501.

Van Dijk, T. A. 'Discourse and society: a new journal for a new research focus'. *Discourse & Society*, 1(1) (1990) 5–16.

Van Maanen, J. *Tales of the Field: On Writing Ethnography*. (Chicago, IL: University of Chicago Press, 1988).

van-Dijk, J. J. M. 'Understanding crime rates: On the interactions between the rational choices of victims and offenders'. *British Journal of Criminology*, 34 (1994) 105–121.

Vanstone, M. *Supervising Offenders in the Community: A History of Probation Theory and Practice*. (Aldershot: Ashgate, 2004).

Varela, F. J. 'Reflections on the Circulation of Concepts between a Biology of Cognition and Systemic Family Therapy'. *Family Process*, 28 (1989) 15–24.

Velody, I. and R. Williams (eds). *The Politics of Constructionism*. (London: Sage Publications, 1998).

Verenne, H. and R. Mcdermott. *Successful Failure: The Schools America Builds*. (Boulder, CO: Westview Press, 1998).

Vieregg, M. *"Wir sind da... und haben etwas zu sagen!" Emanzipatorisch-partizipative Bildungsaspekte von "wohnungs/LOS/theatern" – einem soziokulturellen Theaterprojekt mit wohnungslosen und ehemals wohnungslosen Menschen in Graz*. (Graz: Diplomarbeit, Institut für Erziehungswissenschaft, Universität Graz, 2005).

Von Bertalanffy, L. *General System Theory: Foundations, Development, Application* 2nd ed. (London: Allen Lane The Penguin Press, 1971).

Waldrop, M. M. *Complexity: The Emerging Science at the Edge of Order and Chaos*. (Harmondsworth: Penguin Books, 1992).

Walkerdine, V. *Daddy's Girl: Young Girls and Popular Culture*. (Basingstoke, Hampshire: Palgrave Macmillan, 1997).

Wallerstein, I. 'From sociology to historical social science: Prospects and obstacles'. *British Journal of Sociology*, 51(1) (2000) 25–35.

Wallerstein, I., C. Juma, E. Fox Keller, J. Kocka, V. Y. Mudkimbe, K. Miushakoji, I. Prigogine, P. J. Taylor, and M. R. Trouillet. *Open the Social Sciences: Report of the Gulbenkian Commission on the Restructuring of the Social Sciences*. (Stanford, CA: Stanford University Press, 1996).

Weber, M. *Economy and Society* 2nd ed. (Berkeley, CA: University of California Press, 1978).

Weber, M. *Gesammelte Aufsätze zur Wissenschaftslehre* [originally published in 1922]. (Tübingen: J.C.B. Mohr Verlag, 1988).

Wengraf, T. 'Uncovering the General from within the Particular: From Contingencies to Typologies in the Understanding of Cases'. In P. Chamberlayne, J. Bornat, and T. Wengraf (eds) *The Turn to Biographical Methods in Social Science: Comparative Issues and Examples*. (London: Routledge, 2000), pp. 140–164.

Wengraf, T. 'Historicising the "Socio" Theory, and the Constant Comparative Method, Appendix B'. In P. Chamberlayne, M. Rustin, and T. Wengraf (eds) *Biography and Social Exclusion in Europe: Experiences and Life Journeys*. (Bristol, UK: Policy Press, 2002), pp. 309–328.

Wernet, A. *Einführung in die Interpretatinstechnik der Objektiven Hermeneutik*. (Opladen: Leske + Budrich, 2000).

Wetherell, M. 'Positioning and interpretive repertoires: Conversation analysis and post-structuralism in dialogue'. *Discourse & Society*, 9(3) (1998) 387–412.

Wetherell, M. 'Themes in Discourse Research: The Case of Diana'. In Wetherell. M & Taylor. S. &Yates. S. J. (eds) *Discourse and Theory: A Reader*. (London: Sage Publications, 2001), pp. 14–28.

Wetherell, M. 'Racism and the analysis of cultural resources in interviews'. In H. Van Den Berg, H. Houtkoop-Steenstra, and M. Wetherell (eds) *Analyzing Race Talk: Multidisciplinary Perspectives on the Research Interviews*. (Cambridge: Cambridge University Press, 2003), pp. 11–30.

Wetherell, M., H. Stiven, and J. Potter. 'Unequal egalitarianism: a preliminary study of discourses concerning gender and employment opportunities'. *British Journal of Social Psychology*, 26(1) (1987) 59–71.

Wetherell, M. and J. Potter. *Mapping the Language of Racism: Discourse and the Legitimation of Exploitation*. (Hemel Hempstead: Harvester Wheatsheaf, 1992).

Wetherell, M., S. Taylor, and S. J. Yates (eds). *Discourse as Data: A Guide for Analysis*. (London: Sage Publications, 2001a).

Wetherell, M., S. Taylor, and S. J. Yates (eds). *Discourse, Theory and Practice: A Reader*. (London: Sage Publications, 2001b).

'What the King and Queen saw'. (*North London Record*, 31 March 1939), 10.

Wiener, N. *Cybernetics: Or Control and Communication in the Animal and the Machine*. (New York: John Wiley and Sons, 1948).

Wilkinson, S. 'Prioritizing the political: feminist psychology'. In T. Ibánez and L. Iniguez (eds) *Critical Social Psychology*. (London: Sage Publications, 1997), pp. 178–194.

Williams, F., J. Popay, and A. Oakley (eds). *Welfare Research. A Critical Review*. (London: UCL Press, 1999).

Williams, S. J. *Emotion and Social Theory*. (London: Sage Publications, 2001).

Wise, S. and L. Stanley. 'Having it all: feminist fractured foundationalism'. In K. Davis, M. Evans, and J. Lorber (eds) *Handbook of Gender & Women's Studies*. (London: Sage Publications, 2006), pp. 435–456.

Witkin, S. 'Editorial: Reflections and Farewell'. *Social Work* 47.1 (2002) 5–8.

Wolcott, H. F. 'Posturing in Qualitative Research'. In M. D. Lecompte, W. L. Millroy, and J. Preissle (eds) *The Handbook of Qualitative Research in Education*. (New York: Academic Press, Inc, 1992), pp. 3–52.

Wolf, A. *Does Education Matter?* (London: Penguin Books, 2002).

Wooffitt, R. *Conversation Analysis and Discourse Analysis: A Comparative and Critical Introduction*. (London: Sage Publications, 2005).

Wrentschur, M. 'Forumtheater'. In G. Koch and M. Streisand (eds) *Wörterbuch der Theaterpädagogik*. (Berlin, Milow: Schibri, 2003), pp. 108–110.

Wrentschur, M. 'To Transform Desire into Law: Legislative Theatre with the Homeless as a Tool for Civil Participation and Social Development'. In A. Heimgartner (ed.) *Face of Research on European Social Development. Community Work, Civil Society and Professionalisation in Social Work*. (Wien-Münster: Lit, 2006), pp. 83–94.

Wrentschur, M. with A. Ruckerbauer and M. Vieregg. 'Module Project "Legislative Theatre with Homeless People"'. In B. Cronin, S. Roth, and M. Wrentschur (eds) *Training Manual for Theatre Work in Social Fields*. (Frankfurt am Main: Brandes & Apsel, 2005), pp. 159–184.

Young, J. *The Exclusive Society*. (London: Sage Publications, 1999).

Young, J. 'Merton with energy, Katz with structure: the sociology of vindictive-ness and the criminology of transgression'. *Theoretical Criminology*, 7 (2003) 389–414.

Zima, P. V. *Moderne – Postmoderne*. (Tübingen und Basel: A. Francke Verlag, 1997).

Zizek, S. *Resistance Is Surrender* [Electronic Version]. London Review of Books (2007). Retrieved, 14 March 2008, from http://www.lrb.co.uk/v29/n22/zize01_.html

Index